all
about
cake

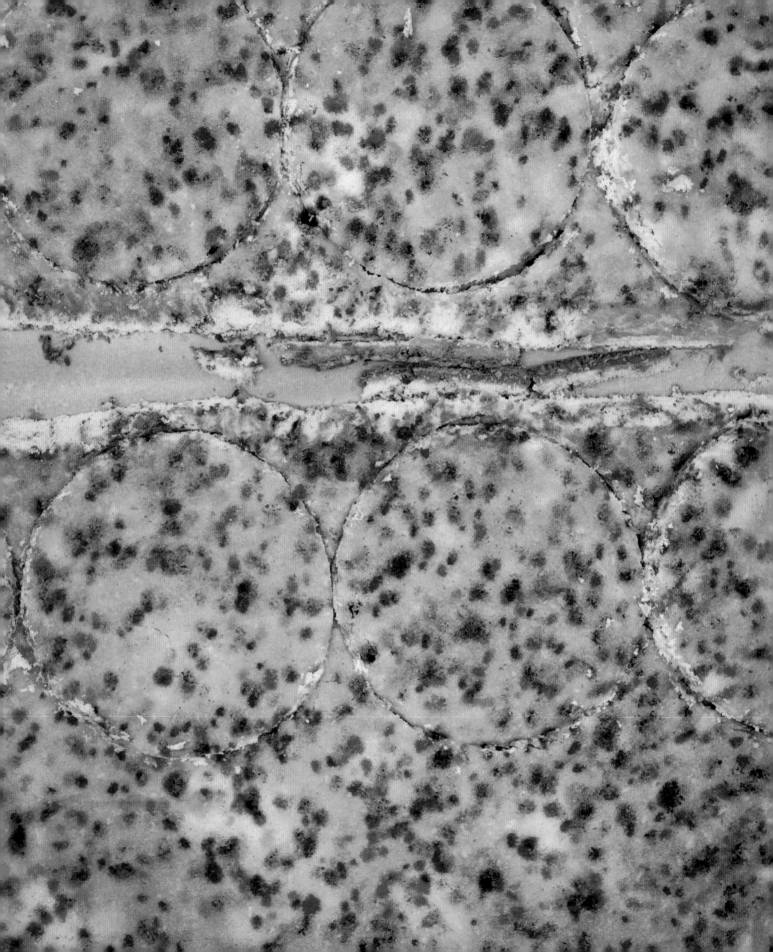

all about cake

christina tosi

with courtney mcbroom
photographs by Gabriele Stabile and Mark Ibold

Clarkson Potter/Publishers
New York

Published in the United States by Clarkson Potter/Publishers, an imprint
of the Crown Publishing Group, a division of Penguin Random House LLC, New York.
crownpublishing.com
clarksonpotter.com

CLARKSON POTTER is a trademark and POTTER with colophon is a
registered trademark of Penguin Random House LLC.

Library of Congress Cataloging-in-Publication Data
Names: Tosi, Christina, author. | Stabile, Gabriele, photographer.
Title: All about cake / Christina Tosi ; photographs by Gabriele Stabile.
Description: First edition. | New York : Clarkson Potter/Publishers, [2018]
Identifiers: LCCN 2017050431 (print) | LCCN 2017052785 (ebook)
    | ISBN 9780451499530 (Ebook) | ISBN 9780451499523 | ISBN 9780451499530 (eISBN)
Subjects: LCSH: Cake. | Desserts. | Quick and easy cooking. | LCGFT: Cookbooks.
Classification: LCC TX771 (ebook) | LCC TX771 .T67 2018 (print) | DDC 641.86/53–dc23
LC record available at https://lccn.loc.gov/2017050431

ISBN 978-0-451-49952-3
Ebook ISBN 978-0-451-49953-0

Printed in China

Book design by Walter Green
Illustrations by Walter Green
Additional photography credits: page 31: courtesy of Crain's Communications, by Buck Ennis;
pages 89, 91, and 200: Milk Bar, Ursula Viglietta and Sarah Crowder.
Cover design by Jen Wang
Cover photographs by Gabriele Stabile

10 9 8 7 6 5 4 3 2 1

First Edition

"Stop leaving me home alone
with so many cakes."

—Will Guidara
(HUSBAND EXTRAORDINAIRE)

contents

the truth . . .
9

tmi
13

bundts, pounds &
a fluffy little cake from heaven
32

hot cakes!
76

sheet cakes for the masses
96

cupcakes (if you must)
122

cake truffles
make the world go 'round
156

BONUS!!!
all about
cake truffle
croquem-
bouches
210

BONUS!!!
all about
ice cream
cakes
266

BONUS!!!
all about
large format
and wedding
cakes
268

get fancy
with layer cakes
212

veganity
276

acknowledgments
282

index
284

the truth . . .

. . . of the matter is that growing up I didn't really love cake. (I KNOW!) I was a fool for dense, fudgy brownies, crazy cookies warm out of the oven, and—my childhood fave—gooey butter cake (which is technically not even a cake! It's a bar cookie.).

Cake was a bit boring to me, almost always the same old formula: a spongy base with some muted flavor, sweet frosting on top. Nine times out of ten, I'd just scrape and eat the frosting off the snooze fest, leaving the cake behind, naked and afraid. To be fair, cake was fun to have at birthdays and celebrations because I do love dessert rituals. And it meant, if I played my cards right, I could finagle enough frosting to keep me going through the afternoon and still have a little for a slumber party pick-me-up. To me, cake was really just a vehicle for a frosting fest.

It wasn't until 2005 that I started really thinking twice about cake. More specifically, layer cake. I had over a decade of home baking under my belt, been to culinary school, and worked my way up in top NYC restaurants, but had still never met a cake that made me swoon. I had started making desserts for the Momofuku restaurants and had found my voice as a pastry chef through the desserts that I adored—ice cream, pie, cookies. The thing I never dared put on the menu was the dessert I never felt was truly lust-worthy. But as my imagination grew, I became obsessed with figuring out how to fall in love with cake.

I sat down and considered the things that bummed me out about cake:

- 😔 Cake flavors are dull and boring.
- 🙄 Cake is usually overbaked to make it sturdy enough to be layered or topped.
- 😞 Cake is usually just one soft, spongy bite. Why take the time to make cake so beautiful on the outside if it's just a snooze fest when you bite in?

Cake, as I knew it, felt like a throwaway, a statue that told no story, and wasn't that awesome to eat. But it's tradition. We're told it's decadent, so we turn a blind eye, or turn off our taste buds, and lift our forks anyhow. We can do better than that! If the world is really going to embrace life and dive face first into a dessert, we deserve more than that. Cake should have personality! Integrity! Texture! And a visual appeal that draws you in and gets you excited about *eating*!

I had a lot of work to do. I believed cake had the potential to be a great vehicle for many things—perspective, point of view, flavor, bits and pieces of goo, graham, glaze, and goodness. But first I had to define a formula for myself, then get the world to trust me and dig in.

I needed to make a direct contradiction to all the reasons cake let me down in the past, and so I decided these would be my cake ground rules:

- **The cake must have a strong point of view, a flavor "story."**
- **Every single layer must be amazingly delicious on its own.**
- **Hidden gems of texture within are key.**
- **And there is no way in H-E-double-hockey-sticks we're going to hide ALL that ingenuity behind a thick coat of frosting. I want to let the people IN, and so I won't frost the sides of the cake.**

And so it began, my little love story with cake. I'd make it every day. Multiple times a day. I'd use ANY cake-worthy opportunity in life to test out this new perspective. A friend's birthday. A dog's birthday. A wedding. First day of vacation. Last day of vacation. A housewarming. I got in there, all for the love of the game, to start loving cake, to make cake lovable.

Once I found someone to bake for, I'd analyze their favorite desserts, and I'd set about devising their cake, layer by layer. Love for strawberry shortcake, lemon chiffon pie, and classic New York cheesecake inspired the Strawberry-Lemon Layer Cake (page 221), a going-away party for someone who loved making tropical cocktails gave birth to the Pineapple Upside-Down Layer Cake (page 237), and someone's love for pancakes, any time of day, paved the way for the Pancake Layer Cake (page 255).

I became a woman possessed in this new universe of layer cakes—curious sponges, soaks, outside-the-box fillings, crumbs, crunches, ganache, unfrosted sides. Occasion by occasion, I baked my way into my now deep and abiding love of cake.

No one teaches you how to be prepared for the things you chase down in life. And so I never really considered that this internal, deep-dive study of mine would be something that inspired others . . . and would maybe change the dessert world forever.

In 2008, when me and my guy and gal pals opened the doors to Milk Bar, we challenged the way lots of people think about baked goods: cookies with sweet and salty bits, cereal-flavored anything, "crack" bars and pie, rainbow-sprinkled "birthday" flavor . . . and especially cakes. I must admit, people were confused at first by the naked-looking sides of our layer cakes, with composed flavors and bits and bobs peeking out. But we gave them the Milk Bar Sweat Down, where resistance is futile, where we keep shoving slices of cake their way until they cave in.

Nowadays, at Milk Bar, it's no secret that we love cake. It has quickly become a way of life. From layer cakes to cake truffles, cake is what makes our operation go 'round. This book is our ode to that. We're so cuckoo for cake, every weekend at our Milk Bar shops, we throw impromptu parties, where we stop the madness for just a moment or two and celebrate over a #cakebreak. We dance, jiggle, and shake alongside our guests and neighbors to celebrate our everyday lives over cake! When our local school needs to raise some funds, our cake shows up, too.

And cake follows us off the clock, beyond the doors of Milk Bar. After all, when you are that obsessed with something, you find it and carry it with you in any and every form. Real Talk: When I'm home, sometimes the last thing I want to do is fuss over a layer cake, which is When a simple bundt or pound cake comes in. And if I'm being really honest, even turning on the stove sometimes feels like a chore. So enter: Crock-Pot and microwave cakes—if you're into the warm and fudgy, my friend, I've got your back.

Sometimes your crew of friends is more the sheet-cake crowd. And other times, the young 'uns in your kitchen, dying to get up in the mix, are more the cupcake type (the only reason we'll allow for them). We're so into spreading the love of cake that we have recipes for those who don't have a baking bone in their body. As for cake balls, cake pops, or call them what you will, we whisper our secrets for transforming bites of cake into our legendary "cake truffles" in the pages that follow, too.

And, for those fussier perfectionists and pros who just can't get enough, we'll get down in there, too, with recipes, processes, tips, and tricks from our classic 6-inch layer cake all the way up to our insane multitier wedding cake architectural feat, if you're really set on going for it!

I went from being a cake hater to a cake revolutionary. And if there's one more thing you must know about me, it's that talk is cheap, especially in the kitchen. Seeing, tasting, is believing. Come on in, tie that apron 'round your waist. A headscarf for flair will get your imagination in the right place, or put on some tunes to get you bouncing. Heat the oven and start nosing around in your fridge and cupboards. I want you all in, as I welcome you into our wild, wonderful world of CAKES!

tmi

The beauty of too much information is that, depending on your personality, mood, or desire to absorb, it can be *just the right amount* of information. If you're up for it, dive into the depths of this section for an assessment of your gear, and set yourself up for success when writing out your shopping list for our world-of-cake essentials. If you've baked your way through any of our books and/or make cakes from scratch, you already know much of what's to come. But here's a refresher. And if you need a little dose of life advice, there's some of that here, too.

the goods

We choose the ingredients or "goods" we use in our cake recipes wisely—we know WAY too much about the vast world of chocolate chips, which is how we know which brand and size we like best. This section is your guide when you grocery shop or take inventory of your kitchen cabinets.

Can't find an ingredient at your local grocery store? Never underestimate the power of amazon.com—we're their unofficial spokes-bakery. (Don't worry, our payday is near . . .)

Bananas, rrrrrrrrripe
Bananas are easy to procure, but ripened bananas is an art we take quite seriously. Buy them a few days before you plan to use them. Ripen them on the counter, in a brown paper bag, or in the freezer (my fave pro tip!), until the skins are jet-black and the fruit has turned to mush. Though visually unappealing, this is when bananas are at their absolutely most flavorful! If you're

a household that keeps a heavy stock of bananas, pay it forward and always keep an airtight container of very ripe bananas frozen (still in their skins), so you never have to wait to make the Banana-Chocolate–Peanut Butter Crock-Pot Cake (page 90) or Banana-Chocolate-Hazelnut Cupcakes (page 153). Just remember to defrost and remove the banana from its blackened skin before using!

Butter

I know you know what butter is. We love butter at Milk Bar and spend a lot of money on the really good stuff (Plugra). Unsalted, European-style butter is the best of the best for these recipes; it's higher in fat, typically 82 percent.

Chocolate, all of it

Generally, we stand by Valrhona for 55% feves, 72% feves, and cocoa powder, and suggest you do the same. Baller chocolate in a recipe = insanely delicious cake out of the oven. (Also "feves" = flat wide disks of chocolate that make melting easy. If you can only find chocolate in a block or brick, just be sure to chop it down well for even melting.)

Mini Chocolate Chips: Semisweet mini chocolate chips are our chip of choice for flavor and distribution. Nestlé and Barry Callebaut do the job just right.

White Chocolate: . . . is not even technically chocolate because it contains cocoa butter, but no cocoa solids (the stuff that makes chocolate brown and delicious). We use it as a thin shell around the cake truffles, and as a base for certain cake swirls, but mostly rely on it for its technical properties like setting a glaze and giving a great mouthfeel without adding a competing flavor. Feel free to choose whatever white chocolate (even in chip form) you can get your hands on.

Citric or ascorbic acid

You can find citric or ascorbic acid powders marketed as "sour salt" in the spice aisle, or as vitamin C powder in the vitamin aisle, or just buy them by their own name online. We use them interchangeably to enhance the flavor in many of our citrus-based recipes.

Corn powder

We invented corn powder, but we'll give away our secret: It's freeze-dried corn kernels you can buy online or at a Whole Foods near you. Then in a blender, grind it into a flour-like consistency, and store it in an airtight container. It is yellow gold, this I promise you. It is the hard-to-put-your-finger-on flavor in our cereal milk ice cream and crack pie filling and adds an insanely fresh and natural depth whether the flavor goal is straight-up corn or not, without disrupting texture or consistency. There is absolutely no substitute for it, and we use so much of it that we figured we should start selling it in our stores and at milkbarstore.com, too!

Dulce de leche

Dulce de leche is sometimes called "milk jam" and it's exactly as delicious as that sounds. There are a ton of different ways to make dulce de leche, but we prefer simmering an unopened can of sweetened condensed milk, label removed, fully submerged in a pot of water for 2 hours. Make sure the water level is always 2 inches above the can, or the can might explode in your face! Cool the can completely before opening, or another in-your-face explosion could occur.

You can also find cans of dulce de leche in the international aisle or at a Latin supermarket. La Lechera is our favorite brand. If you want to get a little adventurous, use *cajeta* in lieu of dulce de leche. It's quite similar, but made with goat's milk so it has more of a funk to it.

Extracts

We're not into using flavor extracts as a crutch, but when used wisely and sparingly, they can help impart certain flavors without affecting the science of baking in a recipe. When we call for them, it's for good reason.

Vanilla Extract: This is the extract you know and love and can find anywhere. It's a dark vanilla color and scent, and awesome in almost any baked good (except where clear vanilla extract is called for; see below). McCormick will always do right by us.

Clear Vanilla Extract: Find it online. Some grocery stores carry it, but most don't. DO NOT substitute regular vanilla extract for it; it is a vastly different flavor experience. Think about that dark, warming vanilla flavor in a chocolate chip cookie—that's regular vanilla extract. Then think about the light, creamy vanilla flavor you find in a Creamsicle. That's clear vanilla extract. Awesome in its own right, for different flavor reasons!

Cola Extract: We love Amoretti brand cola extract. Find it online. There is no substitution.

Banana, Butter, Lemon, and Peppermint Extracts: Most grocery stores carry these extracts, but if you're uncertain, take it to the Internet.

Flours

All-Purpose (AP) Flour: This one is pretty self-explanatory. Any brand will do, though we like King Arthur.

Cake Flour: Softasilk or Purasnow are the brands to choose. AP flour is *not* a substitute, nor is self-rising cake flour—your cakes will not sponge and rise the same way unless you use cake flour.

Corn Flour: We use corn flour to deepen a corny flavor profile. If you can't find corn flour, you can use half cake flour and half corn powder (pulverized freeze-dried corn) by volume or weight in a recipe.

Gluten-Free Flour: Bob's Red Mill or Cup4Cup work great. If you make your own blend at home, high five! We can't vouch for your formula, but have our fingers crossed!

Food coloring

Much like extracts, we use food coloring sparingly and only when necessary. We don't use an ungodly amount; and if you don't want to use food coloring, you don't have to.

Gelatin

Sheet Gelatin: This is easier to work with than the powdered stuff, but ironically more difficult to find as a home cook. If you're buying sheets, note that all our recipes call for the "silver" grade of strength.

Powdered Gelatin: A cinch to find in the baking aisle of your local grocery store and it can be substituted for sheets in every application. We'll give you the conversion in any recipe that requires it. You will by no means sacrifice the quality of the product if you use powdered gelatin, but the quality of the product will definitely falter if you don't follow the instructions correctly for blooming gelatin (see page 27).

Lipton tea and Lipton tea powder

An Arnold Palmer isn't really an Arnold Palmer unless you stick to classic Lipton tea: It's full of tannin, it's bitter, and it holds the flavor of lemonade perfectly. We generally use tea leaves (you know, the stuff in the tea bags) to fold into batters before baking and instant iced tea drink mix in raw applications. Every grocery store I've been to carries both.

Nonfat milk powder

Think of nonfat milk powder as the secret-weapon ingredient in the recipes that call for it. It gives an amazing depth of flavor; it just makes things taste better, even if it doesn't taste so great on its own. Find it in the powdered drink mix aisle or baby food aisle of your grocery store. It's often labeled as "instant nonfat dry milk." Any brand will do.

Oil

We use grapeseed oil in all our baking. It is a little more viscous than most oils, it doesn't impart any flavor, and it has an amazing emulsifying quality. If you have canola or vegetable oil, or another neutral (odorless/flavorless) oil in the house, feel free to use that, too.

Pectin NH

Though there are several types available depending on one's need and application, we use pectin NH in our liquid fruit applications. It sets well (especially with fruits that are low in sugar) and is thermo-irreversible, which means it maintains its body whether it is hot or cold. Pectin gives fruit a really great consistency (perfect for a layer in a cake!) without making it jiggly like Jell-O. Once you start jamming with it, you won't stop. Find it online.

Purees
Fruit can be purchased already pureed or you can buy fruit whole and puree it at home. I don't consider purchasing fruit purees cheating, especially if I need puree from a fruit that is out of season. Passion fruit puree is definitely worth buying, as is cherry, unless you live in a sweet cherry state and they're in season. Amazon.com is your go-to here. Boiron or Capfruit are our preferred brands.

If you choose to make purees at home, it is essential that you use the ripest fruit possible; if you don't, there is no way your puree will taste good. Never use fruit juice or fruit nectar in place of puree. It's totally different.

Salt
We use Diamond Crystal kosher salt for everything. It's not iodized and has larger granules than table salt. There is something about iodized salt that I don't like the flavor of, plus table salt is really small and it looks like sugar, and that confuses and scares me. Kosher salt is usually located on the shelf right below the table salt shelf at the grocery store. Be aware, however, that Morton's brand kosher salt is about 66 percent heavier by volume than Diamond Crystal kosher salt. This is a nonissue if you're weighing your salt, but if you're using freedom (volume) measurements, just know that you will need about half the volume of Morton's salt as the recipe calls for.

Yellow cake mix
Yellow cake mix is absolutely delicious. We never use the mix to bake an actual cake; we use it to re-create the familiar flavor of boxed cakes in different ways, like Yellow Cake Crumbs (page 111) and Yellow Cake Frosting (page 111).

When it comes to choosing yellow cake mix, please believe me that Pillsbury is the way to go. Pillsbury did not pay me to say this; it is legitimately the best one. We tested recipes calling for yellow cake mix with every possible brand and, again, I can't stress enough that Pillsbury wins. Duncan Hines is a close second, but that's it. No other brand will give you that boxed yellow cake flavor that we all know and love.

the 'wares

You don't need much, but there are some key pieces of kitchen equipment—or "'wares" as we call them—that are essential to executing recipes in this book. Often the 'wares called for are what set some of our techniques and final cakes apart. We've simplified our equipment needs to the necessities, plus their substitute counterparts.

Acetate
We use acetate when assembling a layer cake. Acetate—a thick, shiny strip of plastic—allows us to build up, layer by layer, in a cake ring (see page 20) and ensures a smooth and shiny edge to the finished cake, giving that signature peek-a-boo unfrosted-side vibe. Acetate is often sold at specialty cake stores, but can always be found online. Buy it in a 3-inch-wide roll or sheet.

Baking pans/vehicles
Angel Food Pan: You thought we'd just leave you high and dry with all those extra egg whites? Not us! Use a 10-inch round (18-cup) angel food (aka tube) cake pan. Hopefully you have one at home. If not, a standard kitchen supply store will have you covered.

Bundt Pan: All our bundt cake recipes were developed to fit a standard 12-cup bundt pan. We love using the classic bundt pans handed down by our grandmas, or the ones that we picked up at last weekend's yard sale (they're very retro). Bundt pans are easy enough to come by on eBay and Etsy if you can't find one at your local kitchen supply store. Bundts do come in a 6-cup variety and even smaller, so if you use them, please be sure to scale down the ingredients and baking time. My general rule of thumb is to scale the baking time down on the same scale as the baking vehicle (i.e., if the bundt pan is half the size, I cut baking time in half. For mini bundt pans that are about 1 cup, divide the baking time by 12), then add on 3- to 5-minute increments until the cake skewers come out clean. And above all else, promise me you'll grease them, then flour them well before baking. Those fellas can get super sticky!

Crock-Pot: Whether you use a vintage Crock-Pot or a new baller Breville slow cooker, your sweet and savory life will never be the same. When making hot cakes, use the low setting. In a vintage variety, expect your hot cake to "bake" with a darker outer ring. Though we always get excited when using our aunt's old Crock-Pot, the results with the newer machines were out of control—they have better heat distribution, which means a more evenly cooked cake with a golden brown bottom!

Cupcake Pan: All cupcake (if you must) recipes in this book are designed for 12-cup muffin/cupcake pans. Feel free to size the cupcakes up or down into maxis or minis, but be sure to choose the corresponding paper cups and adjust the baking time (use the rule of thumb for bundt pans; see above).

Loaf or Pound Cake Pan: Every pound cake recipe here uses a 1-pound rectangular loaf pan. A medium-size heavy-bottomed pan works best: we swear by our OXO Pro Nonstick Loaf Pan. Thin-walled pans will color the exterior quicker, but the center will take just as long to bake through, or some pans will just cook quicker in general.

And don't freak out, but there are often very small variations in the actual dimensions of a 1-pound loaf pan—some are 8.5 inches while others 9 inches. Our recipes work in all 1-pound loaf pans. Just remember to grease, then flour them well, and if this is your first time baking one of these recipes with a pan other than the OXO Pro Nonstick, just test the cake to see if it's done 5 or 10 minutes early. If you use a ½-pound loaf pan, your cake will bake in approximately half the time, and so on. I'm pretty sure you've got it. Right?

Mug: We love standard 11-ounce mugs, because every microwave cake recipe makes two perfect mugs. Any microwaveable mug will do, but if your mug is bigger or smaller and you fill it up with batter, you may end up needing to cook it for more or less time.

Sheet Pan: Invest in two quality quarter-sheet pans (aka 13 × 9-inch jelly-roll pans) and treat them with integrity and respect. That sheet pan is the only thing that guarantees you success! We don't bake our cakes in cake pans because cakes never bake evenly in them—they either end up jiggly in the center and baked perfectly on the outside or baked perfectly in the center and overbaked on the outside, so we bake them in sheet pans, then cut rounds out afterward. Quarter-sheet pans are the secret to a layer cake or sheet cake's success. We love OXO pans— they're heavy-bottomed and perfect for every use.

If you've got a monster kitchen at home (or work), a huge oven, and a dream for larger layer or sheet cakes, you are welcome to upgrade to a half- or even full-sheet pan. (Just remember to double or quadruple a recipe that calls for a quarter-sheet pan!)

Cake rings

A cake ring is basically a cake pan with no top or bottom. Every layer cake recipe in this book requires baking the batter in a quarter-sheet pan, then using a 6-inch cake ring to cut out rounds. The ring is then used as a base in which to build the cake. If you already have a 6-inch cake pan, you can use that to cut the rounds and to build the cake (just don't bake the cake in it).

If you're going for a bigger kahuna, 10-inch, 14-inch, and on up, cake rings are easy to find. Specialty kitchen supply stores typically carry all cake ring sizes. They're easy to find in stock online, too.

Gloves

We use disposable latex gloves, especially when truffling, to keep our nail art on point and for germ-free, easy cleanup. Though they're not mandatory, they will make your life VERY awesome when making those dense, sandy little gems from heaven. Pick up a box next time you're wheeling your cart down the household cleaning aisle of your supermarket.

Measuring cups and spoons

If you choose to forgo the precision that using a scale brings, measuring cups will do. Your end product will be a tad less accurate, but perfectly fine and tasty. You'll also find that your ¼-cup measure will be useful in other parts of this book, like when portioning cupcake batter into pans, and your trusty tablespoon measure will be your new cake truffle sidekick! Old or new measuring cups will do (they all vary in the slightest ways, which is why we're all about that scale life).

Microwave

We use our microwave for everything from melting butter and chocolate to making microwave cakes. Though it is one of man's greatest inventions, like unicorns every microwave is different. Take heed when setting 15- or 30-second bursts of heat. Keep your eye on the batter or butter or chocolate. Items can overheat or burn quickly when left unattended!

Mixer and attachments

We love using our stand mixer with the paddle and whisk attachments that go along with it for many of the recipes in this book. A hand-held granny mixer will work, but is less baller (sorry, Gram). For other recipes, two bowls, a whisk, and a rubber spatula work great, too, and is so noted.

Offset spatula

Your best friend when smoothing cake batter into a quarter-sheet pan is a 4½-inch offset spatula. Easy to find online and at specialty kitchen stores, this little fella is also a great help when decorating cupcakes or spreading frostings on a layer cake. Not having one is not a deal breaker, however. A rubber spatula combined with a bent spoon will get any job done, too.

Oven

Whoa. Did you know, much like microwaves, every oven is different, too? Get to know yours. Convection, convention. The hot spots, the cold spots, the unleveled spots. Play to your oven's strengths, and pretty please use an oven thermometer so your cakes come out as pro as you!!!

Oven thermometers

Turns out the temperature on the dial of most ovens is different from the actual internal temperature. The world is not out to get you, I promise. Just buy an oven thermometer from a kitchen supply store or online. Clip or hang the oven thermometer on the middle rack in your oven all the way toward the door so you can read it easily.

Heat the oven to the temperature noted in the recipe. When the oven sensor (usually a light) says the oven is properly heated, consult the oven thermometer and adjust the temperature dial until the thermometer tells you you're at the temperature your recipe requires. Note that there will still be hotter and cooler spots in the oven (your thermometer will be sitting in what is likely the coolest zone), but you'll be on the right track.

Pan spray (nonstick cooking spray)

There are lots of approaches to grease. My grandmother would save the back of butter papers and use the residual butter on them to grease her pans. We use pan spray to grease baking pans.

For bundts and pound cakes, spray and then flour the pans (a crucial step in the unmolding process). For sheet cakes and layer cakes, we use pan spray to help a piece of parchment paper settle in, then spray the parchment with more pan spray. An ungreased baking pan, unless it's for cupcakes, is a disaster waiting to happen. Stock up on pan spray in the baking aisle of your local grocery. We prefer Pam.

Parchment paper

We line every quarter-sheet pan with parchment paper, a waxless wax paper, for easy unmolding and cleanup. You can get by with using wax paper or a silicone baking mat (Silpat) instead. Just don't use aluminum foil, since it conducts more heat and it will burn the bottom of your cake. Parchment paper is also a great work surface (no sticking, easy cleaning) when cutting cake rounds or making sheet cakes. Grocery stores stock parchment paper, usually sold in rolls, in the baking aisle. For precut sheets of parchment that lie flat, try a kitchen supply store or go online.

(Heatproof "rubber") Spatula

A sturdy heatproof "rubber" spatula is (1) actually made of silicone and (2) a great investment and a necessity for scraping down the sides of a mixing bowl, transferring batters to baking pans, and making a fruit jam or a nut brittle. OXO makes a ton in fun colors and sizes. We're of the opinion you can never have too many.

Scale

Precision is key, my friend. Precision makes a huge difference in scaling ingredients for a recipe. If you spend the money on this cookbook and take the time to read it, do yourself a favor and invest in a $20 scale that measures in grams, found in any cookware store or online. To be nice, we will still give you the freedom (volume) measurement for each weight, but I can't stress enough how much better and more precise your product will turn out if you weigh in grams. Treat your scale with love and respect. Never store anything on top of it and make sure it stays calibrated. We check our scales once a week by placing a pound of butter on all of them to make sure they read 453 grams (that's 1 pound to all of you nongram speakers).

Silicone baking mat/silpat

Silicone baking mats are like pieces of parchment paper, except that they're made of silicone and you can use them repeatedly. You can use them to bake cookies, or to pour caramel or brittle onto. Basically, they are great and you should invest in two or three. Make sure the sizes match the sizes of the sheet pans you have at home. Hand-wash them in warm soapy water with a nonabrasive sponge or dishcloth.

Spoons

The cheaper the better for this book, believe it or not. We go out of our way to get the least sturdy, most bendable spoons. Though we use spoons to taste everything we make to be sure the flavor is on point, we also love to bend and then use said bent spoons to apply frostings and spread fillings. Don't use the spoons you got for your registry or your partner will hate us. Instead spend $5 on a new set of cheapos at the dollar store. That way we'll all be friends for life.

Timer

Unless you keep an inner timer that's on par with the atomic clock, you are going to need a timer for everything that goes into the oven, except of course if you have a dependable timer that's already attached to your oven. Whatever way, you need to keep track of how long everything has been a-baking. We strongly support obnoxious ringtones cued up on an iPhone.

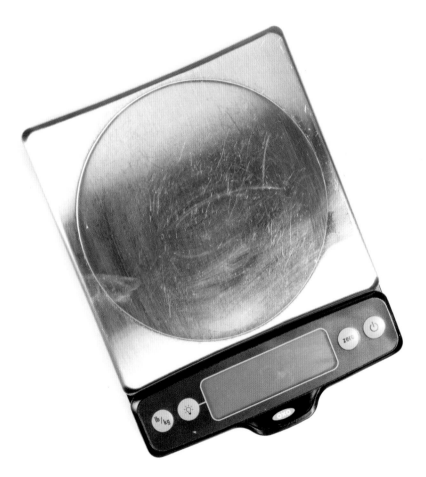

the techniques

Listen, we're only really fussy about the techniques that are tried and true in our kitchen. There's a lot you can wing, but the following are some of the foundations that've made many a novice into great bakers, chefs, and thinkers of food.

Blooming gelatin: get it right, or do it twice

In order to incorporate it seamlessly into a mixture, gelatin must be softened, or "bloomed," first.

For Sheet Gelatin: To bloom any amount of sheet gelatin, soak it in a small bowl of cold water. The gelatin is bloomed when it has become soft, after about 2 minutes. If the gelatin still has hard bits to it, it needs to bloom longer. If it is so soft it is falling apart, it is overbloomed; discard the gelatin and start over. Gently squeeze the bloomed gelatin to remove any excess water before using.

For Powdered Gelatin: To bloom powdered gelatin (any amount between ½ teaspoon and 2 teaspoons), sprinkle it evenly onto the surface of 2 tablespoons cold water in a small cup. If you dump the powdered gelatin into a pile on top of the water, the granules in the center will remain hard and will not bloom. If you use too much water to bloom the gelatin, its consistency will be looser than intended. Allow the granules to soften entirely in the cold water for 3 to 5 minutes, then scoop the gelatin out of the water (it will have absorbed a fair bit of it, and that's OK).

To incorporate either kind of gelatin into a mixture, you need to dissolve the bloomed gelatin in hot, but not boiling, liquid—usually a bit of whatever it will be mixed into. If the gelatin gets too hot, it will lose its strength and you will have to start over again.

Creativity and interchangeability

You will learn very quickly that interchangeability in our kitchen when creating is all part of our process. We love Milk Crumbs (page 129) SO much, we use them as a textural layer, a truffle coating, a cupcake topping, and beyond. Because we didn't score a cookbook deal for an 800-page book, and because we know how smart you are, we want to take the time to remind you that many of these frostings, fillings, soaks, crumbs, and cake batters can be used in a variety of ways, far beyond how we use them in our favorite recipes here. The batter for Corn Sheet Cake (page 115) would make a fantastic microwave cake or Crock-Pot cake topped with chocolate, caramel, or fresh strawberries, and the Creamsicle Crock-Pot Cake (page 86) would make a killer sheet cake when topped with a frosting along the lines of Strawberry Frosting (page 143), but using orange jam instead!

Same mentality goes for leftover bits and pieces of crumbs, crunches, and fillings: Look at them as the jumping-off point to your next killer cake creation.

Iteration and discovery are vital in our world, so much so that we started a line at Milk Bar called MilkID where you can design your own layer cake by diving into our arsenal of go-to flavors and fillings. Please, please, please, get creative! Make us proud!

Tasting for yourself, baking for yourself

Precision is key in baking, but so is remembering you are making delicious food for yourself or someone else. That's why it's important to taste every step of the way and love the flavor of what you're making. This may or may not include shamelessly licking the spatula before you put the cake in the oven. (I've caught plenty an improperly measured-out cake recipe this way.) Taste to know what tastes good to you. Learn how to use sugars, salt, and citrus or acid to balance flavors in any recipe. Tweak each recipe if you want it sweeter, saltier, or more acidic. We like punch-you-in-the-face flavors; you may want something mellower. If you taste as you go, you'll know to adjust Strawberry Frosting (page 143) to mellow it out or give it more of a kick.

Unless you're making angel food cake, sifting is a waste of time

We don't sift 99 percent of the flour in our kitchen. We believe it to be a waste of time in our recipes. Mixing the flour in without sifting does deflate the batter ever so slightly, but we bake buttery, moist American cakes, not delicate French soufflés. The only exception to this rule: Mommala's Angel Food Cake (from Heaven) (page 74).

cake freshness and storage

In our large kitchens, we typically take three days to make a layer cake. On day one, we bake cake. On day two, we make the fillings, soaks, and crumbs. On day three, we layer and set the cakes. Then on day four, we sell—or eat—the cake!

Keeping baked cake and any corresponding frostings, fillings, and textural pizzazz fresh until it's ready to be used is crucial. Maybe you want to stockpile layers of chocolate chip cake you'll top with frosting later for a bat mitzvah coming up? Maybe you want to make three layer cakes for your triplets' birthday next week. Alternatively, maybe your latest dinner party guests ate only half the pretzel cake truffles and one quarter of the corn and blueberry sheet cake. What does one do to ensure these beautiful baked goods, either in process or not fully consumed, stay fresh and bring sweetness to another day in the future?

Our mantra is: up to one week in the fridge, up to one month in the freezer (covered well in plastic wrap or secured in a clean, odorless, airtight container), with plenty of room in the fridge or freezer of course.

the life lessons

Be happy

Decide what happiness means to you. Then decide to be happy. It doesn't just happen. It's a decision you make every single day. We're very aware that some of those days are easier than others. Once you decide to be happy enough days in a row, it comes quite easy. Cake also helps.

Be a pro

Decide to do something and do it really well. Believe in the value of hard work. Commit to it. Pursue it. Fall in love with it. Especially when it comes to cake.

Make life a little sweeter

Be an ambassador of life. Get real. Let it in. Embrace the uncomfortable. Do nice things for others. Give back. Surprise people. Trust people. Be the person that people trust. Go above and beyond. Bake more cake.

March to the beat of your own drum

Be a great student. Learn the rules. Learn them well. Then challenge every little bit of them. Own what you know and why you know it. Live life on your terms and don't let anyone tell you who you are or what you can and can't do. Most people will tell you opening a bakery is silly, wearing a bow in your hair ridiculous, and wearing red high-top Converse shoes something teenagers do, not grown women. The pep in our step belongs to us, because we live in the world, but forever and always on our own terms. Our cake is a representation of us and us alone.

Sharing is caring, but do you

We believe in sharing recipes. That's how we learned how to bake! The tips and tricks to our beloved baked goods cannot be chained down. So use them, be inspired by them. But please don't open a Momofiki Moo Bar. Be brilliant, give yourself more credit than that! Come up with your own universe, and remember, you'll always be welcome in ours.

BUNDTS, POUNDS & A FLUFFY LITTLE CAKE FROM HEAVEN

The easiest way to bake a cake is to go to the grocery store, buy a box of cake mix, grab a bowl, whisk in some oil, water, an egg or two, bake—and boom. Or blah!

The easiest way to bake a cake FROM SCRATCH is to grab two bowls, whisk the wet stuff into the dry stuff, pull out your trusty bundt or pound cake pan,

and wait for your apartment building or cul-de-sac to smell like heaven in just over an hour, probably faster than it would take you to go to the store in the first place. Plus you make instant friends with plenty of cake to go around, this I promise you.

A killer cake doesn't have to come with muss, fuss, or a fancy stand mixer (though great ones do also come with all three later in this book). A terrific, simple cake can

celebrate the fruits and vegetables of the season, turn any day into a really good day, and require very little dish washing (provided you grease and flour that pan properly!).

Get a youngster or novice baker involved in these simple bundts and pounds and slices from heaven. Or just throw a spur-of-the-moment bundt party for breakfast, tea-or-coffee time, or late at night (my personal fave).

lemon poppy seed bundt cake

makes one 12-cup bundt cake/serves 10 to 12

I got my very sweet tooth from my mother. I don't know where she got it from, but for as long as I can remember, my mother has been a lemon poppy seed cake fanatic. We will meet at Starbucks for a cup of coffee in any town, city, or state supposedly because we need caffeine, but truthfully, because we're guaranteed a slice of lemon pound cake. If I'm baking for her at home, a batch of this cake is a requirement. I am not an only child, but for the 60+ minutes this cake is in the oven, I like to believe I'm the favorite child.

7 to 10	lemons	2 pounds
210g	unsalted butter, melted	1¾ sticks
275g	buttermilk	1¼ cups
145g	honey	¼ cup + 3 T
95g	grapeseed or other neutral oil	½ cup + 2 T
6	large eggs	
1	egg yolk	
530g	ap flour	3¾ cups
440g	sugar	2 cups + 3 T
25g	poppy seeds	3 T + 1 tsp
5g	baking powder	1¼ tsp
5g	baking soda	1¼ tsp
5g	kosher salt	1¼ tsp
1 recipe	lemon-honey glaze (opposite)	

1. Heat the oven to 350°F. Grease and flour a 12-cup bundt pan.

2. Using a Microplane or the finest-toothed side of a box grater, zest the lemons. Do your best to grate only as far down as the yellow part of the skin; the white pith has less lemon flavor and can be bitter. Set zest aside.

3. Cut off the tops and bottoms off each zested lemon. Standing the lemon on its newly flat bottom, slice the white peel off following the curve of the fruit until only the fruit itself is left. Over a bowl to collect the juice, run a paring knife along the sides of each segment to release and remove it from the membranes, being sure to also remove all seeds. Roughly chop the lemon segments into 1-inch chunks. Squeeze the lemon membranes to collect the juice. You should have approximately 15g (⅓ cup) lemon zest, 170g (¾ cup) lemon segments, and 70g (⅓ cup) lemon juice. If you have less of any of these amounts, grab a couple more lemons and repeat the process until you have enough. Combine all these lemon items into one bowl. (If you have too much lemon goodness, make lemonade!)

4. Whisk the melted butter, buttermilk, honey, oil, whole eggs, and egg yolk together in a large bowl.

5. Whisk the flour, sugar, poppy seeds, baking powder, baking soda, and salt together in a separate large bowl.

6. Pour the wet ingredients into the dry ones and stir to combine. If the batter looks lumpy, use a whisk to break up all the lumps. Stir in the lemon zest, juice, and segments.

7. Pour the batter into the bundt pan and bake until the cake rises and puffs, 60 to 70 minutes. At 60 minutes, tap the top of the cake with your fingertips: The cake should bounce back firmly and the center should not be jiggly at all. If it doesn't pass this test, leave the cake in the oven for an additional 5 to 10 minutes.

8. Let the cake cool in the pan for 45 minutes, then run a small butter knife or offset spatula between the edge of the cake and the pan to help release it. Invert the pan onto a wire rack to fully release the cake and let it cool completely before glazing. Put a rimmed baking pan underneath the wire rack to catch the excess glaze.

9. With the cake still on the wire rack, pour the lemon-honey glaze in an even stream all over the top of the cake. (Don't feel like you need to use all the glaze. Save any leftover glaze to serve on the side when you slice the cake.) Let the glaze set up for 15 minutes, then dig in!

10. The cake will keep in the refrigerator, wrapped, for up to 1 week. Let the refrigerated cake sit at room temperature for 1 hour before serving.

lemon-honey glaze

makes about 350g (1 cup)

250g	**confectioners' sugar**	2 cups
2	**lemons, juiced**	60g (¼ cup)
40g	**honey**	2 T

Put the confectioners' sugar in a medium bowl and gently whisk in the lemon juice and honey until a thick, smooth glaze forms. Cover until you're ready to use it.

This is a killer glaze for bundt cakes, donuts, and beyond. I even like sneaking some into a cup of hot water or tea for some zing and a kick! Add a little more or less lemon juice to change the viscosity of the glaze, depending on your preference.

If you make the glaze in advance, nuke it for 5 to 10 seconds to bring it back to a pourable state.

raspberry bundt cake

makes one 12-cup bundt cake/serves 10 to 12

This gal is pretty in pink! She's light, bright, and brilliant for any season or occasion. Raspberry and grapefruit make a killer flavor duo, but feel free to substitute strawberry, rose, or more raspberry or grapefruit, in the puree or glaze. I was never the kind of little one who was into tea parties, but this one inspires me to collect some hilariously floral china, buy fancy gloves for my friends, and get the calligraphied invitations out!

225g	unsalted butter, melted	2 sticks (16 T)
220g	buttermilk	1 cup
150g	grapeseed or other neutral oil	¾ cup
25g	vanilla extract	2 T
5	large eggs	
2	large egg yolks	
450g	cake flour	3½ cups
450g	sugar	2¼ cups
100g	light brown sugar	⅓ cup + 2 T (packed)
8g	baking powder	2 tsp
8g	kosher salt	2 tsp
1 recipe	raspberry puree (page 38)	
1 recipe	grapefruit glaze (page 38)	

1. Heat the oven to 350°F. Grease and flour a 12-cup bundt pan.

2. Whisk the melted butter, buttermilk, oil, vanilla extract, whole eggs, and egg yolks together in a large bowl.

3. Whisk the cake flour, sugar, brown sugar, baking powder, and salt together in a separate large bowl.

4. Pour the wet ingredients into the dry ones and stir to combine. If the batter looks lumpy, use a whisk to break up all the lumps.

5. Pour half of the batter into the bundt pan. Drizzle half of the raspberry puree in an even layer along the batter and use a toothpick to swirl it around. Pour the remaining cake batter on top, then drizzle the remaining raspberry puree on top and swirl it around with a toothpick.

6. Bake until the cake rises and puffs, 60 to 70 minutes. At 60 minutes, tap the top of the cake with your fingertips: The cake should bounce back firmly and the center should not be jiggly at all. If it doesn't pass this test, leave the cake in the oven for an additional 5 to 10 minutes.

7. Let the cake cool in the pan for 45 minutes, then run a small butter knife or offset spatula between the edge of the cake and the pan to help release it. Invert the pan onto a wire rack to fully release the cake and let it cool completely before glazing. Put a rimmed baking pan underneath the wire rack to catch the excess glaze.

(recipe continues)

8. With the cake still on the wire rack, pour the grapefruit glaze in an even stream all over the top of the cake. (Don't feel like you need to use all the glaze. Save any leftover glaze to serve on the side when you slice the cake.) Let the glaze set up for 15 minutes, then dig in!

9. The cake will keep in the refrigerator, wrapped, for up to 1 week. Let the refrigerated cake sit at room temperature for 1 hour before serving.

raspberry puree

makes about 280g (1¼ cups)

340g	raspberries	12 ounces
50g	sugar	¼ cup
0.5g	kosher salt	⅛ tsp

Put the raspberries, sugar, and salt in a blender and buzz until the raspberries are broken down. Pour the raspberry puree through a fine-mesh sieve and set aside until ready to use.

grapefruit glaze

makes about 515g (1½ cups)

1	grapefruit	
360g	confectioners' sugar	3 cups
1g	kosher salt	¼ tsp

1. Using a Microplane or the finest-toothed side of a box grater, zest the grapefruit. Do your best to grate only as far down as the yellow-pink part of the skin; the white pith has less grapefruit flavor and can be bitter. Set zest aside.

2. Cut off the top and bottom of the grapefruit. Standing the grapefruit up on its newly flat bottom, slice off the white peel following the curve of the fruit until only the fruit itself is left. Over a bowl, run a paring knife along the sides of each segment to release and remove it from the membranes, being sure to also remove all seeds. Chop the segments up into small chunks, about the size of peas. Weigh out 130g (½ cup) of the segments and put them in a bowl with the zest. (Eat the leftover segments or save them for a late-night snack.)

3. Squeeze all of the remaining juice from the grapefruit membranes into a separate bowl. Measure out 25g (2 tablespoons) and add that juice to the bowl with the grapefruit segments and zest.

4. Whisk the confectioners' sugar and salt into the grapefruit concoction and use immediately to glaze the bundt cake.

This glaze adds extra fresh flavor and a little surprise texture!

If you make the glaze in advance, nuke it for 5 to 10 seconds to bring it back to a pourable state.

Add a little more or less grapefruit juice to change the viscosity of the glaze, depending on your preference.

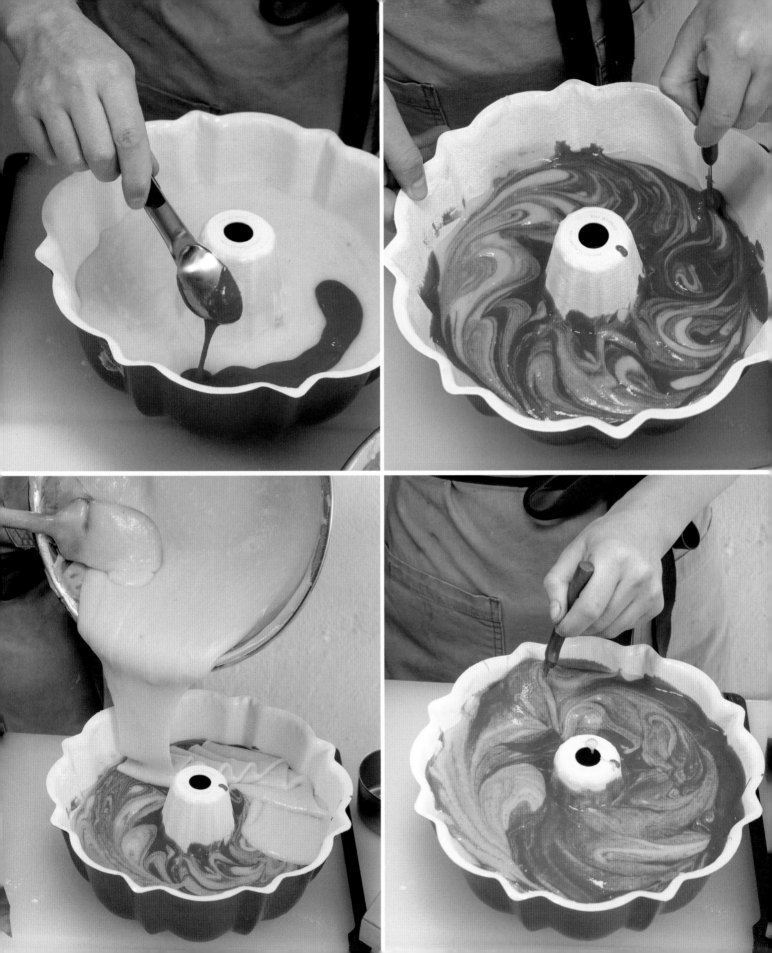

cherry cola bundt cake

makes one 12-cup bundt cake/serves 10 to 12

Though I grew up in the Midwest and with somewhat Southern sensibilities, I was never allowed to drink real soda as a kid, so you can imagine how far my eyes popped out of my head when I found out there was such thing as 7-Up cake—and even more so, Coca-Cola cake. I wanted to love them so, but I was always underwhelmed by soda cakes. Turns out, extracts were the secret ingredients for this magnificent idea of a cake. Cherry cola feels like my spirit animal more days than not, so it felt mandatory to make a cherry cola bundt cake a reality.

Read up on cherry puree (see page 17) and cola extract (see page 15).

230g	unsalted butter, melted	2 sticks (16 T)
150g	cherry cola	⅔ cup + 1 T
150g	cherry puree	⅔ cup
100g	grapeseed or other neutral oil	½ cup
30g	molasses	2 T
10g	vanilla extract	2½ tsp
10g	cola extract	2½ tsp
5	large eggs	
2	large egg yolks	
450g	cake flour	3½ cups
450g	sugar	2¼ cups
100g	light brown sugar	⅓ cup + 2 T (packed)
8g	baking powder	2 tsp
8g	kosher salt	2 tsp
1 recipe	cherry cola glaze (page 42)	

1. Heat the oven to 350°F. Grease and flour a 12-cup bundt pan.

2. Whisk the melted butter, cherry cola, cherry puree, oil, molasses, vanilla extract, cola extract, whole eggs, and egg yolks together in a large bowl.

3. Whisk the cake flour, sugar, brown sugar, baking powder, and salt together in a separate large bowl.

4. Pour the wet ingredients into the dry ones and stir to combine. If the batter looks lumpy, use a whisk to break up all the lumps.

5. Pour the batter into the bundt pan and bake until the cake rises and puffs, 60 to 70 minutes. At 60 minutes, tap the top of the cake with your fingertips: The cake should bounce back firmly and the center should not be jiggly at all. If it doesn't pass this test, leave the cake in the oven for an additional 5 to 10 minutes.

6. Let the cake cool in the pan for 45 minutes, then run a small butter knife or offset spatula between the edge of the cake and the pan to help release it. Invert the pan onto a wire rack to fully release the cake and let it cool completely before glazing. Put a rimmed baking pan underneath the wire rack to catch the excess glaze.

(recipe continues)

7. With the cake still on the wire rack, pour the cherry cola glaze in an even stream all over the top of the cake. (Don't feel like you need to use all the glaze. Save any leftover glaze to serve on the side when you slice the cake.) Let the glaze set up for 15 minutes, then dig in!

8. The cake will keep in the refrigerator, wrapped, for up to 1 week. Let the refrigerated cake sit at room temperature for 1 hour before serving.

cherry cola glaze

makes about 300g (1 cup)

60g	cream cheese	2 ounces
30g	unsalted butter	2 T
180g	confectioners' sugar	1½ cups
30g	cherry cola	2 T
2g	cola extract	½ tsp
1g	vanilla extract	¼ tsp
0.5g	kosher salt	⅛ tsp
1 or 2 drops	red food coloring (optional)	

If you make the glaze in advance, nuke it for 5 to 10 seconds to bring it back to a pourable state.

Feel free to use a little more or less cherry cola to change the viscosity of the glaze, depending on your preference.

1. Heat the cream cheese and butter together in the microwave for 30 seconds. At this point the butter should be mostly melted and the cream cheese should be soft. (If it's not, zap it for an additional 10 seconds.) Stir the mixture together vigorously until you have a smooth concoction.

2. Put the cream cheese mixture in a medium bowl and whisk in the confectioners' sugar, cherry cola, cola extract, vanilla extract, salt, and food coloring (if using). Whisk everything together until you have a smooth, lump-free glaze. Use immediately.

pistachio bundt cake

makes one 12-cup bundt cake/serves 10 to 12

Hello, old friend. You've been with me since the great cake pursuit of 2005. I never grew up with pistachios (way too far-out fancy for my taste as a kiddo), so I thought the birthday cake victim who enthusiastically told me of an earth-shatteringly delicious pistachio cake was just plain cray. Boy, was I wrong. I now make you for special occasions *and* the everyday because. You're. That. Good. I also like to convince myself you're a reasonable post-run snack since you have so many nuts in you. Protein, am I right?!

260g	pistachios	2 cups
75g	grapeseed or other neutral oil	⅓ cup + 1 T
130g	grapeseed or other neutral oil	⅔ cup
75g	heavy cream	⅓ cup + 1 tsp
55g	light corn syrup	3 T + 1 tsp
330g	large egg whites	from 11 large eggs
260g	confectioners' sugar	2 cups + 2 T
220g	ap flour	1½ cups + 3 T
210g	almond flour	2¼ cups
150g	sugar	¾ cup
100g	instant pistachio pudding mix	one 3.4-ounce package
11g	baking powder	1 T
9g	kosher salt	2¼ tsp
1 recipe	pistachio glaze (page 46)	
75g	chopped toasted pistachios, for garnish	½ cup

1. Heat the oven to 350°F. Grease and flour a 12-cup bundt pan.

2. Put the pistachios in a microwave-safe bowl and zap them for 30 seconds to warm them. (Warming them helps them break down into a paste more easily.) In a blender, puree the warm pistachios and the 75g (⅓ cup + 1 tablespoon) oil until a coarse paste forms, with pistachio bits no larger than the size of sesame seeds.

3. Whisk the pistachio paste, the 130g (⅔ cup) oil, heavy cream, and corn syrup together in a large bowl.

4. Add the egg whites to the wet ingredients and whisk everything together until you have an evenly combined concoction.

5. Whisk the confectioners' sugar, AP flour, almond flour, sugar, pudding mix, baking powder, and salt together in a separate large bowl.

6. Pour the wet ingredients into the dry ones and stir to combine. If the batter looks lumpy, use a whisk to break up all the lumps.

For a gluten-free hack, substitute gluten-free flour for the AP flour (just as you can in any recipe in this book), but since this recipe already features almond flour, just use all almond flour.

(recipe continues)

7. Pour the batter into the bundt pan and bake until the cake rises and puffs, 60 to 70 minutes. At 60 minutes, tap the top of the cake with your fingertips: The cake should bounce back firmly and the center should not be jiggly at all. If it doesn't pass this test, leave the cake in the oven for an additional 5 to 10 minutes.

8. Let the cake cool in the pan for 45 minutes, then run a small butter knife or offset spatula between the edge of the cake and the pan to help release it. Invert the pan onto a wire rack to fully release the cake and let it cool completely before glazing. Put a rimmed baking pan underneath the wire rack to catch the excess glaze.

9. With the cake still on the wire rack, pour the pistachio glaze in an even stream all over the top of the cake. (Don't feel like you need to use all the glaze. Save any leftover glaze to serve on the side when you slice the cake.) Let the glaze sit for 5 minutes, then sprinkle the top of the cake with the toasted pistachios. Let the glaze continue to set up for 10 more minutes, then dig in!

10. The cake will keep in the refrigerator, wrapped, for up to 1 week. Let the refrigerated cake sit at room temperature for 1 hour before serving.

pistachio glaze

makes about 360g (1¼ cups)

95g	pistachios	¾ cup
50g	grapeseed or other neutral oil	¼ cup
160g	confectioners' sugar	1⅓ cups
45g	whole milk	3 T
10g	grapeseed or other neutral oil	1 T
0.5g	kosher salt	⅛ tsp

1. Put the pistachios in a microwave-safe bowl and zap them for 30 seconds to warm them. (Warming them helps them break down into a paste more easily.) In a blender, puree the warm pistachios and 50g (¼ cup) oil until a smooth paste forms (this is purposefully a different consistency than the pureed pistachio element for the cake batter itself).

2. Whisk the pistachio paste, confectioners' sugar, milk, 10g (1 tablespoon) oil, and salt together in a medium bowl just before you are ready to glaze the cake.

Though I love a good GI-Joe, shades of green, pistachio-on-pistachio moment, I really love this cake with a green-white zebra glaze vibe using the Lemon-Honey Glaze (page 35) to make the white stripes.

If you make the glaze in advance, nuke it for 5 to 10 seconds to bring it back to a pourable state. Feel free to use a little more or a less milk to change the viscosity of the glaze, depending on your preference.

mint julep bundt cake

makes one 12-cup bundt cake/serves 10 to 12

Though I've never been to the Kentucky Derby IRL, I love to craft a killer fascinator every spring and raucously root for a horse I only just met on TV minutes before. I like to fancy myself a Southerner at heart, because they have such soul, and of course, because their cocktail claim to fame is the mint julep. I'm not typically one to mix booze with baking, but I just can't deny the oaky bourbon notes and how they make the fresh muddled mint sing, even in a simple bundt cake.

240g	unsalted butter, melted	2 sticks (16 T) + 1 T
90g	lemon juice	⅓ cup
70g	buttermilk	¼ cup + 1 T
70g	bourbon	¼ cup + 1 T
75g	grapeseed or other neutral oil	¼ cup + 1½ T
7g	lemon extract	2 tsp
5	large eggs	
3	large egg yolks	
600g	sugar	3 cups
450g	cake flour	3½ cups
8g	baking powder	2 tsp
8g	kosher salt	2 tsp
1 recipe	bourbon-lemon glaze (page 48)	
15	fresh mint leaves, torn	
15	fresh mint leaves, whole	

1. Heat the oven to 350°F. Grease and flour a 12-cup bundt pan.

2. Whisk the melted butter, lemon juice, buttermilk, bourbon, oil, lemon extract, whole eggs, and egg yolks together in a large bowl.

3. Whisk the sugar, cake flour, baking powder, and salt together in a separate large bowl.

4. Pour the wet ingredients into the dry ones and stir to combine. If the batter looks lumpy, use a whisk to break up all the lumps.

5. Pour the batter into the bundt pan and bake until the cake rises and puffs, 60 to 70 minutes. At 60 minutes, tap the top of the cake with your fingertips: The cake should bounce back firmly and the center should not be jiggly at all. If it doesn't pass this test, leave the cake in the oven for an additional 5 to 10 minutes.

6. Let the cake cool in the pan for 45 minutes, then run a small butter knife or offset spatula between the edge of the cake and the pan to help release it. Invert the pan onto a wire rack to fully release the cake and let it cool completely before glazing. Put a rimmed baking pan underneath the wire rack to catch the excess glaze.

If you're a sober or underage friend, substitute lemon for bourbon! I'm not really a drinker, either. (I'm much more interested in cake!)

(recipe continues)

7. With the cake still on the wire rack, pour the bourbon-lemon glaze in an even stream all over the top of the cake. Immediately garnish the cake with the torn mint leaves by adhering them to the glaze. (Don't feel like you need to use all the glaze. Save any leftover glaze to serve on the side when you slice the cake.) Let the glaze set up for 15 minutes.

8. Just before serving, take the whole mint leaves and stack them on top of each other. Roll the leaves up into a small tube, like a fruit roll-up, then use a chef's knife to thinly slice the mint-tube crosswise into a chiffonade. Garnish each serving with some extra glaze and a little mint chiffonade to show you care.

9. The cake will keep in the refrigerator, wrapped, for up to 1 week. Let the refrigerated cake sit at room temperature for 1 hour before serving.

bourbon mint soak

makes about 220g (1 cup)

100g	sugar	½ cup
60g	water	¼ cup
20	fresh mint leaves, washed	
60g	bourbon	¼ cup

If you really need to take the edge off, this leftover soak works great on the rocks with an extra splash of bourbon!

1. Bring the sugar and water to a boil in a small saucepan. Once it boils, remove it from the heat and add the mint leaves. Cover the saucepan and let the mint leaves steep for 10 minutes.

2. Pour the syrup and mint into a blender, add the bourbon, and blend for 30 seconds, until the mint is broken down. Strain the mixture through a fine-mesh sieve. The soak will keep in the refrigerator, covered, for 1 month.

bourbon-lemon glaze

makes about 175g (⅔ cup)

130g	confectioners' sugar	1 cup + 1 T
40g	bourbon mint soak (at right)	¼ cup
4g	lemon extract	1 tsp
2g	kosher salt	½ tsp

If you make the glaze in advance, nuke it for 5 to 10 seconds to bring it back to a pourable state.

Feel free to use a little more or less bourbon mint soak to change the viscosity of the glaze, depending on your preference.

Whisk all of the ingredients together in a bowl and use immediately.

molasses-rye bundt cake

makes one 12-cup bundt cake/serves 10 to 12

Real Talk: This cake is deep. It is not for the faint of heart. It speaks to the kooky, crazy, savory-yet-sweet side of the kitchen. Be brave, give it a try. We love to eat it with a glass of rich, thick stout beer, sitting in a well-worn leather chair.

10g	caraway seeds	1 T
230g	unsalted butter, melted	2 sticks (16 T) + ½ T
220g	buttermilk	1 cup
150g	grapeseed or other neutral oil	¾ cup
55g	molasses	¼ cup
6	large eggs	
600g	sugar	3 cups
200g	light brown sugar	¾ cup + 2 T (packed)
360g	cake flour	2¾ cups + 2 T
120g	rye flour	1 cup
20g	ground caraway	¼ cup
20g	kosher salt	1 T + 2 tsp
8g	baking powder	2 tsp
1 recipe	molasses-stout glaze (page 52)	

1. Heat the oven to 350°F. Grease and flour a 12-cup bundt pan.

2. Put the caraway seeds on a sheet pan and toast them in the oven until they darken and become insanely fragrant, about 10 minutes. Leave the oven on.

3. Whisk the melted butter, buttermilk, oil, molasses, and eggs together in a large bowl.

4. Whisk both sugars, the cake flour, rye flour, ground caraway, salt, baking powder, and toasted caraway seeds together in a separate large bowl.

5. Pour the wet ingredients into the dry ones and stir to combine. Use a whisk to break up the lumps if needed.

6. Pour the batter into the bundt pan and bake until the cake rises and puffs, 60 to 70 minutes. At 60 minutes, tap the top of the cake with your fingertips: The cake should bounce back firmly and the center should not be jiggly at all. If it doesn't pass this test, leave the cake in the oven for an additional 5 to 10 minutes.

7. Let the cake cool in the pan for 45 minutes, then run a small butter knife or offset spatula between the edge of the cake and the pan to help release it. Invert the pan onto a wire rack to fully release the cake and let it cool completely before glazing. Put a rimmed baking pan underneath the wire rack to catch the excess glaze.

(recipe continues)

8. With the cake still on the wire rack, pour the molasses-stout glaze in an even stream all over the top of the cake. (Don't feel like you need to use all the glaze. Save any leftover glaze to serve on the side when you slice the cake.) Let the glaze set up for 15 minutes, then dig in!

9. The cake will keep in the refrigerator, wrapped, for up to 1 week. Let the refrigerated cake sit at room temperature for 1 hour before serving.

molasses-stout glaze

makes about 385g (¾ cup)

110g	cream cheese	4 ounces
15g	molasses	1 T
220g	confectioners' sugar	2 cups
40g	stout beer	2 T + 1½ tsp
1g	kosher salt	¼ tsp

1. Heat the cream cheese and molasses in the microwave for 30 seconds.

2. Put the cream cheese mixture in a medium bowl and use a whisk to stir in the confectioners' sugar, stout, and salt. Use immediately to glaze the cake.

If you want to make your glaze booze-free, just use milk instead of stout. You can even do half milk, half stout if you prefer just a hint of booze.

If you make the glaze in advance, nuke it for 5 to 10 seconds to bring it back to a pourable state.

Feel free to use a little more or less beer (or milk) to change the viscosity of the glaze, depending on your preference.

sesame pound cake

makes 1 pound cake/serves 8 to 10

I never really understood the beauty and nuance of the flavor of sesame seeds until I once accidentally bought a bar of halvah instead of a Snickers. I was busy multitasking—'gramming a killer pic while also picking up a sugar-fix snack. I figured any candy bar that sat right next to a Snickers must be in great company. How different could it be?! Turns out wildly so. The feel of halvah is light and airy, textured with curious sugary splinters. And its flavor, bitter yet nutty, is much more sophisticated than peanut butter. It's made from sesame seeds ground into a paste called tahini, and it opened me up to a world of baking with tahini. This cake is part toffee, part sesame, and out of control with some fresh fruit jam and a pat of butter.

Choose your pan wisely for this bad boy. See page 20.

115g	unsalted butter, melted	1 stick (8 T)
110g	buttermilk	½ cup
75g	tahini	⅓ cup
3	large eggs	
250g	sugar	1¼ cups
60g	light brown sugar	¼ cup + 1 tsp (packed)
185g	cake flour	1½ cups + 2 T
4g	baking powder	1 tsp
4g	kosher salt	1 tsp
170g	sesame seed brittle (opposite)	1½ cups
5g	cake flour	1½ tsp

1. Heat the oven to 350°F. Grease and flour a loaf pan.

2. Whisk the melted butter, buttermilk, tahini, and eggs together in a large bowl.

3. Whisk both sugars, the 185g (1½ cups plus 2 tablespoons) cake flour, baking powder, and salt together in a separate large bowl.

4. Pour the wet ingredients into the dry ones and stir to combine. If the batter looks lumpy, use a whisk to break up all the lumps.

5. Toss 112g (1 cup) of the sesame seed brittle with the 5g (1½ teaspoons) cake flour, then stir into the batter.

6. Pour the batter into the loaf pan and sprinkle the remaining brittle on top. Bake until the cake rises and puffs, 60 to 70 minutes. At 60 minutes, tap the top of the cake with your fingertips: The cake should bounce back firmly and the center should not be jiggly at all. If it doesn't pass this test, leave the cake in the oven for an additional 5 to 10 minutes.

7. Let the cake cool in the pan for 45 minutes, then run a small butter knife or offset spatula between the edge of the cake and the pan to help release it. Invert the pan onto a wire rack to fully release the cake. Turn the cake right side up and let it cool completely before slicing and serving.

8. The cake will keep in the refrigerator, wrapped, for up to 1 week.

sesame seed brittle

makes about 170g (1½ cups)

100g	sugar	½ cup
70g	sesame seeds, untoasted	½ cup

1. Line a quarter-sheet pan with a silicone baking mat.

2. Make a dry caramel by heating the sugar in a heavy-bottomed saucepan over medium-high heat. As soon as the sugar starts to melt, use a heatproof spatula to move it constantly around the pan so that it melts evenly. Cook and stir until the caramel is a deep, dark amber, 3 to 5 minutes after it just starts to melt.

3. Once the caramel has reached the target color, take it off the heat and quickly stir in the sesame seeds. Once the sesame seeds are completely covered in sugar, pour them out onto the sheet pan and use a spatula to spread them out as thinly as possible. Work quickly because the caramel will set fast and become impossible to spread around. Let the sesame seed brittle cool completely.

4. Once cooled, use a rolling pin or mallet to break up the sesame brittle into tiny lentil-size pieces. Use a blender or food processor to break it up further into a sandy consistency.

rhubarb-elderflower pound cake

makes 1 pound cake/serves 8 to 10

This pound cake makes me want to sing all about *Spring!* from the mountaintops. It transports me and makes me feel like I'm an extra in the closing scene of *The Sound of Music*. I make as much rhubarb-elderflower jam as possible during the few short weeks rhubarb is in season in New York, so I can schmear and goo to my heart's desire and never worry about saying auf Wiedersehen to rhubarb or worrying when we'll meet again.

Choose your pan wisely for this bad boy. See page 20.

125g	unsalted butter, melted	1 stick (8 T) + 1 T
125g	buttermilk	½ cup + 1 T
85g	grapeseed or other neutral oil	⅓ cup + 2 T
12g	vanilla extract	1 T
3	large eggs	
1	large egg yolk	
250g	sugar	1¼ cups
60g	light brown sugar	¼ cup (packed)
245g	cake flour	2 cups
4g	baking powder	1 tsp
4.5g	kosher salt	1 tsp
1 recipe	rhubarb-elderflower goo (page 60)	

1. Heat the oven to 350°F. Grease and flour a 1-pound loaf pan.

2. Whisk the melted butter, buttermilk, oil, vanilla extract, whole eggs, and egg yolk together in a large bowl.

3. Whisk both sugars, the cake flour, baking powder, and salt together in a separate large bowl.

4. Pour the wet ingredients into the dry ones and stir to combine. Use a whisk to break up the lumps if needed.

5. Pour the batter into the loaf pan and bake until the cake rises and puffs, 60 to 70 minutes. At 60 minutes, tap the top of the cake with your fingertips: The cake should bounce back firmly and the center should not be jiggly at all. If it doesn't pass this test, leave the cake in the oven for an additional 5 to 10 minutes.

6. Let the cake cool in the pan for 45 minutes, then run a small butter knife or offset spatula between the edge of the cake and the pan to help release it. Invert the pan onto a wire rack to fully release the cake.

7. Use a spoon or offset spatula to smear the rhubarb-elderflower goo all over the top of the cake. Don't feel like you must use all of the goo; save some to serve on the side.

8. The cake will keep in the refrigerator, wrapped, for up to 1 week. Let the refrigerated cake sit at room temperature for 1 hour before serving.

(recipe continues)

rhubarb-elderflower goo

makes about 330g (1 cup)

25g	unsalted butter	2 T
60g	cream cheese	2 ounces
110g	confectioners' sugar	1 cup
1g	kosher salt	¼ tsp
2g	vanilla extract	½ tsp
135g	rhubarb-elderflower jam (at right)	½ cup

1. Heat the butter and the cream cheese together in the microwave for 30 seconds, or until the cream cheese has softened and the butter has melted.

2. Put the cream cheese mixture in a medium bowl and stir in the confectioners' sugar, salt, and vanilla extract.

3. Whisk in the rhubarb-elderflower jam. Continue to whisk everything together until you have a smooth, gooey glaze. Use immediately.

rhubarb-elderflower jam

makes about 265g (1 cup)

280g	fresh rhubarb	10 ounces
100g	sugar	½ cup
2g	pectin NH	½ tsp
0.5g	kosher salt	⅛ tsp
20g	lemon juice	1 T + 1½ tsp
25g	elderflower syrup	1 T + 1½ tsp

1. Wash the rhubarb and slice each stalk crosswise into ¼-inch chunks.

2. Whisk together the sugar, pectin, and salt in a medium pot or saucepan. Add the rhubarb and toss everything together until the rhubarb is well coated. Slowly stir in the lemon juice and bring the mixture to a full, rolling boil over medium-high heat. Reduce the heat and cook at a simmer to activate the pectin. Continue cooking until the jam coats the back of a spoon and everything has reduced to 1 cup, about 25 minutes.

3. Remove the jam from the heat and whisk in the elderflower syrup. Let cool completely before using it. (You need only 135g [½ cup] of the jam for the rhubarb-elderflower goo, so save the remaining jam to serve with the cake or with toast!) The jam can be stored in an airtight container in the fridge for up to 2 weeks.

Fear not, you are just a few clicks and a day away from elderflower syrup showing up at your doorstep. We love d'Arbo or Belvoir. This jam should not be made without it—it makes it special, I'm talking next level. Leftover elderflower syrup (if you don't go crazy making huge batches of jam) is an incredible flavor agent in any mock(cock)tail.

compost pound cake

makes 1 pound cake/serves 8 to 10

We often dream in skies studded with compost cookies, and just can't control when pretzels, potato chips, coffee, oats, graham crackers, chocolate, and butterscotch chips make their way down to earth and into a bowl of pound cake batter.

This cake is an homage to the team of hardbodies at Milk Bar who have been mixing this seemingly odd collection of cookie mixins since November 15, 2008. That's when we opened the doors to our little bakery, having no clue what the world outside would think of this kitchen-sink, fudgy-on-the-inside, crispy-on-the-outside, salty-yet-sweet cookie. This pound cake version is pretty darn special, too.

Choose your pan wisely for this bad boy. See page 20.

90g	unsalted butter, melted	7 T
90g	buttermilk	⅓ cup
30g	grapeseed or other neutral oil	3 T
10g	vanilla extract	2½ tsp
3	large eggs	
240g	cake flour	2 cups
180g	sugar	¾ cup + 3 T
30g	light brown sugar	2 T (packed)
30g	old-fashioned rolled oats	¼ cup
4g	ground coffee	1 T
4g	baking powder	1 tsp
4g	kosher salt	1 tsp
75g	mini chocolate chips	⅓ cup + 1 T
75g	mini butterscotch chips	⅓ cup + 1 T
50g	graham crackers, crumbled	⅓ cup
10g	ap flour	1 T + 1 tsp
65g	mini chocolate chips	⅓ cup
2.5g	grapeseed or other neutral oil	½ tsp
75g	mini butterscotch chips	⅓ cup + 1 T

10g	grapeseed or other neutral oil	2 tsp
25g	potato chips	1 cup
25g	mini pretzels	½ cup

1. Heat the oven to 350°F. Grease and flour a 1-pound loaf pan.

2. Whisk the melted butter, buttermilk, 30g (3 tablespoons) oil, vanilla extract, and eggs together in a large bowl.

3. Whisk the cake flour, sugar, brown sugar, oats, coffee, baking powder, and salt together in a separate large bowl.

4. Pour the wet ingredients into the dry ones and stir to combine. If the batter looks lumpy, use a whisk to break up all the lumps.

5. In a separate bowl, toss the 75g (⅓ cup + 1 T) chocolate chips, 50g (¼ cup) butterscotch chips, and graham cracker crumbles, with the AP flour. (Tossing them in flour first helps to keep them from sinking to the bottom of the cake while it bakes.)

(recipe continues)

6. Pour half of the compost batter into the loaf pan, then fold the remaining batter into the bowl with the chocolate chips, butterscotch chips, and graham cracker crumbles. Pour this mixture on top of the batter in the loaf pan.

7. Bake until the cake rises and puffs, about 70 minutes. At 60 minutes, tap the top of the cake with your fingertips: The cake should bounce back and the center should no longer be jiggly. If it doesn't pass this test, leave the cake in the oven for an additional 5 to 10 minutes.

8. Let the cake cool in the pan for 45 minutes, then run a small butter knife or offset spatula between the edge of the cake and the pan to help release the cake from the pan. Invert the pan onto a wire rack to fully release the cake. Turn the cake right side up and let it cool completely.

9. Melt the 65g (⅓ cup plus 1 teaspoon) mini chocolate chips and 2.5g (½ teaspoon) of oil in the microwave in 30-second increments. Repeat this step with the 75g (⅓ cup plus 1 tablespoon) butterscotch chips and 10g (2 teaspoons) oil in a separate container.

10. Decorate the top of the compost pound cake by dipping the potato chips and pretzels, broken up if desired, in the melted chocolate and butterscotch, using each as a glue to stick the chips and pretzels to the top. Put the cake in the fridge and let the chocolate harden and cool for 5 minutes, then dig in!

11. The cake will keep in the refrigerator, wrapped, for up to 1 week. Let the refrigerated cake sit at room temperature for 1 hour before serving.

pretzel pound cake

makes 1 pound cake/serves 8 to 10

Pretzel cake came later to us in life at Milk Bar—2011, I believe it was. When you hang around sweet things so often, it's pretty standard to always be in pursuit of a salty bite to help balance out your sugar-laced belly. Pretzels, as you can imagine, are a hot commodity. But after a few years of eating a bite of cake and then a pretzel and then a bite of cake and then a pretzel . . . you start to really question why you're not just eating pretzel cake. It is my absolute favorite way to get both my sweet and salty fix. The Pretzel Layer Cake (page 246) and Pretzel Cake Truffles (page 200) are also quite epic.

Choose your pan wisely for this bad boy. See page 20.

200g	mini pretzels	4 cups
150g	unsalted butter, melted	1 stick (8 T) + 3 T
110g	grapeseed or other neutral oil	½ cup + 2 tsp
100g	buttermilk	⅓ cup + 2 T
20g	molasses	1 T + 1 tsp
4	large eggs	
330g	sugar	1½ cups + 3 T
120g	cake flour	1 cup
17g	kosher salt	1 T + 1 tsp
7g	baking powder	1¾ tsp
3g	baking soda	¾ tsp
1 recipe	burnt honey glaze (opposite)	

1. Heat the oven to 350°F. Grease and flour a 1-pound loaf pan.

2. In a blender or food processor, grind the pretzels into a fine powder. You should have about 2 cups of pretzel powder. Set the powder aside.

3. Whisk the melted butter, oil, buttermilk, molasses, and eggs together in a large bowl.

4. Whisk the sugar, cake flour, salt, baking powder, baking soda, and pretzel powder together in a separate large bowl.

5. Pour the wet ingredients into the dry ones and stir to combine. If the batter looks lumpy, use a whisk to break up all the lumps.

6. Pour the batter into the loaf pan and bake until the cake rises and puffs, 60 to 70 minutes. At 60 minutes, tap the top of the cake with your fingertips: The cake should bounce back firmly and the center should not be jiggly at all. If it doesn't pass this test, leave the cake in the oven for an additional 5 to 10 minutes.

7. Let the cake cool in the pan for 45 minutes, then run a small butter knife or offset spatula between the edge of the cake and the pan to help release it. Invert the pan onto a wire rack to fully release the cake. Turn the cake right side up. Put a rimmed baking pan under the wire rack to catch the excess glaze.

8. With the cake still on the wire rack, pour the burnt honey glaze in an even stream all over the top of the cake. (Don't feel like you need to use all the glaze! Save any left over to serve on the side when you slice the cake.) Let the glaze continue to set up for 15 more minutes, then dig in!

9. The cake will keep in the refrigerator, wrapped, for up to 1 week. Let the refrigerated cake sit at room temperature for 1 hour before serving.

burnt honey glaze

makes about 420g (¾ cup)

310g	**honey**	⅔ cup
110g	**heavy cream**	½ cup
2g	**kosher salt**	½ tsp

Once cooled, or if you make the glaze in advance, nuke it for 5 to 10 seconds to bring it back to a pourable state.

Feel free to use a little more or a little less cream to change the viscosity of the glaze, depending on your preference.

1. Put the honey in a large heavy-bottomed pot. (Use a much larger and deeper pot than you think you will need; the honey will bubble up and rise in the cooking process.) Heat the honey over high heat until it darkens in color and begins to smell a little nutty, 6 to 7 minutes.

2. Slowly and carefully drizzle in the heavy cream. The honey will really start to bubble up at this point and a bunch of steam will come pouring out of the pot. Be careful, because steam burns are the worst.

3. Once the honey has settled down and the steam has dissipated, use a heatproof spatula to stir the concoction together until everything is smooth, and stir in the salt.

4. Transfer the burnt honey glaze to a small container and put it in the refrigerator for at least 1 hour, until it has thickened to an ooey-gooey glazey consistency.

5. The glaze will keep in the refrigerator, in an airtight container, for up to 2 weeks.

burnt miso pound cake

makes 1 pound cake/serves 8 to 10

In all honesty, I would never have even contemplated putting miso (a deeply flavored fermented soybean paste) into a dessert until I challenged myself to try every ingredient in the Momofuku dry storage prep kitchen in 2006. Wowza, was I surprised by the incredible flavor miso brought to sweet, butter-based sauces like butterscotch and buttery pound cakes. I quickly learned that the combination of savory miso, the bright yet homey flavor of an apple, and the rich vibe of sour cream made an unstoppable flavor trio. I use shiro miso when I bake. Also referred to as white miso, it is the mildest on the market and has the perfect amount of saltiness to go along with sweet concoctions.

100g	shiro miso	5 T
145g	buttermilk	⅔ cup
100g	grapeseed or other neutral oil	½ cup
150g	unsalted butter, melted	1 stick (8 T) + 3 T
5	large eggs	
310g	sugar	1½ cups + 1 T
290g	cake flour	2⅓ cup
65g	light brown sugar	¼ cup + 1 tsp (packed)
5g	baking powder	1¼ tsp
1g	kosher salt	¼ tsp
1 recipe	apple compote (page 175)	
1 recipe	sour whipped cream (page 68)	

1. Heat the oven to 400°F. Line a baking sheet with a silicone baking mat.

2. Spread the miso out in an even layer, about ¼ inch thick, on the lined baking sheet. Bake it until the miso is browned and quite burnt around the edges, 10 to 15 minutes. Don't be a ninny! The edges should be quite burnt and there should be patches of burnt spots all over the top. Remove it from the oven and let it cool slightly.

3. Reduce the oven to 350°F. Grease and flour a 1-pound loaf pan.

4. Scrape the miso into a blender. Add the buttermilk and oil and blend until smooth. Pour the mixture into a large bowl. Whisk the melted butter and eggs into the miso mixture.

5. Whisk the sugar, cake flour, brown sugar, baking powder, and salt together in a separate large bowl.

6. Pour the wet ingredients into the dry ones and stir to combine. If the batter looks lumpy, use a whisk to break up all the lumps.

7. Pour the batter into the loaf pan and bake until the cake rises and puffs, about

Choose your pan wisely for this bad boy. See page 20.

Shiro miso is easy to nab in the international aisle of your grocery store.

(recipe continues)

80 minutes. At 75 minutes, tap the top of the cake with your fingertips: The cake should bounce back and the center should no longer be jiggly. If it doesn't pass this test, leave the cake in the oven for an additional 3 to 5 minutes.

8. Let the cake cool in the pan for 45 minutes, then run a small butter knife or offset spatula between the edge of the cake and the pan to help release it. Invert the pan onto a wire rack to fully release the cake. Turn the cake right side up and let it cool completely before slicing.

9. Before serving, toast the slices lightly then dollop each with apple compote and sour whipped cream.

sour whipped cream

makes about 245g (1 cup)

110g	heavy cream	½ cup
110g	sour cream	½ cup
20g	confectioners' sugar	¼ cup
4g	vanilla extract	1 tsp

Add all of the ingredients to a medium bowl and use a whisk to whip them into soft peaks, about 2 minutes, depending on how fast and furious a whisker you are.

banana green curry pound cake

makes 1 pound cake/serves 8 to 10

This spicy-sweet combo was something the world's first "Milk man" (the rest of us were women), James Mark, dreamed up in individual mini-loaf form. It's exotic, great for breakfast, and edgy in all the right ways. Toasting and serving it with black pepper butter makes it even more heavenly.

280g	*rrrrrrrrripe* **bananas**	2 medium
170g	**unsalted butter, melted**	1½ sticks (12 T)
165g	**sour cream**	¾ cup
18g	**green curry paste**	1 T
2g	**banana extract**	½ tsp
2	**large eggs**	
1	**large egg yolk**	
200g	**sugar**	1 cup
135g	**ap flour**	1 cup
120g	**cake flour**	1 cup
6g	**baking powder**	1½ tsp
6g	**baking soda**	1 tsp
5g	**kosher salt**	1¼ tsp
1 recipe	**black pepper butter, softened** (page 259)	

1. Heat the oven to 350°F. Grease and flour a 1-pound loaf pan.

2. Put the mushy, ripe bananas in a bowl. Mash with a whisk or spoon, if your bananas aren't ripe enough to nearly be liquid already.

3. Whisk the melted butter, sour cream, green curry paste, banana extract, whole eggs, and egg yolk together in a large bowl. Add the bananas and stir to combine.

4. Whisk the sugar, AP flour, cake flour, baking powder, baking soda, and salt together in a separate large bowl.

5. Pour the wet ingredients into the dry ones and stir to combine. If the batter looks lumpy, use a whisk to break up all the lumps.

6. Pour the batter into the loaf pan and bake until the cake rises and puffs, 60 to 70 minutes. At 60 minutes, tap the top of the cake with your fingertips: The cake should bounce back firmly and the center should not be jiggly at all. If it doesn't pass this test, leave the cake in the oven for an additional 5 to 10 minutes.

7. Let the cake cool in the pan for 45 minutes, then run a small butter knife or offset spatula between the edge of the cake and the pan to help release it. Invert the pan onto a wire rack to fully release the cake and let it cool completely before serving.

8. To serve, choose to toast it (or not) and slather each slice with black pepper butter.

9. The cake will keep in the refrigerator, wrapped, for up to 1 week. Let the refrigerated cake sit at room temperature for 1 hour before serving.

Read up on the pro art of ripening bananas (see page 13)!

Green curry paste is easy to nab in the international aisle of your grocery store.

The combo of AP and cake flour keeps this cake light but still banana-bread–like.

Choose your pan wisely for this bad boy. See page 20.

celery root pound cake

makes 1 pound cake/serves 8 to 10

Growing up, I was never one to eat my vegetables, and I can't quite figure out why my mom didn't pull a fast one like this on me. My favorite part of this cake is that it has a secret dose of vegetables in it. Whole wheat flour, too. A healthy-ish cake?! What virtuosity! And beyond that, the root vegetable is highly interchangeable—if you're into beets, sub them in one-for-one for the celery root! Same goes for parsnips, carrots, rutabaga. (OK, maybe that's living too far on the edge . . . or is it?!) Take this cake even further and plate it with some pickled celery, celery leaves, and a strawberry whipped cream—I adore the combo of celery root and strawberry!

145g	unsalted butter, melted	1 stick (8 T) + 2 T
50g	grapeseed or other neutral oil	¼ cup
2	large eggs	
1	large egg yolk	
255g	whole wheat flour	1¾ cups + 3T
150g	light brown sugar	⅔ cup (packed)
130g	sugar	½ cup + 2 T
7.5g	kosher salt	1¾ tsp
5g	baking powder	1¼ tsp
2g	baking soda	½ tsp
0.5g	ground cinnamon	¼ tsp
400g	celery root	2 small
1 recipe	strawberry whipped cream (opposite)	
1 recipe	pickled celery (opposite)	
	celery leaves, for garnish	

1. Heat the oven to 350°F. Grease and flour a 1-pound loaf pan.

2. Whisk the melted butter, oil, whole eggs, and egg yolk together in a large bowl.

3. Whisk the whole wheat flour, brown sugar, sugar, salt, baking powder, baking soda, and cinnamon together in a separate large bowl.

4. Pour the wet ingredients into the dry ones and stir to combine. The mixture will be really thick and hard to stir. This is okay; it will loosen up once you add the celery root, which you should do now.

5. Peel and shred the celery root. Measure out 290g (2½ cups) and stir it into the batter until it is evenly combined.

6. Scrape the batter into the loaf pan and bake until the cake rises and puffs, 60 to 70 minutes. At 60 minutes, tap the top of the cake with your fingertips: The cake should bounce back firmly and the center should not be jiggly at all. If it doesn't pass this test, leave the cake in the oven for an additional 5 to 10 minutes.

Substitute AP flour for whole wheat flour one-for-one, if needed. Or get really deep and go for rye or pumpernickel flour, even!

Choose your pan wisely for this bad boy. See page 20.

7. Let the cake cool in the pan for 45 minutes, then run a small butter knife or offset spatula between the edge of the cake and the pan to help release it. Invert the pan onto a wire rack to fully release the cake. Turn the cake right side up and let it cool completely before slicing and serving.

8. Top each slice with a dollop of strawberry whipped cream, a few slices of pickled celery, and some torn celery leaves.

9. Any leftover cake can be kept, well-wrapped, in the refrigerator for up to a week.

strawberry whipped cream

makes about 300g (1¾ cups)

100g	strawberry jam (page 143)	½ cup
200g	heavy cream	¾ cup + 2½ T

1. When you are ready to serve the celery root pound cake, put the jam in a large bowl and use a spatula to loosen it up. If needed, stir the jam vigorously to be sure there are no lumps.

2. Pour the heavy cream into the bowl of jam and whisk the mixture together until it has reached soft peaks. Use immediately.

pickled celery

makes about 130g (1 cup), plus brine

130g	celery	4 ounces (2 large stalks)
100g	rice vinegar	½ cup
45g	sugar	¼ cup
40g	water	3 T
0.5g	kosher salt	⅛ tsp

1. Slice the celery on an angle across the stalk into ⅛-inch-thick slices. Put the slices in a heatproof bowl.

2. Combine the vinegar, sugar, water, and salt in a small saucepan and bring to a boil. Pour the pickling liquid over the celery while it is still hot.

3. Cover and refrigerate the celery for at least 4 hours before using. The pickled celery will keep in the refrigerator, in an airtight container, for up to 1 week.

mommala's angel food cake (from heaven)

makes one 10-inch angel food cake/serves 10 to 12

Occasionally in life, you end up with extra egg whites and we've found that the best thing to do in this case is save them until you have amassed enough to make our girl Hilary Fann's classic angel food cake recipe, which is based on the one her mom (aka Mommala) used to make. It's light and fluffy and the perfect base recipe to go along with any of the glazes in this chapter. Get creative when you make this: Play around with different extracts and pair your little cake from heaven with a glaze that you think would be rad. We love adding a little rose water and pairing it with the Rhubarb-Elderflower Goo (page 60). Or try adding some almond extract and use the Pistachio Glaze (page 46). Or get imaginative and substitute the cola extract with lime extract in the Cherry Cola Glaze (page 42).

180g	confectioners' sugar	1½ cups
120g	cake flour	1 cup
1g	kosher salt	¼ tsp
360g	large egg whites	from 12 large eggs
5g	cream of tartar	1½ tsp
200g	sugar	1 cup
4g	vanilla extract	1 tsp
1 recipe	your glaze of choice	

1. Heat the oven to 375°F. Make sure your 10-inch angel food cake pan is very clean and very dry.

2. Whisk the confectioners' sugar, cake flour, and salt together in a medium bowl, then sift them together into a large, dry bowl.

3. Put the egg whites and cream of tartar in the bowl of a stand mixer fitted with the whisk attachment. Beat the whites on medium-high for 2 to 3 minutes, until the mixture is very foamy and you can't see any liquid egg white in the bottom of the bowl.

4. Increase the mixer speed to high and begin adding the sugar very gradually, 1 teaspoon at a time. Take it easy here; it should take about 5 minutes to add all the sugar.

5. Continue to beat the egg whites and sugar for another 2 to 3 minutes on high speed. During this time, add the vanilla extract and any additional flavoring or coloring you want. The mixture should look voluminous and glossy, and hold soft peaks.

Swap out the vanilla extract for another extract, if you're feeling adventurous!

Do *not* grease the baking pan for this recipe. Angel food cake is delicate and will collapse if the sides of the pan are not clean and dry!

6. Gently transfer the egg whites to the largest bowl you own. The larger the bowl, the easier it will be to thoroughly fold in the dry ingredients without deflating the whites. Carefully sprinkle half of the sifted dry ingredients as evenly as possible on top of the egg whites. Use a flexible spatula to gently fold the egg white mixture over the dry, starting from the bottom center of the bowl and dragging the spatula along the bottom of the bowl toward you, folding it over the dry ingredients and rotating the bowl as you go, and breaking up any large pockets of dry ingredients along the way.

7. As soon as the largest pockets of dry ingredients are incorporated, go ahead and add the rest of the dry ingredients and fold them into the mixture.

8. The second you feel confident that the dries are incorporated with no large pockets remaining (small pea-size lumps are OK), gently pour the batter into the pan and bake until it is puffy, slightly browned, and springs back when touched, 30 to 35 minutes.

9. Remove the cake from the oven, remove the bottom of the pan if there is one, or quickly flip the pan upside down onto a wire rack and let it hang for 2 to 3 hours, until cool.

10. Run a small butter knife or offset spatula between the edge of the cake and the pan to help release it, getting as far down to the bottom as you can. Shake the cake pan a little bit to make sure the cake is loosened on all sides before inverting to fully release the cake.

11. If you choose to glaze your beautiful angel food cake, put it on a wire rack with a rimmed baking dish underneath and pour your glaze of choice in an even stream all over the top of the cake. (If you have any leftover glaze, serve it on the side when you slice the cake.) Let the glaze set up for 15 minutes, then dig in!

12. The angel food cake will keep in the refrigerator, wrapped, for up to 1 week. Let the refrigerated cake sit at room temperature for 1 hour before serving.

HOT CAKES!

Honestly, my biggest beef with cake these days is: How come no one eats their cake hot?! I know, it sounds like a *Seinfeld* episode, but I'm serious. Warm, slightly dense cakes, especially when ever-so-slightly underbaked, are one of life's greater gifts. They aren't much to look at, but they soothe the soul like nothing else.

BEST BOSS EVER

HOME SWEET HOME

I say it's high time we embrace this simple, obvious fact. I learned all about fancy French technique, studying under masters of the culinary arts. I've worked and dined in some of the most high-end joints in the world. I know the rules say that you're supposed to serve cakes cool. But I refuse to abide. (And why do you think molten lava cakes are so . . . HOT?!)

Instead, I've written an entire chapter about my love for devilishly and deliciously warm, gooey cakes, or as I like to call them generally, Hot Cakes!

When I was younger, though I could whisk up a batter easily without supervision, turning on the oven solo was completely out of the question as far as my mother was concerned. So I beat her at her own game and warmed my favorite batters in the microwave. I've been friends with microwave cake for a long time.

And then there's my set-it-and-forget-it love: the Crock-Pot. When I was opening Milk Bar, working insane hours as one does when getting a business off the ground, I realized that the only way to ensure a warm meal when I finally made it home was to load up the Crock-Pot in the morning.

After enough batches of mexichili and cornbake, I started wondering what wild world of desserts the Crock-Pot could produce, too. So we made extra cake batter from each layer cake we baked and piloted it in our retro friend. We layered one batter on top of the other, swirled in curds and crumbs to push the limits, we even threw leftover bread and custards in there, too. Within a week, I had bought Crock-Pots for the entire team at nearby thrift stores and yard sales. It's a joke that we laugh about still nearly a decade later: "Do you still have the vintage Crock-Pot Tosi gave you?"

oatmeal-apple-brown sugar microwave mug cake

makes two 11-ounce mugs of cake/serves 2

Oatmeal cookies and apples are the two most prominent snacks and desserts of my childhood. I didn't have a great from-scratch cake recipe up my sleeve when I was young and microwaving strange batters for fun, but I like to think this is the recipe I'd make for my mom, grandma, or aunts if I did. It's deeply nurturing and tugs at the heartstrings of some of my favorite early food memories. I also like to think it's not too far off from a mug full of oatmeal, but I can really convince myself of anything in order to get a little more butter and sugar into a bite of warm, oaty goodness.

75g	buttermilk	⅓ cup + 2 tsp
40g	unsalted butter, melted	2½ T
25g	grapeseed or other neutral oil	2 T
4g	vanilla extract	1 tsp
1	large egg	
45g	quick oats	½ cup
40g	sugar	3 T
40g	light brown sugar	2 T + 2 tsp (packed)
40g	cake flour	¼ cup + 1 T
1g	baking powder	¼ tsp
1g	kosher salt	¼ tsp
0.25g	ground cinnamon	⅛ tsp
1 recipe	green apple matchsticks (page 80)	
1 recipe	brown sugar glaze (page 80)	

1. Find your two best 11-ounce mugs and set them aside.

2. Whisk the buttermilk, melted butter, oil, vanilla extract, and egg together in a bowl.

3. Whisk the oats, sugar, brown sugar, cake flour, baking powder, salt, and cinnamon together in a separate bowl.

4. Pour the wet ingredients into the dry ones and stir to combine. If the batter looks lumpy, use a whisk to break up all the lumps.

5. Divide the batter between the mugs and top each mug with a generous amount of the apple matchsticks.

6. Microwave the mugs until the cakes rise and puff up and look like they are about to spill out over the mugs. Start with 1 minute, and if they look too raw, continue to microwave in 15-second increments until the sides and top have set, leaving hot gooey cake batter hidden inside (up to 2½ minutes).

Use quick oats instead of rolled oats in this recipe—if you do use rolled oats, they will be delicious, but will remain slightly "al dente" due to the short cooking time in the microwave.

(recipe continues)

7. Remove the mugs from the microwave, drizzle the brown sugar glaze all over the top, and garnish each oatmeal cake with more apple matchsticks.

8. This will take every ounce of self-control you have, but wait 1 minute before stirring it up and digging in with a spoon.

brown sugar glaze

makes about 40g (2 tablespoons)

1 recipe	liquid reserved from green apple matchsticks (at right)	
5g	unsalted butter	1 tsp

1. Put the liquid reserved from the apple matchsticks into a small pot and bring to a boil over high heat. Reduce the temperature to low and continue to cook until the liquid darkens and coats the back of a spoon, about 1½ minutes. Stir the butter into the mixture until melted.

2. Let the glaze cool to room temperature before using.

green apple matchsticks

makes about 100g (1 cup)

5g	lemon juice	1 tsp
1	granny smith apple	
60g	light brown sugar	¼ cup (packed)
0.5g	kosher salt	⅛ tsp

1. Heat the oven to 250°F. Line a sheet pan with parchment paper.

2. Put the lemon juice in the bottom of a small bowl. Cut the apple into matchsticks, by first slicing one side of the apple into ⅛-inch slices starting at the edge and working your way to the core. Stack the slices on top of each other and slice them again into long ⅛-inch-wide matchsticks. Add these matchsticks to the bowl with the lemon juice and toss to coat. Repeat with all sides of the apple until all that's left is the core.

3. Toss the matchsticks with the light brown sugar and salt and let them sit for 10 minutes to release their juices.

4. Gently squeeze the apples to release more of their juices. Reserve the brown sugar and apple juice liquid for the brown sugar glaze (at left).

5. Spread the apple matchsticks evenly across the lined sheet pan and bake until they dry out and start to caramelize, about 40 minutes. The apples can be stored at room temperature, in an airtight container, for up to 3 days.

mint chocolate chip molten microwave mug cake

makes two 11-ounce mugs of cake/serves 2

I can never quite shake my obsession with mint chocolate chip ice cream, but eating those flavors warm, late at night from a mug, makes me believe I CAN give up the ice cream if I can keep my gooey, molten microwave cake. Sidecar this snack with a cup of peppermint tea or a hot cocoa or both, and you'll be the hero of your household.

5	**starlight peppermint candies**	
40g	**unsalted butter, melted**	2½ T
35g	**buttermilk**	2 T
25g	**grapeseed or other neutral oil**	2 T
4g	**peppermint extract**	1 tsp
1	**large egg**	
80g	**sugar**	⅓ cup + 1 T
20g	**light brown sugar**	1 T + 1 tsp (packed)
60g	**cake flour**	½ cup
1g	**baking powder**	¼ tsp
1g	**kosher salt**	¼ tsp
40g	**mini chocolate chips**	3 T
6g	**cake flour**	1 tsp

1. Find your two best 11-ounce mugs.

2. Unwrap the peppermint candies and place them in a zip-seal freezer bag. Use a rolling pin to crush them into small, pea-size pieces.

3. Whisk the melted butter, buttermilk, oil, peppermint extract, and egg together in a large bowl.

4. Whisk both sugars, the 60g (½ cup) cake flour, baking powder, and salt together in a separate large bowl.

5. Pour the wet ingredients into the dry ones and stir to combine. If the batter looks lumpy, use a whisk to break up all the lumps.

6. Toss the chocolate chips in the 6g (1 teaspoon) cake flour and stir them into the batter. Divide the batter between the mugs.

7. Microwave the mugs until the cakes rise and puff up and look like they are about to spill out over the mugs. Start with 1 minute, and if it looks too raw, continue to microwave in 15-second increments until the sides and top have set, leaving hot gooey cake batter hidden inside (up to 2½ minutes).

8. Remove the mugs from the microwave and garnish them with the crushed peppermint bits (they give a great toffee-like texture). This will take every ounce of self-control you have, but wait 1 minute before stirring it up and digging in with a spoon.

molten chocolate microwave mug cake

makes two 11-ounce mugs of cake/serves 2

This is like a combination of a warm-out-of-the-oven brownie, a square of cake, and all of your deepest chocolate dreams come true. Scoop your favorite ice cream atop this gooey masterpiece and you'll drift peacefully to sleep, like you just had a boring old glass of warm milk, but better.

Read up on our cocoa powder and chocolate of choice (see page 14).

40g	**unsalted butter, melted**	2½ T
35g	**buttermilk**	2 T
20g	**grapeseed or other neutral oil**	1 T + 1 tsp
1g	**vanilla extract**	¼ tsp
1	**large egg**	
100g	**sugar**	½ cup
50g	**cake flour**	⅓ cup + 2 tsp
20g	**cocoa powder**	2 T + 2 tsp
2g	**baking powder**	½ tsp
2g	**kosher salt**	½ tsp
45g	**mini chocolate chips**	3 T

1. Find your two best 11-ounce mugs and set them aside.

2. Whisk the melted butter, buttermilk, oil, vanilla extract, and egg together in a bowl.

3. Whisk the sugar, cake flour, cocoa powder, baking powder, and salt together in a separate bowl.

4. Pour the wet ingredients into the dry ones and stir to combine. If the batter looks lumpy, use a whisk to break up all the lumps. Stir in the chocolate chips.

5. Divide the batter evenly between the mugs. Microwave the mugs until the cakes rise and puff up and look like they are about to spill out over the mugs. Start with 1 minute. If it looks too raw, continue to microwave in 15-second increments until the sides and top have set, leaving hot gooey cake batter hidden inside (up to 2½ minutes).

6. Remove the mugs from the microwave. This will take every ounce of self-control you have, but wait 1 minute before stirring it up and digging in with a spoon.

creamsicle crock-pot cake

makes 1 crock of cake/serves 8 to 10

The hot, sticky summers of my childhood in Ohio and Virginia gave me full-on rights to become a Popsicle aficionado. I liked cherry and blue raspberry, and was always happy with a great Bomb Pop, but my real jam was a Creamsicle. I loved the combination of orange and its unique, dreamy, creamy version of vanilla . . . one that was different from what I knew to be the vanilla flavor in, say, a chocolate chip cookie.

The blend of orange and this "new" vanilla flavor—which comes from clear vanilla extract—is one I love to riff on when creating a new dessert. Clear vanilla lacks depth—it has that baseline vanilla flavor and that's it. It's simple, straightforward, and is the nostalgic flavor of birthday cake and the cool, milky vibes of an ice pop. In this warm, gooey, Crock-Pot form, I must say it gets VERY high scores from the team.

1	**orange**	
115g	**unsalted butter, melted**	1 stick (8 T)
110g	**buttermilk**	½ cup
60g	**grapeseed or other neutral oil**	¼ cup
12g	**clear vanilla extract**	1 T
2	**large eggs**	
2	**large egg yolks**	
315g	**sugar**	1½ cups
200g	**cake flour**	1⅔ cups
6g	**baking powder**	1½ tsp
4g	**kosher salt**	1 tsp
1 recipe	**creamsicle swirl** (opposite)	

1. Plug in a 4- to 6-quart Crock-Pot. Grease the interior with pan spray and set the temperature to low.

2. Using a Microplane or the finest-toothed side of a box grater, zest the orange. Do your best to grate only as far down as the orange part of the skin; the white pith has less orange flavor and can be bitter. Set aside.

3. Juice the orange and put both the zest and the juice in a large bowl. Whisk in the melted butter, buttermilk, oil, vanilla extract, whole eggs, and egg yolks.

4. Whisk the sugar, cake flour, baking powder, and salt together in a separate large bowl.

5. Pour the wet ingredients into the dry ones and stir to combine. If the batter looks lumpy, use a whisk to break up all the lumps.

6. Pour the cake batter into the Crock-Pot, then drizzle half of the creamsicle swirl all over the top of the batter. Use a spatula to swirl the creamsicle mixture throughout the batter.

Read up on extracts (see page 15) and take the time to procure clear vanilla extract for all things "birthday" and Creamsicle flavored.

Read up on Crock-Pots and their heat settings (see page 19).

7. Partially cover the Crock-Pot and cook the cake on high for 4 to 6 hours, until it has set and is cooked through in the center.

8. While it's still hot, spoon the cake directly from the Crock-Pot onto plates and drizzle each scoop with the remaining creamsicle swirl.

creamsicle swirl

makes about 225g (1 cup)

110g	**cream cheese**	4 ounces
30g	**heavy cream**	2 T
80g	**confectioners' sugar**	½ cup
4g	**clear vanilla extract**	1 tsp
1g	**kosher salt**	¼ tsp

1. Heat the cream cheese in the microwave for 30 seconds.

2. Stir the cream, confectioners' sugar, vanilla extract, and salt into the cream cheese until everything is evenly combined and silky smooth. Set the mixture aside until you are ready to swirl it into the creamsicle cake batter. It will keep in the refrigerator, in an airtight container, for up to 2 weeks.

black sesame crock-pot cake

makes 1 crock of cake/serves 8 to 10

When I first tasted black sesame paste, I was a woman possessed. Awesome peanut butter notes, but fancier and with an unexpected color and depth?! Sign me up! Black sesame paste is not cheap, but boy-oh-boy do I think it's worth it.

This cake is nutty and rich. If you've got gourmands coming over for a food-themed Halloween party, it also makes a great "cauldron" of delicious black stuff.

And feel free to sub black sesame paste into any recipe that calls for peanut butter, or throw a tablespoon into your next smoothie. Don't fear the seemingly sullen jet-black vibes, just close your eyes and go with it.

115g	**unsalted butter, melted**	1 stick (8 T)
110g	**buttermilk**	½ cup
60g	**grapeseed or other neutral oil**	¼ cup
8 g	**vanilla extract**	2 tsp
2	**large eggs**	
2	**large egg yolks**	
315g	**sugar**	1½ cups
200g	**cake flour**	1⅔ cups
6g	**baking powder**	1½ tsp
3 g	**kosher salt**	¾ tsp
1 recipe	**black sesame swirl** (opposite)	

1. Plug in a 4- to 6-quart Crock-Pot. Grease the interior with pan spray and set the temperature to low.

2. Whisk the melted butter, buttermilk, oil, vanilla extract, whole eggs, and egg yolks together in a large bowl.

3. Whisk the sugar, cake flour, baking powder, and salt together in a separate large bowl.

4. Pour the wet ingredients into the dry ones and stir to combine. If the batter looks lumpy, use a whisk to break up all the lumps.

5. Pour the cake batter into the Crock-Pot, then partially cover it and cook the cake on high for 2 hours. At this point the cake will be partially set but still quite raw, especially in the center. Drizzle all of the black sesame swirl over the top of the batter. Partially cover the Crock-Pot again, drop the temperature to low, and continue cooking for an additional 2 to 3 hours, until the cake has set and is cooked through in the center.

6. While it's still hot, spoon the cake directly from the Crock-Pot onto plates and devour.

Though attempting to make your own is a near impossible feat, specialty grocery stores often sell black sesame paste as "black tahini" or "black sesame spread." Otherwise, you know the Internet has you covered.

Read up on Crock-Pots and their heat settings (see page 19).

black sesame swirl

makes about 160g (1 cup)

85g	**white chocolate**	3 ounces
75g	**black sesame paste**	¼ cup + 1 T
1g	**kosher salt**	¼ tsp

Put the white chocolate, sesame paste, and salt in a microwave-safe container and microwave in 30-second increments, stirring in between, until the chocolate has melted and you have a smooth mixture. The black sesame swirl will keep in the refrigerator, in an airtight container, for up to 2 weeks. Just rewarm it in the microwave, again in short increments, until it's pourable before using.

banana-chocolate-peanut butter crock-pot cake

makes 1 crock of cake/serves 8 to 10

My nieces will do just about anything for any combo of banana, chocolate chips, and peanut butter. This hot cake is like a warm hug for even the youngest palate in the house. Perfect for a snow day or a sleepover, it's also a great place for *rrrrrripe* bananas!

Read up on the pro art of ripening bananas (see page 13)!

Read up on Crock-Pots and their heat settings (see page 19).

110g	buttermilk	½ cup
85g	unsalted butter, melted	6 T
1	large egg	
20g	grapeseed or other neutral oil	2 T
2g	banana extract	½ tsp
340g	*rrrrrripe* bananas	3 medium
220g	ap flour	1½ cups + 3 T
200g	sugar	1 cup
3 g	baking powder	¾ tsp
3 g	baking soda	¾ tsp
2g	kosher salt	½ tsp
150g	mini chocolate chips	¾ cup + ½ T
3g	ap flour	1 tsp
1 recipe	peanut butter goo (opposite)	

1. Plug in a 4- to 6-quart Crock-Pot. Grease the interior with pan spray and set the temperature to low.

2. Whisk the buttermilk, melted butter, egg, oil, and banana extract together in a large bowl.

3. Mush 225g (2) of the bananas into a paste with your hands and stir the banana paste into the bowl of wet ingredients. Chop the remaining 115g (1) banana into small bite-size chunks and set them aside.

4. Whisk the 220g (1½ cups + 3 tablespoons) flour, the sugar, baking powder, baking soda, and salt together in a separate large bowl.

5. Pour the wet ingredients into the dry ones and stir to combine. If the batter looks lumpy, use a whisk to break up all the lumps.

6. Pour half of the cake batter into the Crock-Pot.

7. Toss the mini chocolate chips with the 3g (1 teaspoon) flour, then stir them, along with the banana chunks, into the remaining cake batter and pour it into the Crock-Pot.

8. Partially cover the Crock-Pot and cook the cake on low for 4 to 6 hours, until it has set and is cooked through in the center.

9. While it's still hot, spoon the cake directly from the Crock-Pot onto plates, drizzle each scoop generously with the peanut butter goo, and devour.

peanut butter goo

makes about 240g (1 cup)

55g	**cream cheese**	2 ounces
55g	**peanut butter**	¼ cup
55g	**whole milk**	¼ cup
40g	**confectioners' sugar**	¼ cup + 1½ T
30g	**unsalted butter, melted**	2 T
2g	**vanilla extract**	¾ tsp
1g	**kosher salt**	¼ tsp

1. Heat the cream cheese in the microwave for 30 seconds to soften.

2. Whisk the peanut butter, milk, confectioners' sugar, melted butter, vanilla extract, and salt into the cream cheese until fully combined and smooth as silk. Peanut butter goo will keep in the refrigerator, in an airtight container, for up to 2 weeks. Just be sure to microwave it for 30 seconds before drizzling it over the cake.

apple cider donut crock-pot pudding

makes 1 crock of cake/serves 8 to 10

Though in my book this is still very much a Crock-Pot *cake*, this recipe is technically more like a bread pudding . . . one that you will never be able to stop eating. It's a love letter to fall in NYC and all the weekends I beg my handsome husband to go apple picking with me. Apple picking is just an excuse for a road trip with unlimited amounts of apple cider and donuts. So call this my excuse for something to do with all the delicious leftovers.

450g	day-old apple cider donuts	1 pound
100g	sugar	½ cup
6g	vanilla extract	1 tsp
2g	kosher salt	½ tsp
2	large eggs	
2	large egg yolks	
200g	whole milk	¾ cup + 2 T
115g	apple cider	½ cup
70g	heavy cream	⅓ cup
1 recipe	apple cider caramel (page 94)	

1. Plug in a 4- to 6-quart Crock-Pot. Grease the interior with pan spray.

2. Break up the donuts into bite-size pieces, about the size of walnuts, and place them in the Crock-Pot.

3. Whisk the sugar, vanilla extract, salt, whole eggs, and egg yolks together in a large bowl. Stream in the milk, apple cider, and heavy cream and whisk to combine.

4. Pour the milk and egg mixture into the Crock-Pot, covering the donuts with the liquid. Use a spatula or wooden spoon to stir everything. Cover the Crock-Pot and let it sit without turning it on for 30 minutes, so the donuts can soak up all of the liquid.

5. Stir the donut mixture again, then set the Crock-Pot to low. Partially cover the Crock-Pot and cook the pudding for 4 to 6 hours, until it has set and is cooked through in the center.

6. While it's still hot, spoon the pudding directly from the Crock-Pot onto plates and drizzle each scoop with the apple cider caramel.

If you somehow end up with extra donut bits, slowly toast them in the oven (250°F for 20 minutes) for a crunchy, yummy garnish.

Read up on Crock-Pots and their heat settings (see page 19).

(recipe continues)

apple cider caramel

makes about 200g (¾ cup)

55g	apple cider	¼ cup
15g	unsalted butter, melted	1 T
2g	vanilla extract	½ tsp
2g	kosher salt	½ tsp
100g	sugar	½ cup
55g	heavy cream	¼ cup

1. Combine the apple cider, butter, vanilla extract, and salt in a bowl and set aside.

2. Make a dry caramel: Heat the sugar in a medium heavy-bottomed saucepan over medium-high heat. As soon as the sugar starts to melt, use a heatproof spatula to move it constantly around the pan—you want it all to melt and caramelize evenly. Cook and stir, cook and stir, until the caramel is a deep, dark amber, 3 to 5 minutes from when the sugar starts to melt.

3. Once the caramel has reached the target color, remove the saucepan from the heat. Very slowly and very carefully, pour in the heavy cream. The caramel will bubble up and steam; stand away until the steam dissipates. Use the heatproof spatula to stir the mixture together.

4. Carefully stream in the apple cider mixture and stir it all together. If it is at all lumpy or if there are any clumps of hardened caramel floating around the sauce, put the saucepan back over medium heat and heat the mixture, stirring constantly, until the mixture is smooth.

5. Let the caramel cool before using. It will keep in the refrigerator, in an airtight container, for up to 2 weeks.

⚠ Surface remains hot

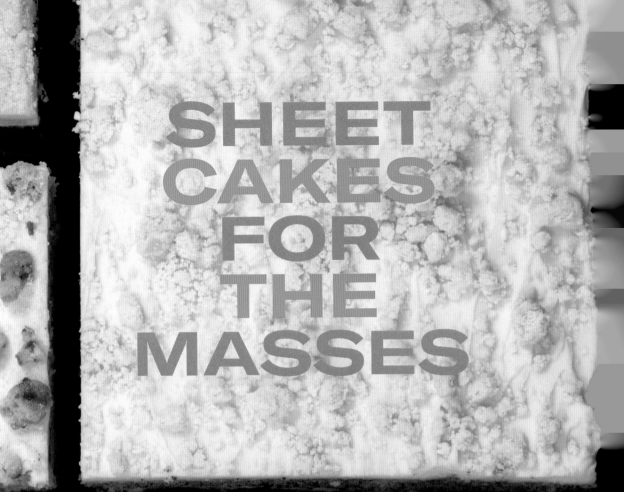

SHEET
CAKES
FOR
THE
MASSES

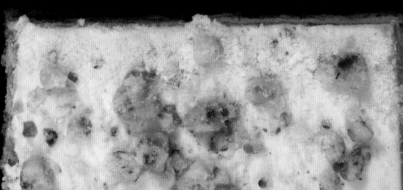

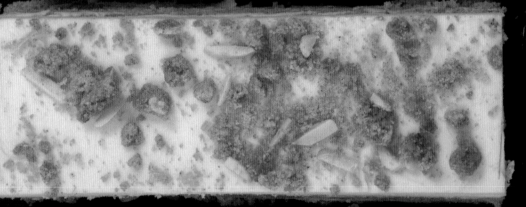

Growing up with a love of baking, but an even stronger sense of community, as a family, we never baked for just ourselves. Don't get me wrong, we always saved a little bit of what we made for home, but mostly we baked for others: neighbors, a PTA meeting, the county fair, churchgoers, a fundraising get-together, and so on.

We weren't focused on the craft of baking, rather the spirit of baking . . . of maximizing happiness for the masses.

Until I left home for culinary school and the bright lights of New York City, I had only ever baked cake in a 9 x 13-inch dish, then covered it in frosting. I could feed twenty people at a time!

And even now, while I love round, fanciful layer cakes, I still live by the approach that a sheet cake always gets the job done for a hungry crowd. It's much easier to slice than a round layer cake, and also makes for a much larger canvas for a thoughtful message like, "Dear Dwayne 'The Rock' Johnson, Will you be our friend?!"

But our approach to sheet cakes here is a step up from my days as a novice baker. There's a little more time, effort, and complexity to it. So you're guaranteed to not just feed the masses, but WOW them with layers and flavors with killers like the Corn and Blueberry Sheet Cake (page 113) or the Inside-Out Chocolate-Yellow Sheet Cake (page 107)!

And since each of the creations that follows is a combination of base cake, frosting, filling, and textural pop, you can easily make your own combinations. And if you just double any of the other quarter-sheet-pan cake recipes in the book, you can use any of those recipes for this chapter, too.

every milk bar sheet cake follows the same formula

layer 1, the bottom

cake: The base of your creation.

cake soak: For moisture and depth of flavor to the bottom layer, anything liquid that tells the "flavor story."

frosting or filling #1: For flavor and structure, this layer is like the stucco to the foundation of your cake. The spread should have body and be delicious enough to stand on its own. When you have two different spreadable fillings, the harder-to-spread one goes down first.

textural layer: Typically a crumb or a crunch; it's all about adding to the "flavor story" while remaining a hidden surprise texture when eaten.

frosting or filling #2: Sometimes the same as frosting or filling #1, this layer is for flavor and structure. It helps keep the layers and crumbs that came before secure in their place and the next layer secure as you build. Filling #2 is also an opportunity to add another flavor and viscosity to the masterpiece. This filling is easier to spread than #1, but can still hold its own.

layer 2, the top

cake: The double decker element of your sheetcake, this layer holds the flavor and beauty of the finishing touches that come next.

frosting or filling #3: Perhaps the same as #1 or #2, this is for flavor and finishing touches. Frost and swirl to your heart's desire when spreading this top layer.

decor: What's left over from your textural layer, the decor is the final POP of color and personality.

baller birthday sheet cake

makes 1 double-layer quarter-sheet cake, 3 to 4 inches tall/serves 15 to 20

This birthday cake is the most popular sheet cake at Milk Bar, probably because celebrating birthdays with cake is a thing, and because people love to eat birthday-flavored cake when celebrating things, even when there's not a birthday to honor in the room.

1 recipe	**birthday sheet cake** (page 104)	
1 recipe	**vanilla milk soak** (page 105)	
1 recipe	**birthday frosting** (page 106)	
280g	**birthday crumbs** (page 106)	2 cups

cake assembly instructions

Put a piece of parchment paper or a silicone baking mat on the counter. Run a knife or offset spatula along the edges of one of the quarter-sheet pans of birthday sheet cake to loosen it from the pan, then invert that cake onto it and peel off the parchment or mat from the bottom of the cake.

layer 1, the bottom

1. Clean the quarter-sheet pan and line it with clean parchment or a silicone baking mat. Place the cake back inside the pan.

2. Dunk a pastry brush in the vanilla milk soak (or use a spoon) and give the cake a good, healthy bath with the soak.

3. Use the back of a spoon to spread one-quarter of the birthday frosting in an even layer over the cake.

4. Sprinkle half of the birthday crumbs evenly over the frosting. Use the back of your hand to press them lightly into the frosting, anchoring them in place.

5. Use the back of a spoon to spread another one-quarter of the birthday frosting as evenly as possible over the crumbs.

layer 2, the top

1. Run a knife or offset spatula along the edges of the second quarter-sheet pan of cake to loosen it from the pan, then invert that cake directly on top of the frosting. Peel off the parchment or silicone baking mat from the bottom of the cake and cover it with the remaining frosting. Give it volume and swirls, or do as we do and opt for a perfectly flat top. Garnish the frosting with the remaining birthday crumbs.

2. Transfer the cake to the freezer and freeze for a minimum of 12 hours to set the cake and filling. Once set, if not serving right away, wrap in plastic and freeze for up to 2 weeks.

3. At least 3 hours before you are ready to serve the cake, pull it out of the freezer and, using an offset spatula or a bench scraper, pop the cake out of the pan.

(recipe continues)

4. Transfer the cake to a cutting board and fill a pitcher with hot water and set it aside. Use a chef's knife to trim the edges of the cake so you are left with flush, smooth sides, submerging the knife in hot water between cuts and wiping the blade clean. This makes for crumb-free, professional-looking cuts every time!

5. Place the cake on a large, rectangular platter. Let it defrost in the fridge for a minimum of 3 hours. (Wrapped well in plastic, the cake can be refrigerated for up to 5 days.)

6. When it's party time, slice the cake into squares and serve!

birthday sheet cake

makes 2 quarter-sheet pans of cake

110g	unsalted butter, softened	1 stick (8 T)
100g	vegetable shortening	½ cup
425g	sugar	2 cups + 2 T
75g	light brown sugar	⅓ cup (packed)
5	large eggs	
180g	buttermilk	¾ cup + 1 T
100g	grapeseed or other neutral oil	½ cup
14g	clear vanilla extract	3½ tsp
420g	cake flour	3½ cups
200g	rainbow sprinkles	1 cup
10g	baking powder	2½ tsp
5g	kosher salt	1¼ tsp
50g	rainbow sprinkles	¼ cup

1. Heat the oven to 350°F. Pan-spray two quarter-sheet pans and line them with parchment paper, or just line them with silicone baking mats.

2. Combine the butter, shortening, and both sugars in the bowl of a stand mixer fitted with the paddle attachment and cream together on medium-high for 2 to 3 minutes, until light and fluffy. Scrape down the sides of the bowl halfway through this process, and again at the end of it.

3. Add the eggs, one at a time, beating on medium-high for 1 minute after each addition. After you add the last egg, scrape down the sides of the bowl, then beat on high for 4 more minutes. Scrape down the sides of the bowl again.

4. Combine the buttermilk, oil, and vanilla extract and with the mixer on medium speed, stream them into the batter very slowly. It should take you approximately 3 minutes to add these liquids. Scrape down the sides of the bowl, increase the mixer speed to medium-high, and paddle for an additional 2 to 3 minutes, until the mixture is practically white, twice the size of your original fluffy butter-and-sugar mixture, and completely homogeneous. Don't rush the process. You're basically forcing too much liquid into an already fatty mixture that doesn't want to make room for that liquid. There should be no streaks of fat or liquid. Stop the mixer and scrape down the sides of the bowl.

5. Whisk together the cake flour, the 200g (1 cup) rainbow sprinkles, the baking powder, and salt in a medium bowl. Set the dry ingredients aside. With the mixer on very low speed, slowly add the dry ingredients and mix for 45 to 60 seconds, just until your batter comes together. Scrape down the sides of the bowl, then mix on low for an additional 45 seconds to make sure no lumps of cake flour get left behind.

6. Divide the batter evenly between the quarter-sheet pans and, using a spatula, spread the cake batter into even layers. Sprinkle the 50 g (¼ cup) rainbow sprinkles evenly on top of the batter in both pans.

7. Bake for 30 to 35 minutes, rotating the pans front to back halfway through baking. The cakes will rise and puff, doubling in size, but will remain slightly buttery and dense. At 30 minutes, gently poke the edge of each cake with your finger: The cakes should bounce back slightly and the centers should no longer be jiggly. If they don't pass these tests, leave the cakes in the oven for an additional 3 to 5 minutes.

8. Let the cakes cool in the pans on a wire rack or, in a pinch, in the fridge or freezer (don't worry, it's not cheating). The cooled cakes can be stored in the fridge, wrapped in plastic wrap, for up to 5 days.

vanilla milk soak

makes about 120g (½ cup)

110g	**whole milk**	½ cup
8g	**clear vanilla extract**	2 tsp

Whisk together the milk and vanilla in a small bowl.

(recipe continues)

birthday frosting

makes about 910g (4 cups)

230g	unsalted butter, softened	2 sticks (16 T)
100g	vegetable shortening	½ cup
110g	cream cheese	4 ounces
55g	light corn syrup	3 T
25g	clear vanilla extract	2 T
400g	confectioners' sugar	2½ cups
4g	kosher salt	1 tsp
0.5g	baking powder	pinch
0.5g	citric acid	pinch

1. Combine the butter, shortening, and cream cheese in the bowl of a stand mixer fitted with the paddle attachment and cream on medium-high for 2 to 3 minutes, until the mixture is smooth and fluffy. Scrape down the bowl.

2. With the mixer on its lowest speed, stream in the corn syrup and vanilla. Crank the mixer up to medium-high and beat for 2 to 3 minutes, until the mixture is glossy white. Scrape down the bowl.

3. Add the confectioners' sugar, salt, baking powder, and citric acid and mix on low speed just to incorporate them. Crank the speed back up to medium-high and beat for 2 to 3 minutes, until you have a brilliant, stark white, beautifully smooth frosting. It should look just like it came out of a plastic tub at the grocery store!

4. Use the frosting immediately, or store it in the refrigerator, for up to 1 week. If you store it in the refrigerator, loosen it up before using it. The easiest way to do this is by putting the frosting in the bowl of a stand mixer fitted with the paddle attachment and beating it on medium speed for 3 to 4 minutes.

birthday crumbs

makes about 630g (4½ cups)

21 g	sugar	1 cup + 1 T
190g	cake flour	1½ cups + 1 T
60g	light brown sugar	¼ cup (packed)
50g	rainbow sprinkles	¼ cup
4g	baking powder	1 tsp
4g	kosher salt	1 tsp
85g	grapeseed or other neutral oil	⅓ cup + 2 T
25g	clear vanilla extract	2 T

1. Heat the oven to 300°F. Line a sheet pan with parchment paper or a silicone baking mat.

2. Combine the sugar, cake flour, brown sugar, sprinkles, baking powder, and salt in the bowl of a stand mixer fitted with the paddle attachment and mix on low speed until well combined.

3. Add the oil and vanilla and paddle again to distribute. The mixture will come together in small clumps.

4. Spread the clumps in a single layer on the lined sheet pan. Bake for 20 minutes, breaking them up occasionally. The crumbs should still be slightly moist to the touch; they will dry and harden as they cool.

5. Let the crumbs cool completely before using in a recipe or scarfing by the handful. The crumbs will keep, in an airtight container, for up to 1 week at room temperature or up to 1 month in the fridge or freezer.

inside-out chocolate-yellow sheet cake

makes 1 double-layer quarter-sheet cake, 3 to 4 inches tall/serves 15 to 20

This ditty is an inside-out version of a classic cake flavor combo, yellow cake with chocolate frosting. We like to keep folks on their toes, so instead, we make a chocolate cake and use yellow cake mix to make texture crumbs and a tasty frosting.

1 recipe	**chocolate sheet cake** (page 108)	
1 recipe	**chocolate milk soak** (page 111)	
200g	**fudge sauce** (page 110)	½ cup
270g	**yellow cake crumbs** (page 111)	2 cups
1 recipe	**yellow cake frosting** (page 111)	

cake assembly instructions

Put a piece of parchment paper or a silicone baking mat on the counter. Run a knife or offset spatula long the edges of the quarter-sheet pans of cake to loosen it from the pan, then invert that cake onto it and peel off the parchment or mat from the bottom of the cake.

layer 1, the bottom

1. Clean the quarter-sheet pan and line it with clean parchment paper or a silicone baking mat. Place the cake you just unmolded back inside the pan. (Trust me.)

2. Dunk a pastry brush in the chocolate milk soak (or use a spoon) and give the cake a good, healthy bath with the soak.

3. Use the back of a spoon to spread all of the fudge sauce in an even layer over the cake.

4. Sprinkle half of the yellow cake crumbs evenly over the fudge sauce. Use the back of your hand to press them lightly into the fudge sauce, anchoring them in place.

5. Use the back of a spoon to spread half of the yellow cake frosting as evenly as possible over the crumbs.

layer 2, the top

1. Run a knife or offset spatula along the edges of the second quarter-sheet pan of cake to loosen it from the pan, then invert that cake directly on top of the frosting. Peel off the parchment or silicone baking mat from the bottom of the cake and cover it with the remaining frosting. Give it volume and swirls, or do as we do and opt for a perfectly flat top. Garnish the frosting with the remaining yellow cake crumbs.

2. Transfer the sheet pan to the freezer and freeze for a minimum of 12 hours to set the cake and filling. Once set, if not serving right

(recipe continues)

away, wrap in plastic and freeze for up to 2 weeks.

3. At least 3 hours before you are ready to serve the cake, pull it out of the freezer and, using an offset spatula or a bench scraper, pop the cake out of the pan.

4. Transfer the cake to a cutting board and fill a pitcher with hot water and set it aside. Use a chef's knife to trim the edges of the cake so you are left with flush, smooth sides, submerging the knife in hot water between cuts and wiping the blade clean. This makes for crumb-free cuts!

5. Place the cake on a large, rectangular platter. Let it defrost in the fridge for a minimum of 3 hours. (Wrapped well in plastic, the cake can be refrigerated for up to 5 days.) When it's party time, slice the cake.

chocolate sheet cake

makes 2 quarter-sheet pans of cake

225g	unsalted butter, softened	2 sticks (16 T)
450g	sugar	2¼ cups
120g	light brown sugar	½ cup (packed)
6	large eggs	
220g	buttermilk	1 cup
210g	grapeseed or other neutral oil	1¼ cups + 2 T
10g	vanilla extract	2½ tsp
310g	cake flour	1½ cups
140g	cocoa powder	1¼ cups
12g	baking powder	1 T
14g	kosher salt	1 T + ½ tsp

1. Heat the oven to 350°F. Pan-spray two quarter-sheet pans and line them with parchment paper, or just line them with silicone baking mats.

2. Combine the butter and both sugars in the bowl of a stand mixer fitted with the paddle attachment and cream together on medium-high for 2 to 3 minutes, until light and fluffy. Scrape down the sides of the bowl halfway through this process, and again at the end of it.

3. Add the eggs, one at a time, beating on medium-high for 1 minute after each addition. After you add the last egg, scrape down the sides of the bowl, then beat on high for 4 more minutes. Scrape down the sides of the bowl again.

4. Combine the buttermilk, oil, and vanilla extract and with the mixer on medium speed, stream them into the batter very slowly. It should take approximately 3 minutes to add these liquids. Scrape down the sides of the bowl, increase the mixer speed to medium-high, and paddle for an additional 2 to 3 minutes, until the mixture is practically white, twice the size of your original fluffy butter-and-sugar mixture, and completely homogeneous. Don't rush the process. You're basically forcing too much liquid into an already fatty mixture that doesn't want to make room for that liquid. There should be no streaks of fat or liquid. Stop the mixer and scrape down the sides of the bowl.

5. Whisk together the cake flour, cocoa powder, baking powder, and salt in a medium bowl.

This recipe is an evolution of the chocolate cake from our first cookbook, with some home-baker efficiencies built in!

Watch the oven diligently when baking this cake. It's already brown, so it's tricky to gauge visually when it's overbaked. (If you overbake it, it becomes crumbly and far less tasty.)

(recipe continues)

6. With the mixer on very low speed, slowly add the dry mixture and mix for 45 to 60 seconds, just until your batter comes together. Scrape down the sides of the bowl, then mix on low for an additional 45 seconds to make sure no lumps of cake flour or cocoa powder get left behind.

7. Divide the batter evenly between the quarter-sheet pans and, using a spatula, spread the cake batter into even layers.

8. Bake for 30 to 35 minutes, rotating the pans front to back halfway through baking. The cakes will rise and puff, doubling in size, but will remain slightly buttery and dense. At 30 minutes, gently poke the edge of each cake with your finger: The cakes should bounce back slightly and the centers should no longer be jiggly. If they don't pass these tests, leave the cakes in the oven for an additional 3 to 5 minutes.

9. Let the cakes cool in the pans on a wire rack or, in a pinch, in the fridge or freezer (don't worry, it's not cheating). The cooled cakes can be stored in the fridge, wrapped in plastic wrap, for up to 5 days.

fudge sauce

makes about 325g (1⅓ cups)

60g	**72% chocolate, chopped**	2 ounces
35g	**cocoa powder**	¼ cup
1g	**kosher salt**	¼ tsp
110g	**heavy cream**	½ cup
70g	**light corn syrup**	¼ cup
50g	**sugar**	¼ cup

1. Combine the chocolate, cocoa powder, and salt in a heatproof medium bowl.

2. Combine the heavy cream, corn syrup, and sugar in a heavy-bottomed saucepan and stir intermittently while bringing to a boil over high heat. The moment it boils, pour it into the bowl holding the chocolate. Let sit for 1 full minute.

3. Slowly, slowly begin to whisk the mixture. Then continue, increasing the vigor of your whisking every 30 seconds, until the mixture is glossy and silky-smooth. This will take 2 to 4 minutes, depending on your speed and strength.

4. You can use the sauce at this point or store it in an airtight container in the fridge for up to 2 weeks. The fudge sauce will be quite solid straight from the fridge. Warm slightly for 30 seconds in the microwave or gently in a saucepan on the stovetop until soft and pourable before using.

chocolate milk soak

makes about 120g (½ cup)

110g	**whole milk**	½ cup
8g	**fudge sauce** (opposite)	2 tsp

Whisk together the milk and fudge sauce in a small bowl. Use immediately.

yellow cake crumbs

makes about 335g (2½ cups)

290g	**yellow cake mix**	2 cups
45g	**unsalted butter, melted**	3 T

1. Heat the oven to 300°F. Line a sheet pan with parchment paper or a silicone baking mat.

2. Combine the yellow cake mix and the melted butter in a bowl and toss, using a spatula, until the mixture starts to come together and form small clusters.

3. Spread the clusters on the lined sheet pan and bake for 20 minutes, tossing halfway through. Your kitchen should smell like buttery heaven. Break up the crumbs and toss them around while they are still warm. Cool the crumbs completely before using.

4. The crumbs will keep in an airtight container in the fridge or freezer for up to 1 month.

yellow cake frosting

makes about 1,075g (4½ cups)

150g	**yellow cake mix**	¾ cup + 3 T
550g	**unsalted butter, softened**	5 sticks (1¼ lb)
300g	**confectioners' sugar**	2½ cups
3g	**kosher salt**	¾ tsp
0.75g	**citric acid**	pinch
85g	**whole milk**	⅓ cup + 1 T

1. Heat the oven to 250°F. Line a sheet pan with parchment paper or a silicone baking mat.

2. Spread the cake mix on the lined sheet pan and bake for 20 minutes. Cool the toasted cake mix completely before using.

3. Combine the butter, confectioners' sugar, salt, citric acid, and the cooled toasted cake mix in the bowl of a stand mixer fitted with the paddle attachment and cream together on medium-high for 6 to 8 minutes, scraping the bowl down once to make sure there are no butter lumps, until the mixture is smooth and fluffy.

4. With the mixer on low, stream in the milk and continue creaming until the puree is fully emulsified and the frosting is smooth and fluffy again.

5. Use the frosting immediately, or store it in an airtight container in the fridge for up to 1 week. If you store it in the refrigerator, be sure to loosen it up before using, otherwise it will be impossible to spread. The easiest way to do this is by putting the frosting in the bowl of a stand mixer fitted with the paddle attachment and beating it on medium speed for 3 to 4 minutes.

There is a brand of yellow cake mix that reigns supreme: It's Pillsbury (see page 17)!

corn and blueberry sheet cake

makes 1 double-layer quarter-sheet cake, 3 to 4 inches tall/serves 15 to 20

This ode to summer was dreamed up by the lovely Jena Derman, a "Milk Maid for life," who stayed late after work one night to make a friend a birthday cake. We became obsessed, immediately. Corn is one of the most underestimated flavors in the pastry world, and with freeze-dried corn ground into corn powder (see page 14), you can make this craveable and colorful sheet cake year-round.

1 recipe	**corn sheet cake** (page 115)	
110g	**whole milk**	½ cup
1 recipe	**sour cream frosting** (page 117)	
1 recipe	**jammy blueberry sauce** (page 116)	
1 recipe	**corn crumbs** (page 117)	

cake assembly instructions

Put a piece of parchment paper or a silicone baking mat on the counter. Run a knife or offset spatula along the edges of one of the quarter-sheet pans of cake to loosen it from the pan, then invert that cake onto it and peel off the parchment or mat from the bottom of the cake.

layer 1, the bottom

1. Clean the quarter-sheet pan and line it anew with clean parchment paper or a silicone baking mat. Place the cake you just unmolded back inside the pan. (Trust me.)

2. Dunk a pastry brush in the milk (or use a spoon) and give the cake a good, healthy bath with the milk.

3. Use the back of a spoon to spread half of the sour cream frosting in an even layer over the cake.

4. Sprinkle half of the corn crumbs evenly over the frosting. Use the back of your hand to press them lightly into the frosting, anchoring them in place.

5. Use the back of a spoon to spread the blueberry jam as evenly as possible over the crumbs.

layer 2, the top

1. Run a knife or offset spatula along the edges of the second quarter-sheet pan of cake to loosen it from the pan, then invert that cake directly on top of the frosting. Peel off the parchment or mat from the bottom of the cake and cover it with the remaining frosting. Give it volume and swirls, or do as we do and opt for a perfectly flat top. Garnish the frosting with the remaining corn crumbs.

2. Transfer the cake to the freezer and freeze for a minimum of 12 hours to set the cake and filling. Once set, if not serving right away, wrap in plastic and freeze for up to 2 weeks.

(recipe continues)

3. At least 3 hours before you are ready to serve the cake, pull it out of the freezer and, using an offset spatula or a bench scraper, pop the cake out of the pan.

4. Transfer the cake to a cutting board and fill a pitcher with hot water and set it aside. Use a chef's knife to trim the edges of the cake so you are left with flush, smooth sides, submerging the knife in hot water between cuts and wiping the blade clean. This makes for crumb-free, professional-looking cuts every time!

5. Place the cake on a large, rectangular platter. Let it defrost in the fridge for a minimum of 3 hours. (Wrapped well in plastic, the cake can be refrigerated for up to 5 days.)

6. When it's party time, slice the cake into squares and serve!

corn sheet cake

makes 2 quarter-sheet pans of cake

230g	unsalted butter, softened	2 sticks (16 T)
500g	sugar	4½ cups
4	large eggs	
220g	buttermilk	1 cup
120g	grapeseed or other neutral oil	⅔ cup
185g	cake flour	1½ cups
110g	corn powder (see page 14)	1¼ cups
40g	corn flour	¼ cup + 1½ T
12g	baking powder	1 T
8g	kosher salt	2 tsp

1. Heat the oven to 350°F. Pan-spray two quarter-sheet pans and line them with parchment paper, or just line them with silicone baking mats.

2. Combine the butter and sugar in the bowl of a stand mixer fitted with the paddle attachment and cream together on medium-high for 2 to 3 minutes, until light and fluffy. Scrape down the sides of the bowl halfway through this process, and again at the end of it.

3. Add the eggs, one at a time, beating on medium-high for 1 minute after each addition. After you add the last egg, scrape down the sides of the bowl, then beat on high for 4 more minutes. Scrape down the sides of the bowl again.

4. Combine the buttermilk and oil, and with the mixer on medium speed, stream them into the batter very slowly. It should take you approximately 3 minutes to add these liquids. Scrape down the sides of the bowl, increase the mixer speed to medium-high, and paddle for an additional 2 to 3 minutes, until the mixture is practically white, twice the size of your original fluffy butter-and-sugar mixture, and completely homogeneous. Don't rush the process. You're basically forcing too much liquid into an already fatty mixture that doesn't want to make room for that liquid. There should be no streaks of fat or liquid. Stop the mixer and scrape down the sides of the bowl.

5. Whisk together the cake flour, corn powder, corn flour, baking powder, and salt in a medium bowl.

6. With the mixer on very low speed, slowly add the dry mixture and mix for 45 to 60 seconds, just until your batter comes together. Scrape down the sides of the bowl, then mix for an additional 45 seconds to make sure no lumps of flour or powder get left behind.

7. Divide the batter evenly between the quarter-sheet pans and, using a spatula, spread the cake batter into even layers.

8. Bake for 30 to 35 minutes, rotating the pans front to back halfway through baking. The cakes will rise and puff, doubling in size, but will remain slightly buttery and dense. At 30 minutes, gently poke the edge of each cake with your finger: The cakes should bounce back slightly and the centers should no longer be jiggly. If they don't pass these tests, leave the cakes in the oven for an additional 3 to 5 minutes.

9. Let the cakes cool in the pans on a wire rack or, in a pinch, in the fridge or freezer (don't worry, it's not cheating). The cooled cakes can be stored in the fridge, wrapped in plastic wrap, for up to 5 days.

(recipe continues)

jammy blueberry sauce

makes about 400g (2 cups)

3g	cornstarch	1½ tsp
7g	water	1½ tsp
½	lemon	
340g	blueberries	12 ounces
50g	sugar	¼ cup
0.5g	kosher salt	⅛ tsp

1. Mix together the cornstarch and water to make a slurry.

2. Juice the lemon into a small saucepan and add the slurry, blueberries, sugar, and salt. Bring everything to a boil over medium heat.

3. Reduce the heat to low and continue cooking until the blueberries blister and the mixture turns dark blue, 5 to 6 minutes. The blueberries should still maintain their shape and not break down completely.

4. Cool the sauce before using. The sauce will keep in the refrigerator, in an airtight container, for up to 2 weeks.

Aptly named, this is more of a sauce than a jam. If you're looking for a thicker blueberry component because you're dreaming up something special, add another 3g (1½ teaspoons) cornstarch in the first step. The saucy consistency here, though, is perfect for this sheet cake.

corn crumbs

makes about 250g (2 cups)

60g	milk powder	⅔ cup
60g	ap flour	½ cup
20g	cornstarch	2 T + 1 tsp
10g	corn powder (see page 14)	2 T
35g	sugar	2 T + 2 tsp
4g	kosher salt	1 tsp
85g	unsalted butter, melted	6 T

1. Heat the oven to 250°F. Line a sheet pan with parchment paper or a silicone baking mat.

2. Combine the milk powder, flour, cornstarch, corn powder, sugar, and salt in a medium bowl. Toss to mix. Add the melted butter and toss, using a spatula, until the mixture starts to come together and form small clusters.

3. Spread the clusters on the lined sheet pan and bake for 20 to 25 minutes. The crumbs should be sandy, but still clumped together, just starting to brown around the edges, and your kitchen should smell like buttery heaven. Cool the crumbs completely. The crumbs will keep in an airtight container in the fridge or freezer for up to 1 month.

sour cream frosting

makes about 800g (4 cups)

205g	unsalted butter, softened	1 stick (8 T) + 7 T
400g	confectioners' sugar	3¼ cups
6g	kosher salt	1½ tsp
200g	sour cream	¾ cup + 1 T
5g	lemon juice	1 tsp

1. Combine the butter, confectioners' sugar, and salt in the bowl of a stand mixer fitted with the paddle attachment and cream together on medium-high for 6 to 8 minutes, scraping the bowl down once to make sure there are no butter lumps, until the mixture is smooth and fluffy.

2. Scrape down the sides of the bowl, then, with the mixer on low, stream in the sour cream and lemon juice and continue creaming until the puree is fully emulsified and the frosting is smooth and fluffy again. Increase the speed of the mixer to medium-high and mix until the entire mass is bright white, silky, and shiny. It should hold medium soft peaks, like whipped cream.

3. Use the frosting immediately or store it in an airtight container in the fridge for up to 1 week. If you store it in the refrigerator, be sure to loosen it up before using, otherwise it will be impossible to spread. The easiest way to do this is by putting the frosting in the bowl of a stand mixer fitted with the paddle attachment and beating it on medium speed for 3 to 4 minutes.

arnold palmer sheet cake

makes 1 double-layer quarter-sheet cake, 3 to 4 inches tall/serves 15 to 20

We're not big golfers. We much prefer double dutch or hopscotch to chasing a little ball around a green landscape ripe for log rolls and cartwheels. But we *do* love the brilliance behind Arnold Palmer and his balancing act of bitter, tannin-forward ice tea with sweet, citrusy lemonade. So much so, that it's a favor profile we love to use as much as possible in our kitchen.

---

1 recipe	**lemon-tea sheet cake**
	(opposite)
1 recipe	**bitter tea soak**
	(page 120)
1 recipe	**citrus milk crumbs**
	(page 120)
1 recipe	**lemon frosting**
	(page 121)

cake assembly instructions

Put a piece of parchment paper or a silicone baking mat on the counter. Run a knife or offset spatula along the edges of one of the quarter-sheet pans of cake to loosen it from the pan, then invert that cake onto it and peel off the parchment or mat from the bottom of the cake.

layer 1, the bottom

1. Clean the quarter-sheet pan and line it with clean parchment paper or a silicone baking mat. Place the cake back inside the pan.

2. Dunk a pastry brush in the bitter tea soak (or use a spoon) and give the cake a good, healthy bath with the soak.

3. Use the back of a spoon to spread one-quarter of the lemon frosting in an even layer over the cake.

4. Sprinkle half of the citrus milk crumbs evenly over the lemon frosting. Use the back of your hand to press them lightly into the frosting, anchoring them in place.

5. Use the back of a spoon to spread one-quarter of the lemon frosting as evenly as possible over the crumbs.

layer 2, the top

1. Run a knife or offset spatula along the edges of the second quarter-sheet pan of cake to loosen it from the pan, then invert that cake directly on top of the frosting. Peel off the parchment or mat from the bottom of the cake and cover it with the remaining frosting. Give it volume and swirls, or do as we do and opt for a perfectly flat top. Garnish the frosting with the remaining citrus milk crumbs.

2. Transfer the cake to the freezer and freeze for a minimum of 12 hours to set the cake and filling. Once set, if not serving right away, wrap in plastic and freeze for up to 2 weeks.

3. At least 3 hours before you are ready to serve the cake, pull it out of the freezer and, using an offset spatula or a bench scraper, pop the cake out of the pan.

4. Transfer the cake to a cutting board and fill a pitcher with hot water and set it aside. Use a chef's knife to trim the edges of the cake so you are left with flush, smooth sides, submerging the knife in hot water between cuts and wiping the blade clean. This makes for crumb-free, professional-looking cuts every time!

5. Place the cake on a large, rectangular platter. Let it defrost in the fridge for a minimum of 3 hours. (Wrapped well in plastic, the cake can be refrigerated for up to 5 days.)

6. When it's party time, slice the cake into squares and serve!

lemon-tea sheet cake

makes 2 quarter-sheet pans of cake

Tear open a bunch of single-serving Lipton tea bags, about 25, or buy Lipton loose black tea online.

60g	Lipton black tea leaves	⅔ cup
230g	unsalted butter, softened	2 sticks (16 T)
625g	sugar	3 cups + 2 T
4	large eggs	
4	large egg yolks	
220g	buttermilk	1 cup
120g	grapeseed or other neutral oil	½ cup + 2 T
400g	cake flour	3⅓ cups
12g	baking powder	1 T
8g	kosher salt	2 tsp
145g	lemon juice	½ cup + ½ T

1. Heat the oven to 350°F. Pan-spray two quarter-sheet pans and line them with parchment paper, or just line the pans with silicone baking mats.

2. Put the tea leaves in a blender or spice grinder and grind them down to a powder.

3. Combine the butter and sugar in the bowl of a stand mixer fitted with the paddle attachment and cream together on medium-high for 2 to 3 minutes, until light and fluffy. Scrape down the sides of the bowl halfway through this process, and again at the end of it.

4. Add the whole eggs and egg yolks, one at a time, beating on medium-high for 1 minute after each addition. After the last addition, scrape down the sides of the bowl, then beat on high for 4 more minutes. Scrape down the sides of the bowl again.

5. Combine the buttermilk and oil, and with the mixer on medium speed, stream them into the batter very slowly. It should take approximately 3 minutes to add these liquids. Scrape down the sides of the bowl, increase the mixer speed to medium-high, and paddle for an additional 2 to 3 minutes, until the mixture is practically white, twice the size of your original fluffy butter-and-sugar mixture, and completely homogeneous. Don't rush the process. You're basically forcing too much liquid into an already fatty mixture that doesn't want to make room for that liquid. There should be no streaks of fat or liquid. Stop the mixer and scrape down the sides of the bowl.

6. Whisk together the tea powder, cake flour, baking powder, and salt in a medium bowl.

7. With the mixer on very low speed, slowly add the dry mixture and mix for 45 to 60 seconds, just until your batter comes together. Scrape down the sides of the bowl, then mix on low for an additional

(recipe continues)

45 seconds to make sure no lumps of cake flour get left behind. Stream in the lemon juice and mix on low until it is fully incorporated.

8. Divide the batter evenly between the quarter-sheet pans and, using a spatula, spread the cake batter into even layers.

9. Bake for 30 to 35 minutes, rotating the pans front to bake halfway through baking. The cakes will rise and puff, doubling in size, but will remain slightly buttery and dense. At 30 minutes, gently poke the edge of each cake with your finger: The cakes should bounce back slightly and the centers should no longer be jiggly. If they don't pass these tests, leave the cakes in the oven for an additional 3 to 5 minutes.

10. Let the cakes cool in the pans on a wire rack or, in a pinch, in the fridge or freezer (don't worry, it's not cheating). The cooled cakes can be stored in the fridge, wrapped in plastic wrap, for up to 5 days.

bitter tea soak

makes 110g (½ cup)

110g	water	½ cup
2	single-serving Lipton black tea bags	

Bring the water to a boil in a small saucepan. Remove it from the heat and add the tea bags. Steep for 5 minutes, or until the tea is very bitter. Discard the tea bags and store the bitter tea soak in an airtight container in the fridge until you're ready to use it.

citrus milk crumbs

makes about 250g (2 cups)

40g	milk powder	½ cup
40g	ap flour	¼ cup
25g	sugar	2 T
12g	cornstarch	2 T
2g	kosher salt	½ tsp
1g	citric acid	¼ tsp
55g	unsalted butter, melted	½ stick (4 T)
20g	milk powder	¼ cup
90g	white chocolate, melted	3 ounces

1. Heat the oven to 250°F. Line a sheet pan with parchment paper or a silicone baking mat.

2. Combine the 40g (½ cup) milk powder, the flour, sugar, cornstarch, salt, and citric acid in a medium bowl. Toss to mix. Add the melted butter and toss, using a spatula, until the mixture starts to come together and form small clusters.

3. Spread the clusters on the lined sheet pan and bake for 20 minutes. The crumbs should be sandy at that point, and your kitchen should smell like buttery heaven. Cool the crumbs completely.

4. Crumble any milk crumb clusters that are larger than ½ inch in diameter and put the crumbs in a medium bowl. Add the 20g (¼ cup) milk powder and toss together until it is evenly distributed throughout the mixture.

5. Pour the white chocolate over the crumbs and toss until your clusters are enrobed. Then continue tossing them every 5 minutes until the white chocolate hardens and the

clusters are no longer sticky. The crumbs will keep in an airtight container in the fridge or freezer for up to 1 month.

lemon frosting

makes about 990g (4 cups)

330g	**unsalted butter, softened**	3 sticks (24 T)
620g	**confectioners' sugar**	5¼ cups
6g	**kosher salt**	1½ tsp
2	**lemons**	

1. Add the butter to the bowl of a stand mixer fitted with the paddle attachment and cream it on medium-high for 2 to 3 minutes, until the mixture is smooth and fluffy. Scrape down the sides of the bowl.

2. Add the confectioners' sugar and salt and mix on low speed just to incorporate them. Crank the speed back up to medium-high and beat for 2 to 3 minutes, until you have a beautifully smooth frosting.

3. Use a Microplane or the finest-toothed side of a box grater to zest the lemons. Do your best to grate only as far down as the yellow part of the skin; the white pith has less lemon flavor and can be bitter. Squeeze 60g (¼ cup) juice from the lemons.

4. Slowly stream lemon juice, along with the zest, into the frosting with the mixer on low speed. Once the zest and juice are incorporated, crank up the mixer once more and beat the lemon frosting for 1 more minute.

5. Use the frosting immediately or store it in an airtight container in the fridge for up to 1 week. If you store it in the refrigerator, be sure to loosen it up before using, otherwise it will be impossible to spread. The easiest way to do this is by putting the frosting in the bowl of a stand mixer fitted with the paddle attachment and beating it on medium speed for 3 to 4 minutes.

CUPCAKES

(IF YOU MUST)

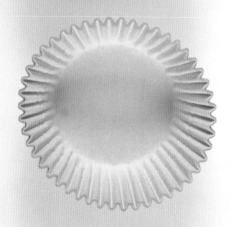

I mean no harm by my feelings on cupcakes.

As a kid, my mom used to make me cupcakes all the time. They were made out of cake mix, with no shame from my go-getting mom, who was out schooling the world on how an intensely focused woman handles business. I was her number one fan, cupcakes and all (and still am).

We don't sell cupcakes at Milk Bar. If anyone stands for bringing the spirit of the home kitchen into professional baking, it's ME! But cupcakes at bakeries are too often a dull cakey muffin with a lifeless goo on top, a fetishized fad, a cliché of the craft I hold so near and dear.

At home, though, my sugar-crazed nieces scream for cupcakes, and there's really no option but to pull out the pastel paper cups, the sea of jimmies and colorful sugar sprinkles in my cupboards, brace myself for the mess

that will quickly follow, and get to baking. I pretend it's a chore, but I also secretly love it.

Cupcakes don't have a place in my bakery, but they do have a place in my home (and are SO much fun there). We would never snub our favorite childhood cake form. Instead, we created some killer recipes to celebrate cupcakes (and, okay, to prove all those stale, bland, too-sweet, overdecorated, and underwhelming cupcakes wrong).

We keep ours VERY simple. A great cupcake needs a delicious cake nub (our recipes are flavorful, moist, and don't dome much at the top, on purpose), a flavorful frosting, and some textural personality. I think you know us well enough by now to know that we're not going to try and sell you on a cupcake that looks like a beautiful pink carnation using four different piping tips. What's really the point? We plan to eat the cupcake, not stare at it for hours, right?

For our cupcakes, you don't need any fancy tools; you can just use a knife or even a spoon to frost. If you want to use a little star tip with a pastry bag, feel free. Or a simple triangle of parchment paper can be rolled into an easy cone-shaped piping bag for a no-fuss frosting application.

Do you have a gaggle of children tugging at your pant leg for their cupcakes NOW? Teach those stinkers the value of hard work. Put a disposable or wipeable tablecloth down on the dinner table, spread out the cupcakes alongside bowls of frosting and decor, and tell them to have at it. Call it a "cupcake decorating party." My mom used to throw them for my sister and my co-birthday party. Pretty brilliant, right?

white album cupcakes

makes 1 dozen cupcakes, plus a few extra just in case

If you asked me as a child what my favorite band was, I would have undoubtedly screamed "The Beatles!" They were the only band that my parents agreed on when I was growing up and, as such, we always listened to them in our home. (I would tell you that, now, my favorite musician is Neil Young, but that's a story for another time.) Although these little cupcake nuggets are made only of plain vanilla ingredients, they are the most moist, delicious cupcakes you'll ever taste. Who would guess that such a basic cupcake could pack such a punch? They are just like the *White Album*, with its unassuming, plain white cover, secretly holding some of the world's greatest songs.

1 recipe	**vanilla cupcakes** (at right)	
125g	**milk crumbs** (page 129), optional	1 cup
430g	**vanilla [aka birthday] frosting** (page 106)	2 cups

cupcake assembly instructions

1. Make sure the cupcakes have cooled completely and the milk crumbs have set.

2. Top each cupcake with a dollop of frosting and use a small offset spatula, knife, or spoon to give it volume and swirls. Garnish each cupcake with milk crumbs, if you must, and serve immediately.

Two cups of frosting is just enough to conservatively top each cupcake. If you LOVE a ton of frosting, feel free to use the entire vanilla frosting recipe and you can pile the frosting as high as you like!

vanilla cupcakes

makes 1 dozen cupcakes, plus a few extra just in case

85g	unsalted butter, softened	6 T
150g	sugar	¾ cup
30g	light brown sugar	2 T (packed)
2	large eggs	
90g	grapeseed or other neutral oil	⅓ cup + 2 T
75g	buttermilk	⅓ cup
55g	whole milk	¼ cup
5g	clear vanilla extract	1¼ tsp
170g	cake flour	1½ cups
4g	baking powder	1 tsp
2g	kosher salt	½ tsp

1. Heat the oven to 350°F. Line a cupcake pan with cupcake liners.

2. Combine the butter and both sugars in the bowl of a stand mixer fitted with the

These make killer gluten-free cupcakes; just substitute gluten-free flour for cake flour and double the salt! Read about gluten-free flours we like (see page 15).

(recipe continues)

paddle attachment and cream together on medium-high for 2 to 3 minutes, until light and fluffy. Scrape down the sides of the bowl halfway through this process, and again at the end of it.

3. Add one of the eggs, beating on medium-high for 1 minute. Add the second egg, scrape down the sides of the bowl, then beat on high for 4 more minutes. Scrape down the sides of the bowl again.

4. Combine the oil, buttermilk, whole milk, and vanilla extract and with the mixer on medium speed, stream it in very slowly. It should take you approximately 3 minutes to add these liquids. Scrape down the sides of the bowl, increase the mixer speed to medium-high, and paddle for an additional 2 to 3 minutes, until the mixture is practically white, twice the size of your original fluffy butter-and-sugar mixture, and completely homogeneous. Don't rush the process. You're basically forcing too much liquid into an already fatty mixture that doesn't want to make room for that liquid. There should be no streaks of fat or liquid. Stop the mixer and scrape down the sides of the bowl.

5. Whisk together the cake flour, baking powder, and salt in a medium bowl.

6. With the mixer on very low speed, slowly add the dry mixture and mix for 45 to 60 seconds, just until your batter comes together. Scrape down the sides of the bowl, then mix on low for an additional 45 seconds to make sure no lumps of cake flour get left behind.

7. Use a heaping ¼ cup to fill the cupcake liners two-thirds to three-quarters full. Do not overfill the liners or the cupcakes will overflow and sink in the middle. (If you have leftover batter, save it and after the first batch bakes, refill the cupcake pan with liners and repeat.)

8. Bake for 25 to 30 minutes. The cupcakes will rise and puff, doubling in size, but will remain slightly buttery and dense. At 25 minutes, gently poke the edge of a few of the cupcakes with your finger: The cake should bounce back slightly and the center should no longer be jiggly. If they don't pass these tests, leave the cupcakes in the oven for an additional 3 to 5 minutes.

9. Let the cupcakes cool on a wire rack or, in a pinch, in the fridge or freezer (don't worry, it's not cheating). The cooled cupcakes can be stored in the fridge, wrapped in plastic wrap, for up to 5 days.

milk crumbs

makes about 250g (2 cups)

40g	milk powder	½ cup
40g	ap flour	¼ cup
25g	sugar	2 T
12g	cornstarch	1 T
2g	kosher salt	½ tsp
55g	unsalted butter, melted	½ stick (4 T)
20g	milk powder	¼ cup
90g	white chocolate, melted	3 ounces

1. Heat the oven to 250°F. Line a sheet pan with parchment paper or a silicone baking mat.

2. Combine the 40g (½ cup) milk powder, the flour, sugar, cornstarch, and salt in a medium bowl. Toss to mix. Add the melted butter and toss, using a spatula, until the mixture starts to come together and form small clusters.

3. Spread the clusters on the lined sheet pan and bake for 20 minutes. The crumbs should be sandy at that point, and your kitchen should smell like buttery heaven. Cool the crumbs completely.

4. Crumble any milk crumb clusters that are larger than ½ inch in diameter and put the crumbs in a medium bowl. Add the 20g (¼ cup) milk powder and toss together until it is evenly distributed throughout the mixture.

5. Pour the white chocolate over the crumbs and toss until your clusters are enrobed. Then continue tossing them every 5 minutes until the white chocolate hardens and the clusters are no longer sticky. The crumbs will keep in an airtight container in the fridge or freezer for up to 1 month.

lemon meringue cupcakes

makes 1 dozen cupcakes, plus a few extra just in case

Everyone loves a lemon meringue pie, so why not build on those flavors and turn them into a cupcake? The lemon cupcake base paired with the lemon meringue is the perfect combo. We top ours with citrus milk crumbs for an extra zangy snap, but Pie Dough Crumbs (page 252) would be great here, too.

1 recipe	**lemon cupcakes** (at right)	
1 recipe	**lemon meringue** (page 132)	
125g	**citrus milk crumbs** (page 120)	1 cup

cupcake assembly instructions

1. Make sure the cupcakes have cooled completely and the citrus milk crumbs have set.

2. Top each cupcake with a dollop of lemon meringue and use a knife, small offset spatula, or spoon to give it volume and swirls. Garnish each cupcake with citrus milk crumbs and serve immediately.

lemon cupcakes

makes 1 dozen cupcakes, plus a few extra just in case

85g	unsalted butter, softened	6 T
180g	sugar	1⅓ cups
2	large eggs	
85g	grapeseed or other neutral oil	⅓ cup + 2 T
50g	buttermilk	¼ cup
50g	whole milk	¼ cup
170g	cake flour	1½ cups
4g	baking powder	1 tsp
3g	kosher salt	¾ tsp
40g	lemon juice	3 T

1. Heat the oven to 350°F. Line a cupcake pan with cupcake liners.

2. Combine the butter and sugar in the bowl of a stand mixer fitted with the paddle attachment and cream together on medium-high for 2 to 3 minutes, until light and fluffy. Scrape down the sides of the bowl halfway through this process, and again at the end of it.

(recipe continues)

3. Add one of the eggs and beat on medium-high for 1 minute. Add the second egg, scrape down the sides of the bowl, then beat on high for 4 more minutes. Scrape down the sides of the bowl again.

4. Combine the oil, buttermilk, and whole milk and with the mixer on medium speed, stream it in very slowly. It should take you approximately 3 minutes to add these liquids. Scrape down the sides of the bowl, increase the mixer speed to medium-high, and paddle for an additional 2 to 3 minutes, until the mixture is practically white, twice the size of your original fluffy butter-and-sugar mixture, and completely homogeneous. Don't rush the process. You're basically forcing too much liquid into an already fatty mixture that doesn't want to make room for that liquid. There should be no streaks of fat or liquid. Stop the mixer and scrape down the sides of the bowl.

5. Whisk together the cake flour, baking powder, and salt in a medium bowl.

6. With the mixer on very low speed, slowly add the dry mixture and mix for 45 to 60 seconds, just until your batter comes together. Scrape down the sides of the bowl, then mix on low for an additional 45 seconds to make sure no lumps of cake flour get left behind.

7. Stream in the lemon juice and mix on low until it is fully incorporated.

8. Use a heaping ¼ cup to fill the cupcake liners two-thirds to three-quarters full. Do not overfill the liners or the cupcakes will overflow and sink in the middle. (If you have leftover batter, save it and after the first batch bakes, refill the cupcake pan with liners and repeat.)

9. Bake for 25 to 30 minutes. The cupcakes will rise and puff, doubling in size, but will remain slightly buttery and dense. At 25 minutes, gently poke the edge of a few of the cupcakes with your finger: The cupcakes should bounce back slightly and the centers should no longer be jiggly. If they don't pass these tests, leave the cupcakes in the oven for an additional 3 to 5 minutes.

10. Let the cupcakes cool on a wire rack or, in a pinch, in the fridge or freezer (don't worry, it's not cheating). The cooled cupcakes can be stored in the fridge, wrapped in plastic wrap, for up to 5 days.

lemon meringue

makes about 350g (2 cups)

4	large egg whites	
1g	cream of tartar	¼ tsp
150g	sugar	¾ cup
1	lemon	
85g	lemon curd (opposite)	¼ cup

1. Make sure your stand mixer bowl, whisk attachment, a medium bowl, and a rubber spatula are very clean and dry. Add the egg whites and cream of tartar to the stand mixer bowl fitted with the whisk attachment and beat them on medium-high until they begin to get foamy.

2. Stream in the sugar and continue to whip the egg whites until they reach stiff, glossy peaks.

3. Using a Microplane or the finest-toothed side of a box grater, zest the lemon. Do your

Two cups is just enough to conservatively top each cupcake. If you LOVE a ton of meringue, feel free to double this recipe and you can pile the frosting up as high as you like!

The meringue topping for these must be made and eaten on the same day, otherwise it deflates and no one wants a sad, deflated cupcake (even if it still tastes delicious, which it would, of course).

You can substitute ½ teaspoon powdered gelatin for the sheet gelatin.

best to grate only as far down as the yellow part of the skin; the white pith has less lemon flavor and can be bitter.

4. Put the lemon zest and lemon curd in a medium bowl and add one-third of the meringue to it. Mix it together vigorously to lighten the lemon curd and to make it easier to incorporate with the remaining meringue.

5. Very gently, add the second third of meringue to the bowl of lemon curd and use a spatula to fold it together. Start by putting the spatula in the middle of the bowl, then gently scrape under and out while you rotate the bowl.

6. Repeat the previous step with the last third of meringue. Continue folding everything together until no white streaks remain. Use the meringue immediately.

a note on meringues

If you dislike the idea of serving raw egg whites, do as the Italians do and make an Italian meringue. You will need a candy thermometer to pull it off. Here's how:

Add the egg whites to the bowl of a stand mixer fitted with the whisk attachment and begin to whip them on medium-high speed. While they are whipping, stir together the sugar and 2 tablespoons water in a small saucepan. Bring the sugar mixture to a boil and continue to heat it until it reaches soft-ball stage (240°F). Once the whites reach soft peaks, turn the mixer speed to low and carefully stream the hot sugar slowly into the egg whites. If the whites reach soft peaks before the sugar syrup has reached soft-ball stage, turn the mixer to low and continue mixing the whites on that speed until the hot sugar syrup is ready. After adding the syrup, continue whipping the egg whites until they cool, 2 to 3 minutes.

lemon curd

makes about 500g (2½ cups)

3	lemons	
100g	sugar	½ cup
4	large eggs	
1	silver gelatin sheet	
115g	unsalted butter, very cold, cut into chunks	1 stick (8 T)
2g	kosher salt	½ tsp

1. Using a Microplane or the finest-toothed side of a box grater, zest the lemons. Do your best to grate only as far down as the yellow part of the skin; the white pith has less lemon flavor and can be bitter. Squeeze 80g (⅓ cup) juice from the lemons.

2. Put the lemon zest, lemon juice, and sugar in a blender and blend until the sugar granules have dissolved. Add the eggs and blend on low until you have a bright-yellow mixture. Transfer the contents of the blender to a medium pot or saucepan. Clean the blender canister.

3. Bloom the gelatin (see page 27).

4. Set the pot of lemon mixture over low heat and whisk regularly as it heats up. Keep a close eye on it as it begins to thicken. Once the mixture starts to bubble up and begin to boil, remove it from the heat and transfer it to the blender. Add the bloomed gelatin, butter, and salt and blend until the mixture is thick, shiny, and super smooth.

5. Pour the mixture through a fine-mesh sieve into a heatproof container and put it in the fridge until the lemon curd has cooled completely, at least 30 minutes. The curd can be refrigerated for up to 1 week; do not freeze.

key lime pie cupcakes

makes 1 dozen cupcakes, plus a few extra just in case

One bite of this cupcake and you will be whisked away to the Florida Keys, on the beach, relaxing with a tropical drink in hand. And you know what goes great with tropical drinks? These cupcakes. There's something special about the chewy consistency of the graham cupcake base after it's baked that is quite addictive, and the key lime whip is perfection.

1 recipe	**graham cracker cupcakes** (at right)	
1 recipe	**key lime whipped cream** (page 139)	
125g	**graham crumbs** (page 219)	1 cup

cupcake assembly instructions

1. Make sure the cupcakes have cooled completely.

2. Top each cupcake with a dollop of key lime whipped cream and use a knife, small offset spatula, or spoon to give it volume and swirls.

3. Garnish each cupcake with graham crumbs and serve immediately.

graham cracker cupcakes

makes 1 dozen cupcakes, plus a few extra, just in case

85g	**unsalted butter, softened**	6 T
215g	**sugar**	1 cup + 1 T
2	**large eggs**	
65g	**grapeseed or other neutral oil**	⅓ cup
100g	**buttermilk**	¼ cup + 3 T
55g	**whole milk**	¼ cup
100g	**cake flour**	¾ cup
30g	**graham cracker crumbs**	¼ cup
3g	**baking powder**	¾ tsp
3g	**kosher salt**	¾ tsp
30g	**key lime juice**	2 T

"Graham cracker crumbs" are graham crackers that have been pulverized into a fine sand in a blender or food processor.

1. Heat the oven to 350°F. Line a cupcake pan with cupcake liners.

2. Combine the butter and sugar in the bowl of a stand mixer fitted with the paddle attachment and cream together on medium-high for 2 to 3 minutes, until light and fluffy. Scrape down the sides of the bowl halfway through this process, and again at the end of it.

(recipe continues)

3. Add one of the eggs, beating on medium-high for 1 minute. Add the second egg, scrape down the sides of the bowl, and beat on high for 4 more minutes. Scrape down the sides of the bowl again.

4. Combine the oil, buttermilk, and whole milk and with the mixer on medium speed, stream it in very slowly. It should take you approximately 3 minutes to add these liquids. Scrape down the sides of the bowl, increase the mixer speed to medium-high, and paddle for an additional 2 to 3 minutes, until the mixture is practically white, twice the size of your original fluffy butter-and-sugar mixture, and completely homogeneous. Don't rush the process. You're basically forcing too much liquid into an already fatty mixture that doesn't want to make room for that liquid. There should be no streaks of fat or liquid. Stop the mixer and scrape down the sides of the bowl.

5. Whisk together the cake flour, graham cracker crumbs, baking powder, and salt in a medium bowl.

6. With the mixer on very low speed, slowly add the dry mixture and mix for 45 to 60 seconds, just until your batter comes together. Scrape down the sides of the bowl, then mix on low for an additional 45 seconds to make sure no lumps of cake flour get left behind.

7. Stream in the key lime juice and mix on low until it is fully incorporated.

8. Use a heaping ¼ cup to fill the cupcake liners two-thirds to three-quarters full. Do not overfill the liners or the cupcakes will overflow and sink in the middle. (If you have leftover batter, save it and after the first batch bakes, refill the cupcake pan with liners and repeat.)

9. Bake for 25 to 30 minutes. The cupcakes will rise and puff, doubling in size, but will remain slightly buttery and dense. At 25 minutes, gently poke the edge of a few of the cupcakes with your finger: The cupcakes should bounce back slightly and the centers should no longer be jiggly. If they don't pass these tests, leave the cupcakes in the oven for an additional 3 to 5 minutes.

10. Let the cupcakes cool on a wire rack or, in a pinch, in the fridge or freezer (don't worry, it's not cheating). The cooled cupcakes can be stored in the fridge, wrapped in plastic wrap, for up to 5 days.

key lime whipped cream

makes about 630g (3 cups)

This toping is a subtle, silkier topping than the others in this book and you'll want to use more of it to top your cupcakes, so we increased the yield on it a tad. If you LOVE a ton of frosting, feel free to double this recipe and you can pile the whip up as high as you like! Any leftovers would be great eaten with fresh berries.

The key lime whip topping must be made and eaten within a day, otherwise it gets a little sad and droopy.

1	lime	
340g	sweetened condensed milk	1 cup + 2 T
70g	key lime juice (bottled)	¼ cup + 2 tsp
1g	kosher salt	¼ tsp
.25g	citric acid	pinch
4 drops	green food coloring	
220g	heavy cream	1 cup

1. Using a Microplane or the finest-toothed side of a box grater, zest the lime. Do your best to grate only as far down as the green part of the skin; the white pith has less lime flavor and can be bitter. Put the zest in a bowl along with the sweetened condensed milk, key lime juice, salt, citric acid, and green food coloring. Stir to combine and watch the sweetened condensed milk thicken before your very eyes!

2. Set the sweetened condensed milk bowl aside and add the heavy cream to the bowl of a stand mixer fitted with the whisk attachment. Whisk it on medium-high until it reaches medium-hard peaks.

3. Remove one-third of the whipped cream and add it to the sweetened condensed milk. Mix it together vigorously to lighten the sweetened condensed milk and to make it easier to incorporate with the remaining whipped cream.

4. Very gently, add the second third of whipped cream to the bowl of sweetened condensed milk and fold it together using a spatula. Start by putting the spatula in the middle of the bowl, then gently scrape under and out while you rotate the bowl.

5. Repeat with the last third of whipped cream. Continue folding everything together until no white streaks remain.

6. Cover the key lime whipped cream and let it sit in fridge for at least 1 hour, or up to overnight, before using it to decorate the cupcakes. The time spent in the fridge gives it a dreamy texture that you'll go bananas for.

strawberry-coconut cupcakes

makes 1 dozen cupcakes, plus a few extra just in case

When we use coconut at Milk Bar, we typically pair it with things like tangerines (see Coconut-Tangerine Cake Truffles, page 193) or pineapples (see Pineapple Upside-Down Layer Cake, page 237). Really, coconut pairs well with anything that lives in the tropical fruit category (if it GROWS together it GOES together is our basic rule of thumb), but for this we decided to get ca-razy and throw strawberries in the mix. Strawberries and coconut are not a super classic flavor combination, but it really works. The frosting here is basically the same as the Pickled Strawberry Frosting (page 225) except without the added vinegar. By all means, if you want a jazzier cupcake, feel free to swap in the pickled strawberry frosting instead.

65g	**shredded, unsweetened coconut**	1 cup
1 recipe	**coconut cupcakes** (at right)	
1 recipe	**strawberry frosting** (page 143)	

cupcake assembly instructions

1. Heat the oven to 250°F. Line a sheet pan with parchment paper.

2. Spread the coconut out on the lined sheet pan and toast in the oven until golden brown, about 20 minutes. Make sure the cupcakes and coconut have cooled completely before moving on to the next step.

3. Top each cupcake with a dollop of strawberry frosting and use a knife or small offset spatula or spoon to give it volume and swirls. Garnish each cupcake with the toasted coconut and serve immediately.

coconut cupcakes

makes 1 dozen cupcakes, plus a few extra just in case

85g	**unsalted butter, softened**	6 T
175g	**sugar**	¾ cup + 2 T
30g	**light brown sugar**	2 T (packed)
2	**large eggs**	
100g	**grapeseed or other neutral oil**	½ cup
70g	**buttermilk**	⅓ cup
70g	**whole milk**	⅓ cup
4g	**vanilla extract**	1 tsp
120g	**cake flour**	1 cup
3g	**baking powder**	¾ tsp
3g	**kosher salt**	¾ tsp
100g	**shredded, unsweetened coconut**	1 cup

1. Heat the oven to 350°F. Line a cupcake pan with cupcake liners.

(recipe continues)

2. Combine the butter and both sugars in the bowl of a stand mixer fitted with the paddle attachment and cream together on medium-high for 2 to 3 minutes, until light and fluffy. Scrape down the sides of the bowl halfway through this process, and again at the end of it.

3. Add one of the eggs, beating on medium-high for 1 minute. Add the second egg, scrape down the sides of the bowl, and beat on high for 4 more minutes. Scrape down the sides of the bowl again.

4. Combine the oil, buttermilk, whole milk, and vanilla extract and with the mixer on medium speed, stream it in very slowly. It should take you approximately 3 minutes to add these liquids. Scrape down the sides of the bowl, increase the mixer speed to medium-high, and paddle for an additional 2 to 3 minutes, until the mixture is practically white, twice the size of your original fluffy butter-and-sugar mixture, and completely homogeneous. Don't rush the process. You're basically forcing too much liquid into an already fatty mixture that doesn't want to make room for that liquid. There should be no streaks of fat or liquid. Stop the mixer and scrape down the sides of the bowl.

5. Whisk together the cake flour, baking powder, and salt in a medium bowl.

6. With the mixer on very low speed, slowly add the dry mixture and mix for 45 to 60 seconds, just until your batter comes together. Scrape down the sides of the bowl, then mix on low for an additional 45 seconds to make sure no lumps of cake flour get left behind. Add the coconut and mix until just combined.

7. Use a heaping ¼ cup to fill the cupcake liners two-thirds to three-quarters full. Do not overfill the liners or the cupcakes will overflow and sink in the middle. (If you have leftover batter, save it and after the first batch bakes, refill the cupcake pan with liners and repeat.)

8. Bake for 25 to 30 minutes. The cupcakes will rise and puff, doubling in size, but will remain slightly buttery and dense. At 25 minutes, gently poke the edge of a few of the cupcakes with your finger: The cupcakes should bounce back slightly and the centers should no longer be jiggly. If they don't pass these tests, leave the cupcakes in the oven for an additional 3 to 5 minutes.

9. Let the cupcakes cool on a wire rack or, in a pinch, in the fridge or freezer (don't worry, it's not cheating). The cooled cupcakes can be stored in the fridge, wrapped in plastic wrap, for up to 5 days.

strawberry frosting

makes about 430g (2 cups)

200g	unsalted butter, softened	1¾ sticks (14 T)
60g	confectioners' sugar	½ cup
175g	strawberry jam (at right)	1 cup
1g	kosher salt	¼ tsp
1g	citric acid	¼ tsp

1. Combine the butter and confectioners' sugar in the bowl of a stand mixer fitted with the paddle attachment and cream together on medium-high for 2 to 3 minutes, until light and fluffy.

2. Meanwhile, whisk together the strawberry jam, salt, and citric acid in a small bowl.

3. Scrape down the sides of the mixer bowl with a spatula. With the mixer on low speed, gradually stream in the strawberry mixture.

4. Use the frosting immediately or store it in an airtight container in the fridge for up to 1 week. If you store it in the refrigerator, be sure to loosen it up before using it, otherwise it will be impossible to spread. The easiest way to do this is by putting the frosting in the bowl of a stand mixer fitted with the paddle attachment and beating it on medium speed for 3 to 4 minutes.

Two cups is just enough to conservatively top each cupcake. If you LOVE a ton of frosting, feel free to double this recipe and you can pile the frosting up as high as you like!

strawberry jam

makes about 650g (3 cups)

450g	ripe strawberries	1 pound
200g	sugar	1 cup
8g	pectin NH	1 T + 1 tsp
2g	kosher salt	½ tsp

1. Wash and hull the strawberries. Put them in a blender and puree until they are fully broken down. Strain through a fine-mesh sieve.

2. Whisk together the sugar, pectin, and salt in a medium pot or saucepan. Slowly whisk in the strawberry puree and bring it to a full, rolling boil over medium-high heat, stirring occasionally with a heatproof spatula. Reduce the heat and cook at a low boil for 2 minutes to activate the pectin and turn the puree into a beautiful jam.

3. Once the pectin has been activated and the jam coats the back of a spoon, remove the jam from the heat. The jam keeps in the refrigerator, in an airtight container, for up to 2 weeks.

Read up on pectin NH (see page 16).

In a pinch, use your favorite store-bought jam instead.

no one hates on a chocolate cupcake

makes 1 dozen cupcakes, plus a few extra just in case

The name for this chocolate dream couldn't be more apt. No joke—nine out of ten taste testers, including myself, declared, "This is the best cupcake I've ever had!" The cake is light and fluffy and the chocolate frosting is extra rich because we add a little melted chocolate to it right at the end. And the final bit that really just pushes these over the edge from good to insane is the chocolate crumb garnish with its deep, rich chocolatey vibes. If you hate on chocolate cupcakes, this one will change your mind and turn you into a believer.

1 recipe	**chocolate cupcakes** (at right)	
1 recipe	**chocolate cupcake frosting** (page 147)	
140g	**chocolate crumbs** (page 147) **or mini chocolate chips**	1 cup

cupcake assembly instructions

1. Make sure the cupcakes have cooled completely.

2. Top each cupcake with a dollop of chocolate frosting and use a knife, small offset spatula, or spoon to give it volume and swirls. Garnish each cupcake with chocolate crumbs or chocolate chips and serve immediately.

chocolate cupcakes

makes 1 dozen cupcakes, plus a few extra just in case

85g	**unsalted butter, softened**	6 T
150g	**sugar**	¾ cup
45g	**light brown sugar**	3 T (packed)
2	**large eggs**	
90g	**grapeseed or other neutral oil**	⅓ cup + 2 T
75g	**buttermilk**	⅓ cup
55g	**whole milk**	¼ cup
3g	**vanilla extract**	¾ tsp
100g	**cake flour**	¾ cup
50g	**cocoa powder**	⅓ cup + 2 T
5g	**kosher salt**	1¼ tsp
4g	**baking powder**	1 tsp

Watch the oven diligently when baking these cupcakes. They're already brown so it's tricky to gauge visually when they're overbaked. (If you overbake them, they become crumbly and far less tasty.)

1. Heat the oven to 350°F. Line a cupcake pan with cupcake liners.

2. Combine the butter and both sugars in the bowl of a stand mixer fitted with the paddle attachment and cream together on

(recipe continues)

medium-high for 2 to 3 minutes, until light and fluffy. Scrape down the sides of the bowl halfway through this process, and again at the end of it.

3. Add one of the eggs, beating on medium-high for 1 minute. Add the second egg, scrape down the sides of the bowl, and beat on high for 4 more minutes. Scrape down the sides of the bowl again.

4. Combine the oil, buttermilk, whole milk, and vanilla extract and with the mixer on medium speed, stream them into the batter very slowly. It should take you approximately 3 minutes to add these liquids. Scrape down the sides of the bowl, increase the mixer speed to medium-high, and paddle for an additional 2 to 3 minutes, until the mixture is practically white, twice the size of your original fluffy butter-and-sugar mixture, and completely homogeneous. Don't rush the process. You're basically forcing too much liquid into an already fatty mixture that doesn't want to make room for that liquid. There should be no streaks of fat or liquid. Stop the mixer and scrape down the sides of the bowl.

5. Whisk together the cake flour, cocoa powder, salt, and baking powder in a medium bowl.

6. With the mixer on very low speed, slowly add the dry mixture and mix for 45 to 60 seconds, just until your batter comes together. Scrape down the sides of the bowl, then mix on low for an additional 45 seconds to make sure no lumps of cake flour or cocoa powder get left behind.

7. Use a heaping ¼ cup to fill the cupcake liners two-thirds to three-quarters full. Do not overfill the liners or the cupcakes will overflow and sink in the middle. (If you have leftover batter, save it and after the first batch bakes, refill the cupcake pan with liners and repeat.)

8. Bake for 25 to 30 minutes. The cupcakes will rise and puff, doubling in size, but will remain slightly buttery and dense. At 25 minutes, gently poke the edge of a few of the cupcakes with your finger: The cupcakes should bounce back slightly and the centers should no longer be jiggly. If they don't pass these tests, leave the cupcakes in the oven for an additional 3 to 5 minutes.

9. Let the cupcakes cool on a wire rack or, in a pinch, in the fridge or freezer (don't worry, it's not cheating). The cooled cupcakes can be stored in the fridge, wrapped in plastic wrap, for up to 5 days.

Two cups is
just enough to
conservatively top
each cupcake. If
you LOVE a ton of
frosting, feel free to
double this recipe
and you can pile the
frosting up as high
as you like!

chocolate cupcake frosting

makes about 420g (2 cups)

125g	unsalted butter, softened	1 stick (8 T) + 1 T
195g	confectioner's sugar	1½ cups + 2 T
2.5g	kosher salt	½ + ⅛ tsp
25g	cocoa powder	¼ cup
30g	whole milk	2 T
40g	55% chocolate, melted and cooled	1½ oz

1. Combine the butter, sugar, salt, and cocoa powder in the bowl of a stand mixer fitted with the paddle attachment and cream everything together on medium-high for 2 to 3 minutes, until the mixture is smooth and fluffy. Scrape down the sides of the bowl.

2. With the mixer on its lowest speed, stream in the milk. Crank the mixer up to medium-high and beat for 2 to 3 minutes, until the mixture is silky smooth and glossy. Scrape down the sides of the bowl.

3. Add the cooled melted chocolate to the frosting and mix on low until it is fully combined and no streaks of chocolate remain.

4. Use the frosting immediately or store it in an airtight container in the fridge for up to 1 week. If you store it in the refrigerator, be sure to loosen it up before using, otherwise it will be impossible to spread. The easiest way to do this is by putting the frosting in the bowl of a stand mixer fitted with the paddle attachment and beating it on medium speed for 3 to 4 minutes.

chocolate crumbs

makes about 700g (5 cups)

200g	sugar	1 cup
200g	ap flour	1½ cups
120g	cocoa powder	1⅓ cups
10g	cornstarch	2 tsp
8 g	kosher salt	2 tsp
170g	unsalted butter, melted	1½ sticks (12 T)

1. Heat the oven to 300°F. Line a sheet pan with parchment paper or a silicone baking mat.

2. Combine the sugar, flour, cocoa powder, cornstarch, and salt in the bowl of a stand mixer fitted with the paddle attachment and paddle on low speed until mixed.

3. Add the melted butter and paddle on low speed until the mixture starts to come together in small clusters.

4. Spread the clusters on the lined sheet pan. Bake for 20 minutes, breaking them up occasionally. The crumbs should still be slightly moist to the touch at that point; they will dry and harden as they cool.

5. Let the crumbs cool completely before using. The crumbs will keep in an airtight container in the fridge or freezer for up to 1 month.

german chocolate cupcakes

makes 1 dozen cupcakes, plus a few extra just in case

The inspiration behind these cupcakes comes from our German Chocolate Jimbo Layer Cake (page 243). Each cupcake is made of a chocolate cupcake base, topped with crack pie frosting, and garnished with pecan crunch. The crack pie frosting is probably the richest frosting known to man, and perhaps the most delicious.

1 recipe	**chocolate cupcakes** (page 145)	
1 recipe	**crack pie frosting** (at right)	
150g	**pecan crunch** (page 150)	1 cup

cupcake assembly instructions

1. Make sure the cupcakes have cooled completely.

2. Top each cupcake with a dollop of crack pie frosting and use a knife, small offset spatula, or spoon to give it volume and swirls. Garnish each cupcake with pecan crunch and serve immediately.

crack pie frosting

makes about 680g (3½ cups)

75g	sugar	⅔ cup
45g	light brown sugar	3 T (packed)
5g	milk powder	1 T
6g	corn powder (see page 14)	1 T
2g	kosher salt	½ tsp
55g	unsalted butter, melted	½ stick (4 T)
40g	heavy cream	3 T
1g	vanilla extract	¼ tsp
2	large egg yolks	
225g	unsalted butter, softened	2 sticks (16 T)
80g	confectioners' sugar	⅔ cup
1g	kosher salt	¼ tsp
175g	shredded, sweetened coconut	1¾ cups

1. Heat the oven to 350°F. Pan-spray a 9 x 5-inch loaf pan.

2. Combine the sugar, brown sugar, milk powder, corn powder, and salt in the bowl of a stand mixer fitted with the paddle attachment and mix on low speed until evenly blended.

This recipe yields more than you'll need to decorate the cupcakes. However, making a smaller batch of this would be a real pain in the behind (trust me). If you LOVE a ton of frosting, this will be the perfect amount for you! If not, you can use any leftovers in lieu of maple syrup on your Saturday morning pancakes and you'll be a happy camper.

(recipe continues)

3. Add the melted butter and paddle for 1 minute on low speed until all the dry ingredients are moist.

4. Add the heavy cream and vanilla extract and continue mixing on low for 1 minute until any white streaks from the cream have completely disappeared into the mixture. Scrape down the sides of the bowl with a spatula.

5. Add the yolks, paddling them into the mixture just to combine; be careful not to aerate the mixture, but be certain the mixture is glossy and homogenous. Mix on low speed until it is.

6. Pour the crack pie filling into the loaf pan and bake for 20 to 25 minutes. At 20 minutes, gently shake the pan: The crack pie filling should be firmer and more set around the edges but slightly jiggly and loose in the center. If the crack pie filling is jiggly all over, give it 2 to 3 minutes more in the oven. It should just start to brown on top.

7. Let the crack pie filling cool to room temperature.

8. Put the softened butter, confectioners' sugar, salt, and cooled crack pie filling in the bowl of a stand mixer fitted with the paddle attachment. Mix on low speed to combine, then bump up the speed to high and cream for about 5 minutes, until the mixture is light and fluffy.

9. Add the shredded coconut and mix on low to combine.

10. Use the frosting immediately or store it in an airtight container in the fridge for up to 1 week. If you store it in the refrigerator, be sure to loosen it up before using, otherwise it will be impossible to spread. The easiest way to do this is by putting the frosting in the bowl of a stand mixer fitted with the paddle attachment and beating it on medium speed for 3 to 4 minutes.

pecan crunch

makes about 245g (1½ cups)

125g	chopped pecans	1 cup
40g	grapeseed or other neutral oil	3 T + 2 tsp
20g	light brown sugar	1 T + 1 tsp (packed)
2g	kosher salt	½ tsp
60g	feuilletine	¾ cup

1. Heat the oven to 325°F.

2. Put the pecans on a sheet pan and toast in the oven until very aromatic and browned, but not burnt, about 15 minutes.

3. Puree the warm pecans in a food processor with the oil, brown sugar, and salt until you have a wet, sandy consistency.

4. In a small bowl, combine the pecan puree with the feuilletine. The crunch will keep in an airtight container at room temperature for 5 days or in the fridge for up to 2 weeks.

Feuilletine has been a secret ingredient of pastry chefs for quite some time now. They are tiny shards of paper thin, caramelized wafers that will add an addictive crunch to any oil-based recipe. (They get super soggy if they interact with water-based liquid.) You can buy them online, or occasionally specialty bakeries will carry them. They will change your life, if you're a texture hound like me.

banana-chocolate-hazelnut cupcakes

makes 1 dozen cupcakes, plus a few extra just in case

If you've baked your way through the original Momofuku Milk Bar cookbook, you may remember the banana-chocolate-hazelnut layer cake recipe. (If you haven't made it yet, what the heck are you waiting for? It's one of our very best recipes!) These cupcakes are our homage to that beloved layer cake. There's something amazing about the way bananas and hazelnuts play off of each other when chocolate is the bridge they get to play on.

1 recipe	**banana cupcakes** (at right)	
1 recipe	**chocolate hazelnut frosting** (page 155)	
140g	**chocolate crumbs** (page 147)	1 cup

cupcake assembly instructions

1. Make sure the cupcakes have cooled completely.

2. Top each cupcake with a dollop of chocolate hazelnut frosting and use a knife, small offset spatula, or spoon to give it volume and swirls. Garnish each cupcake with chocolate crumbs and serve immediately.

We love our chocolate crumbs and use them every chance we get. They make a great garnish for these cupcakes, but if you don't feel like making them, a little dried banana chip and some chopped, toasted hazelnuts would look REAL cute (and also be delicious!).

banana cupcakes

makes 1 dozen cupcakes, plus a few extra just in case

225g	*rrrrrripe* **bananas**	2 medium
85g	**unsalted butter, softened**	6 T
200g	**sugar**	1 cup
1	**large egg**	
110g	**buttermilk**	½ cup
90g	**grapeseed or other neutral oil**	⅓ cup + 2 T
85g	**whole milk**	⅓ cup
2g	**banana extract**	½ tsp
225g	**ap flour**	1¾ cups
3g	**baking powder**	¾ tsp
3g	**baking soda**	½ tsp
2g	**kosher salt**	½ tsp

Read up on the pro art of ripening bananas (see page 13)!

1. Heat the oven to 350°F. Line a cupcake pan with cupcake liners.

2. Put the bananas in a small bowl and use your hands to smoosh them into a mush.

(recipe continues)

3. Combine the butter and sugar in the bowl of a stand mixer fitted with the paddle attachment and cream together on medium-high for 2 to 3 minutes, until light and fluffy. Scrape down the sides of the bowl halfway through this process, and again at the end of it.

4. Add the egg and beat on high for 4 minutes. Scrape down the sides of the bowl.

5. Combine the buttermilk, oil, milk, and banana extract and with the mixer on medium speed, stream them into the batter very slowly. It should take you approximately 3 minutes to add these liquids. Scrape down the sides of the bowl, increase the mixer speed to medium-high, and paddle for an additional 2 to 3 minutes, until the mixture is practically white, twice the size of your original fluffy butter-and-sugar mixture, and completely homogeneous. Don't rush the process. You're basically forcing too much liquid into an already fatty mixture that doesn't want to make room for that liquid. There should be no streaks of fat or liquid. Stop the mixer and scrape down the sides of the bowl.

6. Whisk together the flour, baking powder, baking soda, and salt in a medium bowl.

7. With the mixer on very low speed, slowly add the dry mixture and mix for 45 to 60 seconds, just until your batter comes together. Scrape down the sides of the bowl, then mix on low for an additional 45 seconds to make sure no lumps of AP flour get left behind. Add the banana mush and mix until just combined.

8. Use a heaping ¼ cup to fill the cupcake liners two-thirds to three-quarters full. Do not overfill the liners or the cupcakes will overflow and sink in the middle. (If you have leftover batter, save it and after the first batch bakes, refill the cupcake pan with liners and repeat.)

9. Bake for 25 to 30 minutes. The cupcakes will rise and puff, doubling in size, but will remain slightly buttery and dense. At 25 minutes, gently poke the edge of a few of the cupcakes with your finger: The cupcakes should bounce back slightly and the centers should no longer be jiggly. If they don't pass these tests, leave the cupcakes in the oven for an additional 3 to 5 minutes.

10. Let the cupcakes cool on a wire rack or, in a pinch, in the fridge or freezer (don't worry, it's not cheating). The cooled cupcakes can be stored in the fridge, wrapped in plastic wrap, for up to 5 days.

chocolate hazelnut frosting

makes about 470g (2 cups)

Find 8-ounce tubs of Valrhona *praliné* on amazon.com. It is our hazelnut paste of choice.

Two cups is just enough to conservatively top each cupcake. If you LOVE a ton of frosting, feel free to double this recipe and you can pile the frosting up as high as you like!

40g	55% chocolate	1½ ounces
110g	unsalted butter, softened	1 stick (8 T)
160g	confectioner's sugar	1⅓ cups
30g	cocoa powder	¼ cup
2g	kosher salt	½ tsp
30g	whole milk	2 T
100g	hazelnut praline paste	¼ cup + 1 T

1. Heat the chocolate in 10-second bursts in the microwave until melted and set aside to cool to room temperature.

2. Combine the butter, sugar, cocoa powder, and salt in the bowl of a stand mixer fitted with the paddle attachment and cream together on medium-high for 2 to 3 minutes, until the mixture is smooth and fluffy. Scrape down the sides of the bowl.

3. With the mixer on its lowest speed, stream in the milk. Crank the mixer up to medium-high and beat for an additional 5 minutes, until the mixture is silky smooth and glossy. Scrape down the sides of the bowl.

4. Stir the hazelnut paste into the cooled, melted chocolate and add it to the frosting. Mix the frosting on low until the chocolate-hazelnut mixture has fully combined and no streaks of chocolate remain.

5. Use the frosting immediately or store it in an airtight container in the fridge for up to 1 week. If you store it in the refrigerator, be sure to loosen it up before using, otherwise it will be impossible to spread. The easiest way to do this is by putting the frosting in the bowl of a stand mixer fitted with the paddle attachment and beating it on medium speed for 3 to 4 minutes.

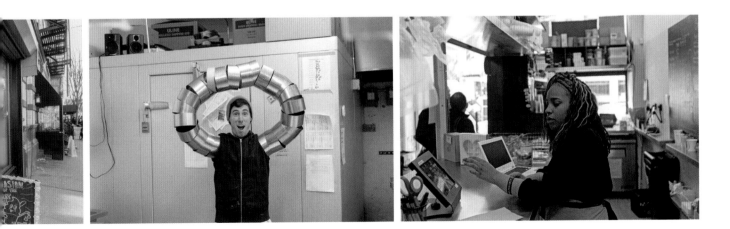

CAKE TRUFFLES MAKE THE WORLD GO 'ROUND

Essentially cake bites or cake hors d'oeuvres (which makes them great for parties), cake truffles were born entirely out of leftovers in our kitchen.

Baking cakes in a flat sheet pan, then cutting them into rounds for the layer cakes in the chapter that follows will always yield cake scraps. In Milk Bar's infancy, we would eat those scraps—there weren't too many and they are delicious, so it was never a problem. Until it became a problem. As certain cakes

grew in popularity—*ahem, birthday cake*—the amount of scraps we amassed became staggering. There was just no way we'd be able to eat them all, let alone give them away. And as a small business owner who was raised with a waste-not-want-not mentality, throwing anything in the trash seemed like the craziest concept around. (Plus we only had one trash can, so it was really an uphill battle all the way.)

We had to get creative. For a time, we dehydrated the scraps, and pretty much every flavor of

dehydrated cake scrap worked great as a soft serve topping. We even went SUPER meta and used them as a crunchy filling for a layer cake. But all of that dehydrating got complicated, so we had to "scrap" that idea. LOLOLOLOL

Next, we blended the scraps into an ice cream base to make cake-flavored ice creams, which were always a winner. We also used them for plated desserts at Momofuku Ko, but even with all that, we grew and the scrap situation grew ever more out of control. I remember looking into our single-door fridges and seeing twenty-quart industrial Cambro containers full of scraps. It was a closing duty to push the scraps down and add more scraps on top. The scraps were coming dangerously close to needing their own zip code in our tiny little kitchen.

Little did we know that the answer to our amassing cake scrap problem had been sitting right in front of us the whole time. In an effort to get people excited about the cake scrap side work, two of the original Milk Maids, Leslie Discher and Helen Jo, always made tiny little cake bites dipped in chocolate and rolled in whatever random crunchies we had lying around, and they would surprise-slip them on different people's stations when they weren't looking. We just thought they were being sweet, and we had not yet considered their brilliance.

Until one day, we were in a meeting talking about the issue at hand: Cambros on Cambros of cake

scraps. Helen Jo went into Real Talk mode. We should put these cake bites on the menu! I was a little hesitant at first and we had a heckuva time coming up with a proper name. "Cake balls" sounded too vulgar, so we landed on cake *truffles*, the ultimate combination of our fancy kitchen backgrounds and our lowbrow Milk Bar life.

They took off like wildfire, and now they pay for our retirement funds. And oh how the tables have turned on our cake scraps: We now bake massive batches of cake just to make the cake truffles! We even use them as our secret code for when the health department comes. If an inspector comes knocking, an employee immediately finds a manager and says, "86 cake truffles"—86 is kitchen-speak for running out of something, but we make cake truffles SO OFTEN we could never possibly actually run out of them. So, if anyone ever runs through the commissary yelling "86 CAKE TRUFFLES!" we'd know the health department has arrived.

(Not that we have anything to hide from the health department, but it's always nice to have a few seconds of a heads-up.)

By the time we wrote the Momofuku Milk Bar cookbook, we had just started to understand the way we thought about cake truffles, and barely had a recipe to share. Nowadays, every layer cake we make at Milk Bar (and every layer cake recipe in this book!) gets a corresponding cake truffle to go along with it. In addition to the cake scrap, sometimes we use the corresponding layer cake components; other times we make elements to enhance the perfect bite of a cake truffle that don't come into play in the layer cake itself. (We have gone through twelve to fourteen tests to get some of our most beloved cake truffle recipes just right.) But one of the beauties of cake truffles is that you don't have to go all the way through the process of baking and assembling a layer cake. They're much easier to make! I love them so much, they orbit my dreams like tiny sugar planets.

every milk bar cake truffle follows the same formula

cake: Newly baked, scrap, or even overbaked, underbaked, or stale cake will do, just make sure it tastes great; it is, after all, the heart of the cake truffle!

soak/binder: Anything that will add moisture to bind the cake and tell the "flavor story" works—from milk to fruit juice to fruit jam to beer.

shell: Typically a very thin covering of white chocolate to lock in the inner freshness of the cake truffle, and to act as a glue for the coat that follows.

coat: Usually a crumb or crunch ground down, anything in a sandy state that will add texture to the outside while also telling the "flavor story."

(If you're ready for extra credit, we've included a BONUS!!! section at the end of this chapter to stack your creations to the sky as cake truffle croquembouches.)

b'day truffles

makes 35 to 40 cake truffles

The birthday cake truffle started it all (i.e., marked our descent into madness). It was the first cake truffle we made and as it gained traction at an ALARMING rate, we knew we were on to something special. It's the cake truffle recipe format in its purest form. (We get a little more elaborate with it later.) But here, we take our classic birthday cake, add a skosh of vanilla-scented milk, roll it into a ball, dip it in white chocolate, and coat it in those delicious birthday crumbs ground down into a sand. It tastes like a really good version of the boxed cake mix that everyone had when they were kids. I don't care who you are—that vanilla flavor mixed with the rainbow sprinkles is unstoppable, and resistance to the sweet, gooey, fudgy, dense center is futile. My favorite way to eat them is straight out of the freezer.

1 recipe	**birthday cake** (page 162)
1 recipe	**vanilla milk soak** (page 105)
1 recipe	**birthday sand** (page 163)
1 recipe	**white chocolate coating** (page 163)

1. Remove the cake from the sheet pan. Break the cake down into crumbs and combine with half the vanilla milk soak in a medium bowl. Toss with your hands until moist enough to knead into a ball. If necessary, slowly add more soak, a little at a time, and knead it in. You want the filling to be quite moist and soft, not chewy. You may or may not end up using all of the soak.

2. Use a tablespoon to scoop even amounts of the cake truffle filling, each scoop approximately half the size of a Ping-Pong ball. Roll each scoop between the palms of your hands to shape and smooth it into a sphere.

3. Put the birthday sand in a medium bowl and set aside.

4. With latex gloves on, put 2 tablespoons of the white chocolate coating in the palm of your hand and roll each ball between your palms, coating it in a thin layer of melted chocolate; add more chocolate to your palm as needed.

5. Put 3 or 4 chocolate-covered balls at a time into the bowl of birthday sand. Immediately toss them with the sand to coat, before the chocolate shell sets and no longer acts as a glue (if this happens, just coat the ball in another thin layer of melted chocolate).

6. Refrigerate for at least 5 minutes to fully set the chocolate shells before eating or storing. The truffles will keep in an airtight container for up to 1 week in the fridge or up to 1 month in the freezer.

(recipe continues)

birthday cake

makes 1 quarter-sheet pan of cake

60g	vegetable shortening	⅓ cup
55g	unsalted butter, softened	½ stick (4 T)
250g	sugar	1¼ cups
50g	light brown sugar	3 T (packed)
3	large eggs	
110g	buttermilk	½ cup
65g	grapeseed or other neutral oil	⅓ cup
8g	clear vanilla extract	2 tsp
245g	cake flour	2 cups
50g	rainbow sprinkles	¼ cup
6g	baking powder	1½ tsp
3g	kosher salt	¾ tsp
25g	rainbow sprinkles	2 T

1. Heat the oven to 350°F. Pan-spray a quarter-sheet pan and line it with parchment paper, or just line the pan with a silicone baking mat.

2. Combine the shortening, butter, and both sugars in the bowl of a stand mixer fitted with the paddle attachment and cream together on medium-high for 2 to 3 minutes, until light and fluffy. Scrape down the sides of the bowl halfway through this process, and again at the end of it.

3. Add the eggs, one at a time, beating on medium-high for 1 minute after each addition. After you add the last egg, scrape down the sides of the bowl, then beat on high for 4 more minutes. Scrape down the sides of the bowl again.

4. Combine the buttermilk, oil, and clear vanilla extract and with the mixer on medium speed, stream them into the cake batter very slowly. It should take you approximately 3 minutes to add these liquids. Scrape down the sides of the bowl, increase the mixer speed to medium-high, and paddle for an additional 2 to 3 minutes, until the mixture is practically white, twice the size of your original fluffy butter-and-sugar mixture, and completely homogeneous. Don't rush the process. You're basically forcing too much liquid into an already fatty mixture that doesn't want to make room for that liquid. There should be no streaks of fat or liquid. Stop the mixer and scrape down the sides of the bowl.

5. Whisk together the cake flour, the 50g (¼ cup) rainbow sprinkles, the baking powder, and salt in a medium bowl.

6. With the mixer on very low speed, slowly add the dry mixture and mix for 45 to 60 seconds, just until your batter comes together. Scrape down the sides of the bowl, then mix on low for an additional 45 seconds to make sure no lumps of cake flour get left behind.

7. Using a spatula, spread the cake batter in an even layer in the pan. Sprinkle the remaining 25g (2 tablespoons) rainbow sprinkles evenly on top of the batter.

8. Bake for 30 to 35 minutes, rotating the pan front to back halfway through baking. The cake will rise and puff, doubling in size, but will remain slightly buttery and dense. At 30 minutes, gently poke the edge of the cake with your finger: The cake should bounce back slightly and the center should no longer be jiggly. If it doesn't pass these

tests, leave the cake in the oven for an additional 3 to 5 minutes.

9. Let the cake cool in the pan on a wire rack or, in a pinch, in the fridge or freezer (don't worry, it's not cheating). The cooled cake can be stored in the fridge, wrapped in plastic wrap, for up to 5 days.

birthday sand

makes about 630g (4 cups)

1 recipe	**birthday crumbs** (page 106)	

Process the birthday crumbs in a food processor until they break down into a fine sand. The sand will keep in an airtight container for 1 week in the fridge or 1 month in the freezer.

You shouldn't stress too much about what kind of white chocolate you use. FYI, some chocolate brands are naturally more viscous when they melt, so if you find that your coating is too thick, just add more grapeseed oil, ½ teaspoon at a time, until it gets to a consistency you like. If you do have a choice, though, try to choose a white chocolate that is less sweet, with less intense vanilla notes, so the overall flavor of the truffle can shine through!

white chocolate coating

makes about 360g (2 cups)

350g	**white chocolate, melted**	6 ounces
10g	**grapeseed or other neutral oil**	1 T

In a small bowl, whisk together the melted white chocolate and oil until homogenous. Keep warm, or remelt if necessary before using.

chocolate malt cake truffles

makes 35 to 40 cake truffles

The chocolate malt cake truffle plays into the chocolate *and* the vanilla person inside everyone with its chocolate cake, malted milk soak (a nod to the chocolate Ovaltine we all drank as kids), thin layer of white chocolate, and malted milk crumbs. It's the nostalgia of childhood with a rich, ooey-gooey center. This, along with the birthday cake truffle, never comes off the menu at any of our stores, because, in my mind, you are either a b'day truffle person or a chocolate malt cake truffle person. You can walk into a Milk Bar, anywhere, anytime, and buy either or BOTH! They are so good, and for a truffle to be able to stand up against our most classic, coveted birthday cake truffle, that's really saying something about its significance.

1 recipe	**chocolate cake** (page 166)
1 recipe	**malted milk soak** (page 167)
1 recipe	**malted milk sand** (page 167)
1 recipe	**white chocolate coating** (page 163)

1. Remove the cake from the sheet pan. Break the cake down into crumbs and combine with half the malted milk soak in a medium bowl. Toss with your hands until moist enough to knead into a ball. If necessary, slowly add more soak, a little at a time, and knead it in. You want the filling to be quite moist and soft, not chewy. You may or may not end up using all of the soak.

2. Use a tablespoon to scoop even amounts of the cake truffle filling, each scoop approximately half the size of a Ping-Pong ball. Roll each scoop between the palms of your hands to shape and smooth it into a sphere.

3. Put the malted milk sand in a medium bowl and set aside.

4. With latex gloves on, put 2 tablespoons of the white chocolate coating in the palm of your hand and roll each ball between your palms, coating it in a thin layer of melted chocolate; add more chocolate to your palm as needed.

5. Put 3 or 4 chocolate-covered balls at a time into the bowl of malted milk sand. Immediately toss them with the sand to coat, before the chocolate shell sets and no longer acts as a glue (if this happens, just coat the ball in another thin layer of melted chocolate).

6. Refrigerate for at least 5 minutes to fully set the chocolate shells before eating or storing. The truffles will keep in an airtight container for up to 1 week in the fridge or up to 1 month in the freezer.

(recipe continues)

chocolate cake

makes 1 quarter-sheet pan of cake

115g	unsalted butter, softened	1 stick (8 T)
225g	sugar	1 cup + 2 T
60g	light brown sugar	¼ cup (packed)
3	large eggs	
110g	buttermilk	½ cup
105g	grapeseed or other neutral oil	½ cup + 3 T
5g	vanilla extract	1¼ tsp
155g	cake flour	1¼ cups
70g	cocoa powder	½ cup
6g	baking powder	1½ tsp
7g	kosher salt	1¾ tsp

1. Heat the oven to 350°F. Pan-spray a quarter-sheet pan and line it with parchment paper, or just line it with a silicone baking mat.

2. Combine the butter and both sugars in the bowl of a stand mixer fitted with the paddle attachment and cream together on medium-high for 2 to 3 minutes, until light and fluffy. Scrape down the sides of the bowl halfway through this process, and again at the end of it.

3. Add the eggs, one at a time, beating on medium-high for 1 minute after each addition. After you add the last egg, scrape down the sides of the bowl, then beat on high for 4 more minutes. Scrape down the sides of the bowl again.

4. Combine the buttermilk, oil, and vanilla extract and with the mixer on medium speed, stream them in very slowly. It should take you approximately 3 minutes to add these liquids. Scrape down the sides of the bowl, increase the mixer speed to medium-high, and paddle for an additional 2 to 3 minutes, until the mixture is practically white, twice the size of your original fluffy butter-and-sugar mixture, and completely homogeneous. Don't rush the process. You're basically forcing too much liquid into an already fatty mixture that doesn't want to make room for that liquid. There should be no streaks of fat or liquid. Stop the mixer and scrape down the sides of the bowl.

5. Whisk together the cake flour, cocoa powder, baking powder, and salt in a medium bowl.

6. With the mixer on very low speed, slowly add the dry mixture and mix for 45 to 60 seconds, just until your batter comes together. Scrape down the sides of the bowl, then mix on low for an additional 45 seconds to make sure no lumps of cake flour or cocoa powder get left behind.

7. Pour the batter into the sheet pan and, using a spatula, spread the cake batter in an even layer in the pan.

8. Bake for 30 to 35 minutes, rotating the pan front to back halfway through baking. The cake will rise and puff, doubling in size, but will remain slightly buttery and dense. At 30 minutes, gently poke the edge of the cake with your finger: The cake should bounce back slightly and the center should no longer be jiggly. If it doesn't pass these tests, leave the cake in the oven for an additional 3 to 5 minutes.

This recipe is an evolution of the chocolate cake from our first cookbook, with some efficiencies for the home baker built in!

Watch the oven diligently when baking this cake. It's already brown, so it's tricky to gauge visually when it's overbaked. (If you overbake it, it becomes crumbly and far less tasty.)

9. Let the cake cool in the pan on a wire rack or, in a pinch, in the fridge or freezer (don't worry, it's not cheating). The cooled cake can be stored in the fridge, wrapped in plastic wrap, for up to 5 days.

malted milk soak

makes about 130g (½ cup)

110g	whole milk	½ cup
20g	Ovaltine, classic malt	¼ cup
1g	kosher salt	½ tsp

Whisk together the milk, Ovaltine, and salt until the Ovaltine is completely dissolved. Use immediately.

malted milk sand

makes about 575g (4 cups)

120g	ap flour	¾ cup
120g	Ovaltine, classic malt	1¼ cups
100g	sugar	½ cup
80g	milk powder	1 cup
40g	cornstarch	¼ cup
2g	kosher salt	½ tsp
115g	unsalted butter, melted	1 stick (8 T)

1. Heat the oven to 275°F.

2. Combine the flour, Ovaltine, sugar, milk powder, cornstarch, and salt in the bowl of a stand mixer fitted with the paddle attachment and mix on low speed until well combined.

3. Add the melted butter and paddle again to distribute. The butter will make the mixture come together in small clumps and then the clumps will break down into a well-combined sand.

4. Spread the sand on a quarter-sheet pan and bake until the sand just starts to darken around the edges, 10 to 12 minutes.

5. Let the sand cool completely before using. The sand will keep in an airtight container for 1 week in the fridge or 1 month in the freezer.

chocolate chip–passion fruit cake truffles

makes 35 to 40 cake truffles

The chocolate chip–passion fruit layer cake from our first book, *Momofuku Milk Bar*, is the unsung hero of Milk Bar cakes, as is its cake truffle sidekick. Folks who love that layer cake are immediately ushered into the Milk Bar circle of trust. Same goes for the truffles.

We found that the chocolate crumbs we use as a textural layer in the cake were too powerful as a truffle coating. We tested and tested and tested, and finally landed on yellow cake mix. It is one of our secret flavor weapons—we never make an actual cake with it, but we use it all the time to bump up flavors in other ways (see Pineapple Upside-Down Layer Cake, page 237). We discovered that if we toast it, it brings out a ton of caramelized notes and lets the flavors of the chocolate chips and passion fruit sing. And thus the chocolate chip–passion fruit truffle was born—vanilla cake, chocolate chips, and passion fruit puree, coated in a thin layer of white chocolate and toasted yellow cake mix. It's a limited menu item and a sleeper hit if there ever was one.

1 box (1 pound)	**yellow cake mix**	3 cups + 2 T
1 recipe	**vanilla cake** (page 190)	
80g	**mini chocolate chips**	½ cup
150g	**passion fruit puree**	¾ cup
1 recipe	**white chocolate coating** (page 163)	

1. Heat the oven to 275°F.

2. Spread the cake mix in an even layer on a quarter-sheet pan. Toast in the oven until the cake mix has the slightest tan color, about 20 minutes. Let cool completely before using.

3. Remove the vanilla cake from the sheet pan. Break the cake down into crumbs and combine them with the chocolate chips and half the passion fruit puree in a medium bowl. Toss with your hands until moist enough to knead into a ball. If necessary, slowly add more puree, a little at a time, and knead it in. You want the filling to be quite moist and soft, not chewy. You may or may not end up using all of the puree.

4. Use a tablespoon to scoop even amounts of the cake truffle filling, each scoop approximately half the size of a Ping-Pong ball. Roll each scoop between the palms of your hands to shape and smooth it into a sphere.

There is a yellow cake mix that reigns supreme: It's Pillsbury!

The more passion fruit juice you can sneak in for an extra zing, the better!

5. Put the toasted yellow cake mix in a medium bowl.

6. With latex gloves on, put 2 tablespoons of the white chocolate coating in the palm of your hand and roll each ball between your palms, coating it in a thin layer of melted chocolate; add more chocolate to your palm as needed.

7. Put 3 or 4 chocolate-covered balls at a time into the bowl of toasted cake mix. Immediately toss them to coat, before the chocolate shell sets and no longer acts as a glue (if this happens, just coat the ball in another thin layer of melted chocolate).

8. Refrigerate for at least 5 minutes to fully set the chocolate shells before eating or storing. The truffles will keep in an airtight container for up to 1 week in the fridge or up to 1 month in the freezer.

apple pie cake truffles

makes 35 to 40 cake truffles

My grandpa was raised on an apple orchard, so growing up, there was always an apple dessert on the table, or in the fridge, or on the counter. Apples were an absolute in my childhood. So I thought it would be a great idea to take apple pie and make it into a layer cake. Milk Maid Alison Roman developed that recipe and it's one of the most delicious celebrations of fall and the harvest I can think of. (It's in the OG Momofuku Milk Bar cookbook.) This truffle is based on it, made with our brown butter cake and bound together with a sticky, cinnamon apple compote. Then we coat it in a thin layer of white chocolate and pie dough sand, which is a sandier version of pie crust.

---

1 recipe	**barely-brown butter cake** (page 174)
1 recipe	**apple compote** (page 175)
1 recipe	**pie dough sand** (page 176)
1 recipe	**white chocolate coating** (page 163)

1. Remove the cake from the sheet pan. Break the cake down into crumbs and combine with half the apple compote in a medium bowl. Toss with your hands until moist enough to knead into a ball. If necessary, slowly add more compote, a little at a time, and knead it in. You want the filling to be quite moist and soft, not chewy. You may or may not end up using all of the compote.

2. Use a tablespoon to scoop even amounts of the cake truffle filling, each scoop approximately half the size of a Ping-Pong ball. Roll each scoop between the palms of your hands to shape and smooth it into a sphere.

3. Put the pie dough sand in a medium bowl and set aside.

4. With latex gloves on, put 2 tablespoons of the white chocolate coating in the palm of your hand and roll each ball between your palms, coating it in a thin layer of melted chocolate; add more chocolate to your palm as needed.

5. Put 3 or 4 chocolate-covered balls at a time into the bowl of pie dough sand. Immediately toss them with the sand to coat, before the chocolate shell sets and no longer acts as a glue (if this happens, just coat the ball in another thin layer of melted chocolate).

6. Refrigerate for at least 5 minutes to fully set the chocolate shells before eating or storing. The truffles will keep in an airtight container for up to 1 week in the fridge or up to 1 month in the freezer.

(recipe continues)

barely-brown butter cake

makes 1 quarter-sheet pan of cake

55g	unsalted butter, softened	½ stick (4 T)
40g	brown butter (see box at right), softened	2 T
250g	sugar	1¼ cups
60g	light brown sugar	¼ cup (packed)
3	large eggs	
110g	buttermilk	½ cup
65g	grapeseed or other neutral oil	⅓ cup
2g	vanilla extract	½ tsp
185g	cake flour	1½ cups
4g	baking powder	1 tsp
4g	kosher salt	1 tsp

1. Heat the oven to 350°F. Pan-spray a quarter-sheet pan and line it with parchment paper, or just line it with a silicone baking mat.

2. Combine both butters and both sugars in the bowl of a stand mixer fitted with the paddle attachment and cream together on medium-high for 2 to 3 minutes, until light and fluffy. Scrape down the sides of the bowl halfway through this process, and again at the end of it.

3. Add the eggs, one at a time, beating on medium-high for 1 minute after each addition. After you add the last egg, scrape down the sides of the bowl, then beat on high for 4 more minutes. Scrape down the sides of the bowl again.

4. Combine the buttermilk, oil, and vanilla extract and with the mixer on medium speed, stream them into the cake batter very slowly. It should take you approximately 3 minutes to add these liquids. Scrape down the sides of the bowl, increase the mixer speed to medium-high, and paddle for an additional 2 to 3 minutes, until the mixture is practically white, twice the size of your original fluffy butter-and-sugar mixture, and completely homogeneous. Don't rush the process. You're basically forcing too much

making brown butter

Know it. Love it. Brown butter is one of the most delicious things to use in any recipe to deepen an already nutty, cinnamon-y, or brown-sugary flavor. The easiest way to make brown butter at home is in bulk, on the stovetop.

Put 1 pound (453g or 4 sticks) of unsalted butter in a large saucepan. Use the largest saucepan you have—the butter will foam up and expand before settling back down into its finished state.

Heat the butter over medium-high heat until it melts, then drop the temperature to medium-low and keep an eye on it. Once melted, the whole process should take approximately 5 minutes. Don't be shy about browning the butter. You want it deep brown in color and super-nutty in aroma. The lighter in color, the lighter in flavor it will be, and vice versa—so get it as dark as possible, until you're nervous about burning it.

Once you heat to your peak color and odor, pour it into a heatproof bowl and cool it completely, stirring it as it cools to distribute the caramelized milk solids evenly. Now you have brown butter available at all times! Store in an airtight container in the fridge for up to 1 week or in the freezer for up to 1 month.

liquid into an already fatty mixture that doesn't want to make room for that liquid. There should be no streaks of fat or liquid. Stop the mixer and scrape down the sides of the bowl.

5. Whisk together the cake flour, baking powder, and salt in a medium bowl.

6. With the mixer on very low speed, slowly add the dry ingredients and mix for 45 to 60 seconds, just until your batter comes together. Scrape down the sides of the bowl, then mix on low for an additional 45 seconds to make sure no lumps of cake flour get left behind.

7. Pour the cake batter into the sheet pan and, using a spatula, spread the batter in an even layer in the pan.

8. Bake for 30 to 35 minutes, rotating the pan front to back halfway through baking. The cake will rise and puff, doubling in size, but will remain slightly buttery and dense. At 30 minutes, gently poke the edge of the cake with your finger: The cake should bounce back slightly and the center should no longer be jiggly. If it doesn't pass these tests, leave the cake in the oven for an additional 3 to 5 minutes.

9. Let the cake cool in the pan on a wire rack or, in a pinch, in the fridge or freezer (don't worry, it's not cheating). The cooled cake can be stored in the fridge, wrapped in plastic wrap, for up to 5 days.

apple compote

makes about 350g (1½ cups)

1	granny smith apple, medium	
200g	sugar	1 cup
4g	pectin NH	½ tsp
2g	ground cinnamon	1 tsp
.25g	kosher salt	pinch

This compote is much more viscous than other soaks in this chapter, which is why you need more of it as a binder for the cake truffles.

Read up on pectin NH (see page 16).

1. Peel and dice the apple into ¼-inch chunks. Measure 200g (1⅔ cups) of the diced apple (eat the rest as a snack!).

2. Stir the sugar, pectin, cinnamon, and salt together in a small bowl. Add the diced apple and toss to combine.

3. Heat the apples in a small, heavy-bottomed saucepan over low heat. The apples will begin to release liquid. Continue to heat the mixture on low until the released liquid begins to boil. Cook the apples on low, stirring occasionally, until they have thickened and softened, but haven't broken down entirely, about 15 minutes.

4. Let the mixture cool completely before using. The apple compote will keep in the refrigerator, in an airtight container, for up to 1 week.

(recipe continues)

pie dough sand

makes about 550g (4 cups)

165g	ap flour	1¼ cups
110g	milk powder	1¼ cups
65g	sugar	¼ cup + 1 T
55g	cornstarch	⅓ cup + 1 tsp
0.5g	ground cinnamon	¼ tsp
4g	kosher salt	1 tsp
85g	unsalted butter, melted	6 T
85g	brown butter (see box, page 174), melted	6 T

1. Heat the oven to 275°F.

2. Combine the flour, milk powder, sugar, cornstarch, cinnamon, and salt in the bowl of a stand mixer fitted with the paddle attachment and mix on low speed until well combined.

3. Add both melted butters and paddle again to distribute. The butter will make the mixture come together in small clumps, then the clumps will break down into a well-combined sand.

4. Spread the sand on a quarter-sheet pan and bake for 12 to 14 minutes. Let the sand get a nice, auburn color. If you take it out too early, it won't have as much depth of flavor, which is key!

5. Let the sand cool completely before using. The sand will keep in an airtight container for 1 week in the fridge or 1 month in the freezer.

MILKSHAKES

CEREAL MILK™ SHAKE

CRACKPIE® SHAKE

CHOCOLATE CEREAL SHAKE

COFFEE SHAKE

CRUNCHY CEREAL SHAKE

BIRTHDAY CAKE SHAKE

CHOCOLATE MALT CAKE SHAKE

CHOCOLATE CHIP PASSIONFRUIT CAKE SHA

PARFAITS

PASSIONFRUIT PARFAIT WITH COMPOST COOKIE GRAN

YUZU PARFAIT WITH THAI TEA GRAN

HOT DRINKS

TEA: BLACK TEA, EARL GREY, GREEN TEA, PEPPERMINT, CINNAMON $2

HOT CHOCOLATE $4

CEREAL MILK™ AFFOGA

SOFT SERVE TWIST

KLES +50¢

ES

GIFT BOX: $20

TRUFFLES

TRUFFLES

popcorn cake truffles

makes 35 to 40 cake truffles

Popcorn cake truffles are based on the popcorn cake, of course, but they *really* taste like a sweet corn cereal cake truffle (I'm looking at you, Corn Pops and Cap'n Crunch). They are sweet, salty, buttery goodness—a guilty pleasure that you can convince yourself is less guilty because corn is a vegetable.

---

1 recipe	**popcorn cake** (page 182)	
120g	**popcorn milk** (page 183)	½ cup
1 recipe	**popcorn sand** (page 183)	
1 recipe	**white chocolate coating** (page 163)	

1. Remove the cake from the sheet pan. Break the cake down into crumbs and combine with half the popcorn milk in a medium bowl. Toss with your hands until moist enough to knead into a ball. If necessary, slowly add more popcorn milk, a little at a time, and knead it in. You want the filling to be quite moist and soft, not chewy. You may or may not end up using all of the popcorn milk.

2. Use a tablespoon to scoop even amounts of the cake truffle filling, each scoop approximately half the size of a Ping-Pong ball. Roll each scoop between the palms of your hands to shape and smooth it into a sphere.

3. Put the popcorn sand in a medium bowl and set aside.

4. With latex gloves on, put 2 tablespoons of the white chocolate coating in the palm of your hand and roll each ball between your palms, coating it in a thin layer of melted chocolate; add more chocolate to your palm as needed.

5. Put 3 or 4 chocolate-covered balls at a time into the bowl of popcorn sand. Immediately toss them with the sand to coat, before the chocolate shell sets and no longer acts as a glue (if this happens, just coat the ball in another thin layer of melted chocolate).

6. Refrigerate for at least 5 minutes to fully set the chocolate shells before eating or storing. The truffles will keep in an airtight container for up to 1 week in the fridge or up to 1 month in the freezer.

(recipe continues)

popcorn cake

makes 1 quarter-sheet pan of cake

1 bag (3.3 oz)	plain microwave popcorn, freshly popped	
115g	unsalted butter, softened	1 stick (8 T)
300g	sugar	1½ cups
3	large eggs	
110g	buttermilk	½ cup
60g	grapeseed or other neutral oil	¼ cup + 1 T
90g	cake flour	¾ cup
5g	corn powder (see page 14)	1 T
5g	baking powder	1¼ tsp
4g	kosher salt	1 tsp

1. Heat the oven to 350°F. Pan-spray a quarter-sheet pan and line it with parchment paper, or just line it with a silicone baking mat.

2. Pulverize the popped popcorn, 1 cup at a time, in a blender until it is a fine powder, then sift it through a regular flour sifter. Continue this process until you have 50g (about 4 cups) of ground, sifted popcorn. Set aside the ground popcorn and put the remaining unground popcorn in a sealable plastic bag to use for the popcorn milk recipe.

3. Combine the butter and sugar in the bowl of a stand mixer fitted with the paddle attachment and cream together on medium-high for 2 to 3 minutes, until light and fluffy. Scrape down the sides of the bowl halfway through this process, and again at the end of it.

4. Add the eggs, one at a time, beating on medium-high for 1 minute after each addition. After you add the last egg, scrape down the sides of the bowl, then beat on high for 4 more minutes. Scrape down the sides of the bowl again.

5. Combine the buttermilk and oil and with the mixer on medium speed, stream them into the cake batter very slowly. It should take you approximately 3 minutes to add these liquids. Scrape down the sides of the bowl, increase the mixer speed to medium-high, and paddle for an additional 2 to 3 minutes, until the mixture is practically white, twice the size of your original fluffy butter-and-sugar mixture, and completely homogeneous. Don't rush the process. You're basically forcing too much liquid into an already fatty mixture that doesn't want to make room for that liquid. There should be no streaks of fat or liquid. Stop the mixer and scrape down the sides of the bowl.

6. Whisk together the ground popcorn, cake flour, corn powder, baking powder, and salt.

7. With the mixer on very low speed, slowly add the dry ingredients and mix for 45 to 60 seconds, just until your batter comes together. Scrape down the sides of the bowl, then mix on low for an additional 45 seconds to make sure no lumps of cake flour get left behind.

8. Pour the cake batter into the sheet pan and, using a spatula, spread the batter in an even layer in the pan.

9. Bake for 30 to 35 minutes, rotating the pan front to back halfway through baking. The cake will rise and puff, doubling in size, but will remain slightly buttery and dense. At 30 minutes, gently poke the edge of the cake with your finger: The cake should bounce back slightly and the center should no longer be jiggly. If it doesn't pass these tests, leave the cake in the oven for an additional 3 to 5 minutes.

Freshly popped microwave popcorn works best in this recipe, but if you have loose popcorn, measure out 90g (about 11 cups) after you've popped it.

10. Let the cake cool in the pan on a wire rack or, in a pinch, in the fridge or freezer (don't worry, it's not cheating). The cooled cake can be stored in the fridge, wrapped in plastic wrap, for up to 5 days.

popcorn milk

makes 275g (1¼ cups)

Use leftover popcorn milk in your next milkshake or as part of the milk in your next bowl of cereal. It will rock your world.

330g	whole milk	1½ cups
20g	popcorn, popped, reserved from popcorn cake (opposite)	2½ cups

1. Put the milk and popcorn into a blender and stir it together. Let the mixture steep for 15 minutes, then blend it together for 30 seconds.

2. Strain the popcorn milk through a fine-mesh sieve. Use immediately or store for a rainy day in an airtight container in the fridge for up to 5 days.

popcorn sand

makes about 490g (4 cups)

Most of the truffle coatings in this book require grinding down a previously made crumb to get it to the right texture. We intentionally developed this recipe as a no-grind one, so skip it here, or you'll end up with a dry, too sandy truffle.

450g	milk sand (at right)	3½ cups
30g	corn powder (see page 14)	⅓ cup
11g	kosher salt	2¾ tsp
2g	sugar	½ tsp

Combine the milk sand, corn powder, salt, and sugar until evenly mixed. The sand will keep in an airtight container for 1 week in the fridge or 1 month in the freezer.

milk sand

makes about 515g (4 cups)

165g	ap flour	1¼ cups
120g	milk powder	1⅓ cups
70g	sugar	⅓ cup
45g	cornstarch	⅓ cup
2.5g	kosher salt	½ + ⅛ tsp
155g	unsalted butter, melted	1 stick (8 T) + 3 T

1. Heat the oven to 275°F.

2. Combine the flour, milk powder, sugar, cornstarch, and salt in the bowl of a stand mixer fitted with the paddle attachment and mix on low speed until well combined.

3. Add the melted butter and paddle again to distribute. The butter will make the mixture come together in small clumps, then the clumps will break down into a well-combined sand.

4. Spread the sand on a quarter-sheet pan and bake until the top of the sand is yellow with a slight tan appearance, 10 to 12 minutes.

5. Let the sand cool completely before using. The sand will keep in an airtight container for 1 week in the fridge or 1 month in the freezer.

dulce de leche cake truffles

makes 35 to 40 cake truffles

These cake truffles are little bite-size love letters to caramel and milk, and they show how powerful those two simple ingredients can be when put together. It's one of my favorite cake truffles because of its simplicity and sweet milkiness. It's my ideal bite of dense, gooey, milky cake with a little bit of caramel, too.

1 recipe **dulce de leche cake**
(opposite)

1 recipe **dulce de leche soak**
(page 186)

1 recipe **milk sand** (page 183)

1 recipe **white chocolate
coating** (page 163)

1. Remove the cake from the sheet pan. Break the cake down into crumbs and combine with half the dulce de leche soak in a medium bowl. Toss with your hands until moist enough to knead into a ball. If necessary, slowly add more soak, a little at a time, and knead it in. You want the filling to be quite moist and soft, not chewy. You may or may not end up using all of the soak.

2. Use a tablespoon to scoop even amounts of the cake truffle filling, each scoop approximately half the size of a Ping-Pong ball. Roll each scoop between the palms of your hands to shape and smooth it into a sphere.

3. Put the milk sand in a medium bowl and set aside.

4. With latex gloves on, put 2 tablespoons of the white chocolate coating in the palm of your hand and roll each ball between your palms, coating it in a thin layer of melted chocolate; add more chocolate to your palm as needed.

5. Put 3 or 4 chocolate-covered balls at a time into the bowl of milk sand. Immediately toss them with the milk sand to coat, before the chocolate shell sets and no longer acts as a glue (if this happens, just coat the ball in another thin layer of melted chocolate).

6. Refrigerate for at least 5 minutes to fully set the chocolate shells before eating or storing. The truffles will keep in an airtight container for up to 1 week in the fridge or up to 1 month in the freezer.

dulce de leche cake

makes 1 quarter-sheet pan of cake

115g	unsalted butter, softened	1 stick (8 T)
150g	sugar	¾ cup
275g	dulce de leche	1 cup
3	large eggs	
1	large egg yolk	
110g	buttermilk	½ cup
75g	grapeseed or other neutral oil	⅓ cup + 1 T
4g	vanilla extract	1 tsp
185g	cake flour	1½ cups
4g	baking powder	1 tsp
4g	kosher salt	1 tsp

1. Heat the oven to 350°F. Pan-spray a quarter-sheet pan and line it with parchment paper, or just line it with a silicone baking mat.

2. Combine the butter and sugar in the bowl of a stand mixer fitted with the paddle attachment and cream together on medium-high for 2 to 3 minutes, until light and fluffy. Scrape down the sides of the bowl halfway through this process, and again at the end of it.

3. Add the dulce de leche and beat on high for another minute.

4. Add the whole eggs and egg yolk, one at a time, beating on medium-high for 1 minute after each addition. After you add the last egg, scrape down the sides of the bowl, then beat on high for 4 more minutes. Scrape down the sides of the bowl again.

5. Combine the buttermilk, oil, and vanilla extract and with the mixer on medium speed, stream them into the cake batter very slowly. It should take approximately 3 minutes to add these liquids. Scrape down the sides of the bowl, increase the mixer speed to medium-high, and paddle for an additional 2 to 3 minutes, until the mixture is practically white, twice the size of your original fluffy butter-and-sugar mixture, and completely homogeneous. Don't rush the process. You're basically forcing too much liquid into an already fatty mixture that doesn't want to make room for that liquid. There should be no streaks of fat or liquid. Stop the mixer and scrape down the sides of the bowl.

6. Whisk together the cake flour, baking powder, and salt in a medium bowl.

7. With the mixer on very low speed, slowly add the dry ingredients and mix for 45 to 60 seconds, just until your batter comes together. Scrape down the sides of the bowl, then mix on low for an additional 45 seconds to make sure no lumps of cake flour get left behind.

8. Pour the cake batter into the sheet pan and, using a spatula, spread the batter in an even layer in the pan.

9. Bake for 30 to 35 minutes, rotating the pan front to back halfway through baking. The cake will rise and puff, doubling in size, but will remain slightly buttery and dense. At 30 minutes, gently poke the edge of the cake with your finger: The cake should bounce back slightly and the center should no longer be jiggly. If it doesn't pass these tests, leave the cake in the oven for an additional 3 to 5 minutes.

Read up on dulce de leche (see page 14).

(recipe continues)

10. Let the cake cool in the pan on a wire rack or, in a pinch, in the fridge or freezer (don't worry, it's not cheating). The cooled cake can be stored in the fridge, wrapped in plastic wrap, for up to 5 days.

dulce de leche soak

makes about 180g (½ cup)

130g	**dulce de leche**	¼ cup + 1 T
50g	**evaporated milk**	¼ cup

Combine the dulce de leche and evaporated milk in a small bowl. Use immediately.

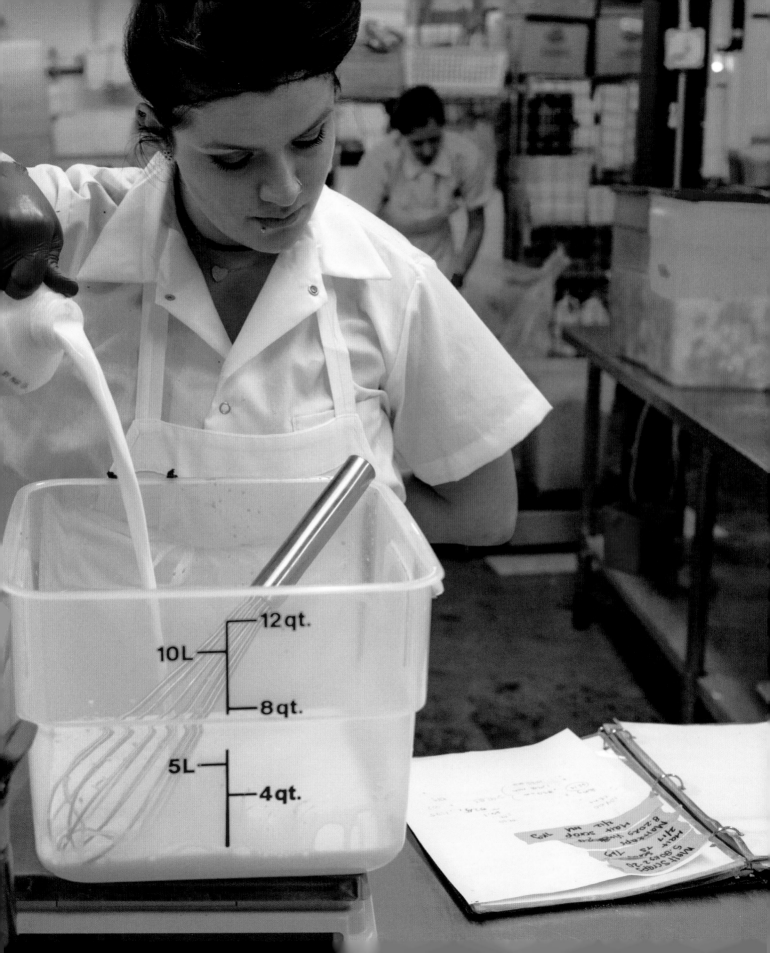

strawberry-lemon cake truffles

makes 35 to 40 cake truffles

These little gems, the kid sister to the Strawberry-Lemon Layer Cake (page 221), come on the menu at Milk Bar each spring, when love is in the air and when gorgeous little wild strawberries start to come into season (even though none of them actually go into these truffles).

Developing this recipe was a little tricky. It's a nod to strawberry season, but our intention was to make strawberry flavor an enhancer, not the star of the show; it's always been a lemon-vanilla cake to us. After a ton of testing with things like Pop Rocks and strawberry Nesquick, we finally landed on a milk-sand-meets-strawberry-drink-mix concoction for the outer coating. We are often proponents of keeping it fancy, but we're also not afraid to celebrate the favorites of our childhood!

1 recipe	**vanilla cake** (page 190)	
120g	**lemon juice**	½ cup
1 recipe	**strawberry sand** (page 191)	
1 recipe	**white chocolate coating** (page 163)	

1. Remove the cake from the sheet pan. Break the cake down into crumbs and combine with half the lemon juice in a medium bowl. Toss with your hands until moist enough to knead into a ball. If necessary, slowly add more juice, a little at a time, and knead it in. You want the filling to be quite moist and soft, not chewy. You may or may not end up using all of the juice.

2. Use a tablespoon to scoop even amounts of the cake truffle filling, each scoop approximately half the size of a Ping-Pong ball. Roll each scoop between the palms of your hands to shape and smooth it into a sphere.

3. Put the strawberry sand in a medium bowl and set aside.

4. With latex gloves on, put 2 tablespoons of the white chocolate coating in the palm of your hand and roll each ball between your palms, coating it in a thin layer of melted chocolate; add more chocolate to your palm as needed.

5. Put 3 or 4 chocolate-covered balls at a time into the bowl of strawberry sand. Immediately toss them with the sand to coat, before the chocolate shell sets and no longer acts as a glue (if this happens, just coat the ball in another thin layer of melted chocolate).

6. Refrigerate for at least 5 minutes to fully set the chocolate shells before eating or storing. The truffles will keep in an airtight container for up to 1 week in the fridge or up to 1 month in the freezer.

(recipe continues)

vanilla cake

makes 1 quarter-sheet pan of cake

115g	unsalted butter, softened	1 stick (8 T)
250g	sugar	1¼ cups
60g	light brown sugar	¼ cup (packed)
3	large eggs	
110g	buttermilk	½ cup
75g	grapeseed or other neutral oil	⅓ cup + 1 T
12g	vanilla extract	1 T
185g	cake flour	1½ cups
4g	baking powder	1 tsp
4g	kosher salt	1 tsp

1. Heat the oven to 350°F. Pan-spray a quarter-sheet pan and line it with parchment paper, or just line it with a silicone baking mat.

2. Combine the butter and both sugars in the bowl of a stand mixer fitted with the paddle attachment and cream together on medium-high for 2 to 3 minutes, until light and fluffy. Scrape down the sides of the bowl halfway through this process, and again at the end of it.

3. Add the eggs, one at a time, beating on medium-high for 1 minute after each addition. After you add the last egg, scrape down the sides of the bowl, then beat on high for 4 more minutes. Scrape down the sides of the bowl again.

4. Combine the buttermilk, oil, and vanilla extract and with the mixer on medium speed, stream them into the cake batter very slowly. It should take you approximately 3 minutes to add these liquids. Scrape down the sides of the bowl, increase the mixer speed to medium-high, and paddle for an additional 2 to 3 minutes, until the mixture is practically white, twice the size of your original fluffy butter-and-sugar mixture, and completely homogeneous. Don't rush the process. You're basically forcing too much liquid into an already fatty mixture that doesn't want to make room for that liquid. There should be no streaks of fat or liquid. Stop the mixer and scrape down the sides of the bowl.

5. Whisk together the cake flour, baking powder, and salt in a medium bowl.

6. With the mixer on very low speed, slowly add the dry ingredients and mix for 45 to 60 seconds, just until your batter comes together. Scrape down the sides of the bowl, then mix on low for an additional 45 seconds to make sure no lumps of cake flour get left behind.

7. Pour the cake batter into the sheet pan and, using a spatula, spread the batter in an even layer in the pan.

8. Bake for 30 to 35 minutes, rotating the pan front to back halfway through baking. The cake will rise and puff, doubling in size, but will remain slightly buttery and dense. At 30 minutes, gently poke the edge of the cake with your finger: The cake should bounce back slightly and the center should no longer be jiggly. If it doesn't pass these tests, leave the cake in the oven for an additional 3 to 5 minutes.

9. Let the cake cool in the pan on a wire rack or, in a pinch, in the fridge or freezer (don't worry, it's not cheating). The cooled cake can be stored in the fridge, wrapped in plastic wrap, for up to 5 days.

strawberry sand

makes about 515g (4 cups)

120g	milk powder	1⅓ cups
120g	ap flour	¾ cup + 3 T
100g	sweetened strawberry drink mix	½ cup
65g	sugar	⅓ cup
30g	cornstarch	¼ cup
115g	unsalted butter, melted	1 stick (8 T)

1. Heat the oven to 275°F.

2. Combine the milk powder, flour, drink mix, sugar, and cornstarch in the bowl of a stand mixer fitted with the paddle attachment and mix on low speed until well combined.

3. Add the melted butter and paddle again to distribute. The butter will make the mixture come together in small clumps, then the clumps will break down into a well-combined sand.

4. Spread the sand on a quarter-sheet pan and bake until the mixture has dried out entirely, about 10 minutes. The sand should remain pink, without any hint of toasting.

5. Let the sand cool completely before using. The sand will keep in an airtight container for 1 week in the fridge or 1 month in the freezer.

coconut-tangerine cake truffles

makes 35 to 40 cake truffles

The sweet tanginess of tangerines pairs perfectly with coconut. It is important to use the ripest in-season tangerines here. You can also use orange jam if you aren't feeling those homemade tangerine confit vibes, though your truffles will be decidedly less exotic.

400g	**shredded, unsweetened coconut**	4 cups
1 recipe	**coconut cake** (page 194)	
200g	**tangerine confit** (page 195)	½ cup + 2 T
1 recipe	**white chocolate coating** (page 163)	

1. Heat the oven to 250°F. Line a sheet pan with parchment paper or a silicone baking mat.

2. Spread the coconut on the lined sheet pan and bake until golden brown, about 30 minutes. Halfway through baking, use a heatproof spatula to toss the coconut around and continue baking. Cool the toasted coconut completely before using.

3. Remove the cake from the sheet pan. Break the cake down into crumbs and combine with half the tangerine confit in a medium bowl. Toss with your hands until moist enough to knead into a ball. If necessary, slowly add more confit, a little at a time, and knead it in. You want the filling to be quite moist and soft, not chewy. You may or may not end up using all of the confit.

4. Use a tablespoon to scoop even amounts of the cake truffle filling, each scoop approximately half the size of a Ping-Pong ball. Roll each scoop between the palms of your hands to shape and smooth it into a sphere.

5. Put the toasted coconut into a medium bowl and set aside.

6. With latex gloves on, put 2 tablespoons of the white chocolate coating in the palm of your hand and roll each ball between your palms, coating it in a thin layer of melted chocolate; add more chocolate to your palm as needed.

7. Put 3 or 4 chocolate-covered balls at a time into the bowl of toasted coconut. Immediately toss them with the coconut to coat, before the chocolate shell sets and no longer acts as a glue (if this happens, just coat the ball in another thin layer of melted chocolate).

8. Refrigerate for at least 5 minutes to fully set the chocolate shells before eating or storing. The truffles will keep in an airtight container for up to 1 week in the fridge or up to 1 month in the freezer.

(recipe continues)

coconut cake

makes 1 quarter-sheet pan of cake

115g	unsalted butter, softened	1 stick (8 T)
260g	sugar	1¼ cups + 1 T
50g	light brown sugar	3 T + 1 tsp (packed)
3	large eggs	
110g	buttermilk	½ cup
75g	grapeseed or other neutral oil	⅓ cup + 1 T
5.5g	vanilla extract	1¼ tsp
185g	cake flour	1½ cups
5g	baking powder	1¼ tsp
4g	kosher salt	1 tsp
150g	shredded, unsweetened coconut	1½ cups

1. Heat the oven to 350°F. Pan-spray a quarter-sheet pan and line it with parchment paper, or just line it with a silicone baking mat.

2. Combine the butter and both sugars in the bowl of a stand mixer fitted with the paddle attachment and cream together on medium-high for 2 to 3 minutes, until light and fluffy. Scrape down the sides of the bowl halfway through this process, and again at the end of it.

3. Add the eggs, one at a time, beating on medium-high for 1 minute after each addition. After you add the last egg, scrape down the sides of the bowl, then beat on high for 4 more minutes. Scrape down the sides of the bowl again.

4. Combine the buttermilk, oil, and vanilla extract and with the mixer on medium speed, stream them into the cake batter very slowly. It should take you approximately 3 minutes to add these liquids. Scrape down the sides of the bowl, increase the mixer speed to medium-high, and paddle for an additional 2 to 3 minutes, until the mixture is practically white, twice the size of your original fluffy butter-and-sugar mixture, and completely homogeneous. Don't rush the process. You're basically forcing too much liquid into an already fatty mixture that doesn't want to make room for that liquid. There should be no streaks of fat or liquid. Stop the mixer and scrape down the sides of the bowl.

5. Whisk together the cake flour, baking powder, and salt in a medium bowl.

6. With the mixer on very low speed, slowly add the dry ingredients and mix for 45 to 60 seconds, just until your batter comes together. Scrape down the sides of the bowl, then mix on low for an additional 45 seconds to make sure no lumps of cake flour get left behind.

7. Add the coconut and mix until just combined.

8. Pour the cake batter into the sheet pan and, using a spatula, spread the batter in an even layer in the pan.

9. Bake for 30 to 35 minutes, rotating the pan front to back halfway through baking. The cake will rise and puff, doubling in size, but will remain slightly buttery and dense. At 30 minutes, gently poke the edge of

the cake with your finger: The cake should bounce back slightly and the center should no longer be jiggly. If it doesn't pass these tests, leave the cake in the oven for an additional 3 to 5 minutes.

10. Let the cake cool in the pan on a wire rack or, in a pinch, in the fridge or freezer (don't worry, it's not cheating). The cooled cake can be stored in the fridge, wrapped in plastic wrap, for up to 5 days.

tangerine confit

makes about 450g (1½ cups)

300g	tangerines	3 large
300g	sugar	1½ cups

1. Wash the tangerines, cut them into quarters, and seed them. Put them into a food processor fitted with the steel blade and pour the sugar on top. Pulse the tangerines and sugar together until there are no pieces larger than a garbanzo bean.

2. Pour the tangerine mixture into a medium pot and cook it over medium heat, stirring occasionally, until it is bubbling and thickened and reaches 220°F, about 10 minutes, skimming the foam off the top along the way. Let the confit cool completely before using it.

3. The tangerine confit will keep in the refrigerator, in an airtight container, for up to 1 month.

pineapple upside-down cake truffles

makes 35 to 40 cake truffles

These truffles are easy to make, and with their gorgeous toasted coconut coating, they are just as easy on the eyes. They're a flavor sneak attack and our hardbody press/marketing specialist and internal communications cheerleader Karla Smith Brown's favorite. Karla will ask the kitchen to make a few extra dozen for an event just so she can stash her share in the office freezer for snack attacks. They're bright, fruity, and appropriate to serve year-round because pineapples are always in season. Well, technically they're not, but since we've never lived anywhere they grow, we just assume they're always growing in a tropical paradise somewhere.

400g	shredded, unsweetened coconut	4 cups
70g	yellow cake mix	¼ cup + 2 T
1 recipe	coconut cake (page 194)	
135g	pineapple juice	½ cup + 1 T
1 recipe	white chocolate coating (page 163)	

There is a yellow cake mix that reigns supreme for this recipe: It's Pillsbury (see page 17)!

1. Heat the oven to 250°F. Line two sheet pans with parchment paper or silicone baking mats.

2. Spread the coconut and cake mix on two separate lined sheet pans and bake until the coconut is golden brown and the cake mix just starts to get color on it, about 30 minutes. Halfway through baking, use a heatproof spatula to toss the coconut and cake mix around and continue baking. Cool them both completely before using.

3. Remove the coconut cake from the sheet pan. Break the cake down into crumbs and combine with the toasted yellow cake mix and half the pineapple juice in a medium bowl. Toss with your hands until moist enough to knead into a ball. If necessary, slowly add more juice, a little at a time, and knead it in. You want the filling to be quite moist and soft, not chewy. You may or may not end up using all of the juice.

4. Use a tablespoon to scoop even amounts of the cake truffle filling, each scoop approximately half the size of a Ping-Pong ball. Roll each scoop between the palms of your hands to shape and smooth it into a sphere.

5. Put the toasted coconut into a medium bowl and set aside.

6. With latex gloves on, put 2 tablespoons of the white chocolate coating in the palm of your hand and roll each ball between your palms, coating it in a thin layer of melted

chocolate; add more chocolate to your palm as needed.

7. Put 3 or 4 chocolate-covered balls at a time into the bowl of toasted coconut. Immediately toss them with the coconut to coat, before the chocolate shell sets and no longer acts as a glue (if this happens, just coat the ball in another thin layer of melted chocolate).

8. Refrigerate for at least 5 minutes to fully set the chocolate shells before eating or storing. The truffles will keep in an airtight container for up to 1 week in the fridge or up to 1 month in the freezer.

german chocolate jimbo cake truffles

makes 35 to 40 cake truffles

The layer cake this truffle is named after (page 243) features a pecan crunch. But for the truffle version, we bind our rich chocolate cake with a *jimbo soak* of milk, brown sugar, and almond butter. It's a classy way of getting a nut element into the truffle without having to go through the hassle of making pecan crunch. The outer covering of toasted coconut makes these look like little snowballs of joy, and that's exactly what they are.

400g	**shredded, unsweetened coconut**	4 cups
1 recipe	**chocolate cake** (page 166)	
1 recipe	**jimbo soak** (opposite)	
1 recipe	**white chocolate coating** (page 163)	

1. Heat the oven to 250°F.

2. Spread the coconut evenly on a quarter-sheet pan and toast in the oven until light golden, 8 to 12 minutes. Then cool it on a wire rack or, in a pinch, in the fridge or freezer.

3. Remove the cake from the sheet pan. Break the cake down into crumbs and combine with half the jimbo soak in a medium bowl. Toss with your hands until moist enough to knead into a ball. If necessary, slowly add more soak, a little at a time, and knead it in. You want the filling to be quite moist and soft, not chewy. You may or may not end up using all of the soak.

4. Use a tablespoon to scoop even amounts of the cake truffle filling, each scoop approximately half the size of a Ping-Pong ball. Roll each scoop between the palms of your hands to shape and smooth it into a sphere.

5. Put the toasted coconut in a medium bowl and set aside.

6. With latex gloves on, put 2 tablespoons of the white chocolate coating in the palm of your hand and roll each ball between your palms, coating it in a thin layer of melted chocolate; add more chocolate to your palm as needed.

7. Put 3 or 4 chocolate-covered balls at a time into the bowl of cooled toasted coconut. Immediately toss them with the coconut to coat, before the chocolate shell sets and no longer acts as a glue (if this happens, just coat the ball in another thin layer of melted chocolate).

8. Refrigerate for at least 5 minutes to fully set the chocolate shells before eating or storing. The truffles will keep in an airtight container for up to 1 week in the fridge or up to 1 month in the freezer.

jimbo soak

makes about 155g (⅔ cup)

110g	**almond butter**	½ cup
5g	**light brown sugar**	1 tsp (packed)
50g	**whole milk**	¼ cup

Combine the almond butter and brown sugar in a bowl, stirring until smooth. Stream in the milk, stirring until the mixture is evenly combined with no lumps. Use immediately.

pretzel cake truffles

makes 35 to 40 cake truffles

These truffles are the ultimate salty-sweet combo in the most dangerous way, because you can eat six of them without really realizing it. Your tummy isn't screaming *too much salt!* or *too much sugar!* We had them on the menu at Noodle Bar for a while and, at first, the Noodle Bar chefs worried that there would be too much salinity between the Noodle Bar ramen broth and the pretzel cake truffles, but then it turned out the truffles were an even bigger hit because they were constantly teasing your tongue, walking that line between salty and sweet. If you are into savory desserts, make this truffle STAT.

1 recipe	**pretzel cake** (opposite)	
110g	**whole milk**	½ cup
1 recipe	**pretzel sand** (page 202)	
1 recipe	**white chocolate coating** (page 163)	

1. Remove the cake from the sheet pan. Break the cake down into crumbs and combine with half the milk in a medium bowl. Toss with your hands until moist enough to knead into a ball. If necessary, slowly add more milk, a little at a time, and knead it in. You want the filling to be quite moist and soft, not chewy. You may or may not end up using all of the milk.

2. Use a tablespoon to scoop even amounts of the cake truffle filling, each scoop approximately half the size of a Ping-Pong ball. Roll each scoop between the palms of your hands to shape and smooth it into a sphere.

3. Put the pretzel sand in a medium bowl and set aside.

4. With latex gloves on, put 2 tablespoons of the white chocolate coating in the palm of your hand and roll each ball between your palms, coating it in a thin layer of melted chocolate; add more chocolate to your palm as needed.

5. Put 3 or 4 chocolate-covered balls at a time into the bowl of pretzel sand. Immediately toss them with the sand to coat them before the chocolate shell sets and no longer acts as a glue (if this happens, just coat the ball in another thin layer of melted chocolate).

6. Refrigerate for at least 5 minutes to fully set the chocolate shells before eating or storing. The truffles will keep in an airtight container for up to 1 week in the fridge or up to 1 month in the freezer.

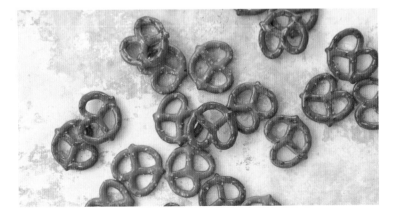

pretzel cake

makes 1 quarter-sheet pan of cake

150g	mini pretzels	3 cups
115g	unsalted butter, softened	1 stick (8 T)
250g	sugar	1¼ cups
15g	molasses	1 T
3	large eggs	
80g	grapeseed or other neutral oil	½ cup
75g	buttermilk	⅓ cup
90g	cake flour	¾ cup
12g	kosher salt	1 T
5g	baking powder	1¼ tsp
2g	baking soda	½ tsp

1. Heat the oven to 350°F. Pan-spray a quarter-sheet pan and line it with parchment paper, or just line the pan with a silicone baking mat.

2. Grind down the pretzels in a blender or food processor into a fine powder; you should have 32g (¼ cup) of pretzel powder. Set aside.

3. Combine the butter, sugar, and molasses in the bowl of a stand mixer fitted with the paddle attachment and cream together on medium-high for 2 to 3 minutes, until light and fluffy. Scrape down the sides of the bowl halfway through this process, and again at the end of it.

4. Add the eggs, one at a time, beating on medium-high for 1 minute after each addition. After you add the last egg, scrape down the sides of the bowl, then beat on high for 4 more minutes. Scrape down the sides of the bowl again.

5. Combine the oil and buttermilk and with the mixer on medium speed, stream it in very slowly. It should take you approximately 3 minutes to add these liquids. Scrape down the sides of the bowl, increase the mixer speed to medium-high, and paddle for an additional 2 to 3 minutes, until mixture is twice the size of your original fluffy butter-and-sugar mixture, and completely homogeneous. Don't rush the process. You're basically forcing too much liquid into an already fatty mixture that doesn't want to make room for that liquid. There should be no streaks of fat or liquid. Stop the mixer and scrape down the sides of the bowl.

6. Whisk together the pretzel powder, cake flour, salt, baking powder, and baking soda.

7. With the mixer on very low speed, slowly add the dry ingredients and mix for 45 to 60 seconds, just until your batter comes together. Scrape down the sides of the bowl, then mix on low for an additional 45 seconds to make sure no lumps of cake flour get left behind.

8. Pour the cake batter into the sheet pan and, using a spatula, spread the batter in an even layer in the pan.

9. Bake for 25 to 30 minutes, rotating the pan front to back halfway through baking. The cake will rise and puff, doubling in size, but will remain slightly buttery and dense. At 25 minutes, gently poke the edge of the cake with your finger: The cake should bounce back slightly and the center should no longer be jiggly. If it doesn't pass these tests, leave the cake in the oven for an additional 3 to 5 minutes.

(recipe continues)

10. Let the cake cool in the pan on a wire rack or, in a pinch, in the fridge or freezer (don't worry, it's not cheating). The cooled cake can be stored in the fridge, wrapped in plastic wrap, for up to 5 days.

pretzel sand

makes about 540g (4 cups)

....

1 recipe   **pretzel crumbs**
              (page 248)

....

Process the pretzel crumbs in a food processor until they break down into a fine sand. The sand will keep in an airtight container for 1 week in the fridge or 1 month in the freezer.

mint cookies and cream cake truffles

makes 35 to 40 cake truffles

This has everything you could ever want in a cake truffle. It is our classic vanilla cake, with chocolate chips folded in after baking, bound together with mint cheesecake coated in that thin layer of white chocolate we all know and love and finished with chocolate sand. Sha-wing! To be honest, even though we only sell these during the holidays, they're delicious year-round. I like to keep some stashed in my freezer and bust them out in the middle of the summer, just because.

---

1 recipe	**vanilla cake** (page 190)	
80g	**mini chocolate chips**	½ cup
125g	**mint liquid cheesecake** (opposite)	½ cup
1 recipe	**chocolate sand** (opposite)	
1 recipe	**white chocolate coating** (page 163)	

1. Remove the cake from the sheet pan. Break the cake down into crumbs and combine with the chocolate chips and half the mint liquid cheesecake in a medium bowl. Toss with your hands until moist enough to knead into a ball. If necessary, slowly add more liquid cheesecake and knead it in. You want the filling to be quite moist and soft, not chewy. You may or may not end up using all of the mint liquid cheesecake.

2. Use a tablespoon to scoop even amounts of the cake truffle filling, each scoop approximately half the size of a Ping-Pong ball. Roll each scoop between the palms of your hands to shape and smooth it into a sphere.

3. Put the chocolate sand in a medium bowl and set aside.

4. With latex gloves on, put 2 tablespoons of the white chocolate coating in the palm of your hand and roll each ball between your palms, coating it in a thin layer of melted chocolate; add more chocolate to your palm as needed.

5. Put 3 or 4 chocolate-covered balls at a time into the bowl of chocolate sand. Immediately toss them with the sand to coat, before the chocolate shell sets and no longer acts as a glue (if this happens, just coat the ball in another thin layer of melted chocolate).

6. Refrigerate for at least 5 minutes to fully set the chocolate shells before eating or storing. The truffles will keep in an airtight container for up to 1 week in the fridge or up to 1 month in the freezer.

mint liquid cheesecake

makes about 460g (2 cups)

A little bit goes a long way when it comes to mint extract. Start with the amount listed, but if you want your peppermint cheesecake to be mintier, by all means, add another small splash. But really be careful with the green food color—an extra drop takes the truffles to a radioactive green state!

2g	**peppermint extract**	½ tsp
1 drop	**green food color**	
1 recipe	**liquid cheesecake** (page 224)	

Use a spatula to mix the peppermint extract and green food color into the cheesecake. The mint cheesecake can be stored in an airtight container in the fridge for up to 1 week.

chocolate sand

makes about 700g (4 cups)

1 recipe	**chocolate crumbs** (page 147)

Process the chocolate crumbs in a food processor until they break down into a fine sand. The sand will keep in an airtight container for 1 week in the fridge or 1 month in the freezer.

liam's #toughcookie cake truffles

makes 35 to 40 cake truffles

This very special recipe was made for my buddy Liam Witt, a brave, #toughcookie of a young guy who embraced every moment of life, loved to bake, and passed away of pediatric cancer. We work closely with Liam's extraordinary family and Cookies for Kids Cancer, the organization they started to help fight for every child's right to a happy, healthy childhood, cancer-free. Liam and I had many things in common, especially our love for Creamsicles and all things orange.

---

1 recipe   **vanilla cake** (page 190)

1 recipe   **vanilla-orange soak**
(page 208)

1 recipe   **vanilla-orange sand**
(page 208)

1 recipe   **white chocolate coating** (page 163)

1. Remove the cake from the sheet pan. Break the cake down into crumbs and combine with half the vanilla-orange soak in a medium bowl. Toss with your hands until moist enough to knead into a ball. If necessary, slowly add more soak, a little at a time, and knead it in. You want the filling to be quite moist and soft, not chewy. You may or may not end up using all of the soak.

2. Use a tablespoon to scoop even amounts of the cake truffle filling, each scoop approximately half the size of a Ping-Pong ball. Roll each scoop between the palms of your hands to shape and smooth it into a sphere.

3. Put the vanilla-orange sand in a medium bowl and set aside.

4. With latex gloves on, put 2 tablespoons of the white chocolate coating in the palm of your hand and roll each ball between your palms, coating it in a thin layer of melted chocolate; add more chocolate to your palm as needed.

5. Put 3 or 4 chocolate-covered balls at a time into the bowl of vanilla-orange sand. Immediately toss them with the sand to coat, before the chocolate shell sets and no longer acts as a glue (if this happens, just coat the ball in another thin layer of melted chocolate).

6. Refrigerate for at least 5 minutes to fully set the chocolate shells before eating or storing. The truffles will keep in an airtight container for up to 1 week in the fridge or up to 1 month in the freezer.

(recipe continues)

vanilla-orange soak

makes about 180g (⅔ cup)

120g	orange juice	½ cup
50g	Tang original drink mix	¼ cup
8g	clear vanilla extract	2 tsp
4g	kosher salt	1 tsp

Combine the orange juice, Tang, vanilla extract, and salt in a small bowl and whisk until the salt and Tang are fully dissolved. Use immediately.

vanilla-orange sand

makes about 545g (4 cups)

120g	milk powder	1½ cups
120g	ap flour	¾ cup + 2 T
100g	Tang original drink mix	½ cup
65g	sugar	⅓ cup
40g	cornstarch	⅓ cup
115g	unsalted butter, melted	1 stick (8 T)
2g	citric acid	½ tsp

1. Heat the oven to 275°F.

2. Combine the milk powder, flour, Tang, sugar, and cornstarch in the bowl of a stand mixer fitted with the paddle attachment and mix on low speed until well combined.

3. Add the melted butter and paddle again to distribute. The butter will make the mixture come together in small clumps, then the clumps will break down into a well-combined sand.

4. Spread the sand on a quarter-sheet pan and bake for 10 to 12 minutes. The sand should remain orange, without any hint of toasting.

5. Let the sand cool completely. Transfer the sand to a bowl and whisk in the citric acid. The sand will keep in an airtight container for 1 week in the fridge or 1 month in the freezer.

all about cake truffle croquembouches

We love to make a croquembouche (a very classy cone-shaped display) out of our cake truffles. It is SO easy to assemble and it always ups the ante of any dessert spread. Our version is different than the classic French version because we use cake truffles instead of the traditional cream puffs. You can use any combination of truffle flavor you like; just make sure the truffles are frozen *solid*, at least overnight, before you assemble the croquembouche or they will break apart in the process.

all you need is

6 ounces	white chocolate
1	12-inch tall, 5-inch-base Styrofoam cone (available online or at most craft stores)
1 tsp	light corn syrup
1	12-inch round serving platter
1	box wooden toothpicks
80	frozen cake truffles, any flavor or combo

here's what you do

1. Melt the chocolate in the microwave.

2. Use a pastry brush to brush the melted chocolate all over the Styrofoam cone, making sure it's covered completely and no Styrofoam is visible.

3. Put the cone in the freezer for 5 minutes to make sure the chocolate has hardened and set.

4. Dollop the corn syrup in the center of the platter and place the cone on top. The corn syrup will act as glue, adhering the cone to the platter.

5. Insert one toothpick into a cake truffle of your choice, concealing half of the toothpick inside the truffle and allowing the other half of it to stick out of the truffle.

6. Start at the bottom. Secure the cake truffle to the cone by sticking the visible part of the toothpick into the cone. Continue doing this until you have covered the entire cone. Work your way up, ending with one cake truffle at the very top.

7. Keep the croquembouche refrigerated until serving.

Here's where we really turn up the temperature on you. (Not literally. Most cakes bake at the same temperature, give or take 50°F.) But layer cakes are not for the in-a-pinch baker, or for someone looking to fill a few lazy hours in the afternoon with kiddos in tow.

These beauts are fancy and require more time, focus, attention to detail, and ingredient sourcing than the (killer) mug cakes or bundts earlier in this book. But they're totally worth it.

Looking back, we were just scratching the surface of layer cakes when we wrote our first book. There is so much more to share here! In the pages that follow, you'll find recipes for some of the most coveted cakes that remain in our repertoire today (like the German Chocolate Jimbo Layer Cake, page 243); cakes we were making when we first opened Milk Bar in 2008 that only the early adopters even know about (like the Key Lime Pie Layer Cake, page 217); and cakes that haven't even graced the menu at Milk Bar . . . yet. Before you continue, though, there is a little mandatory reading. It starts on page 9, and it's a little story on what cake was, and what it is now, why humble cake became fancy, and how a fancy cake can remain humble. And it has all the unspoken rules of the road if you bake the recipes from here on out.

My drive to redefine layer cakes started strong long ago. Now, though, it's all-out madness at Milk Bar. But there is a formula! Because for us, layer cakes are about creativity, but also about architecture, so it's important to understand the formula and building blocks of each layer cake before you get going.

the milk bar layer cake formula

layer 1, the bottom

cake: All roads lead back to how delicious and evenly baked your cake is. Save the scraps for the bottom layer.

cake soak: For moisture and depth of flavor to the bottom layer, anything liquid that tells the "flavor story."

frosting or filling #1: For flavor and structure, this layer is like the stucco to the foundation of your cake. The spread should have body and be delicious enough to stand on its own. When you have two different spreadable fillings, the harder-to-spread one goes down first.

textural layer: Typically a crumb or a crunch; it's all about adding to the "flavor story" while providing a hidden, surprise texture when eating.

frosting or filling #2: Sometimes the same as frosting or filling #1, this layer is for flavor and structure, helping keep the layers and crumbs that came before secure in their place, and helping to keep the next layer secure as you build. This is an opportunity to add another flavor and viscosity to the masterpiece. This filling should be easier to spread than frosting or filling #1.

layer 2, the middle

Repeat!

layer 3, the top

cake: The most perfect round of cake is for the top.

frosting or filling #3: Perhaps the same as #1 or #2, this is for flavor and finishing touches. Frost and swirl to your heart's desire when spreading this top layer.

decor: What's left over from your textural layer, the decor is the final POP of color and personality.

Once we have our inspiration, we use this structure to "build" the layer cake in our imaginations, then get into the kitchen to bring our creativity to life.

In this chapter, we share our favorite layer cakes, but as with all the other chapters in this book, feel free to mix and match the components—or invent your own—to come up with your own layer cake creations. If you have the time, the dedication, and the wherewithal, the world of Milk Bar layer cakes is officially at your fingertips. My advice to you is to plan ahead, do it right or do it twice, and enjoy yourself!

(If you're ready for extra credit, we've included two BONUS!!! sections at the end of this chapter for ice cream cakes and large layer cakes, all the way up to tiered wedding cakes!)

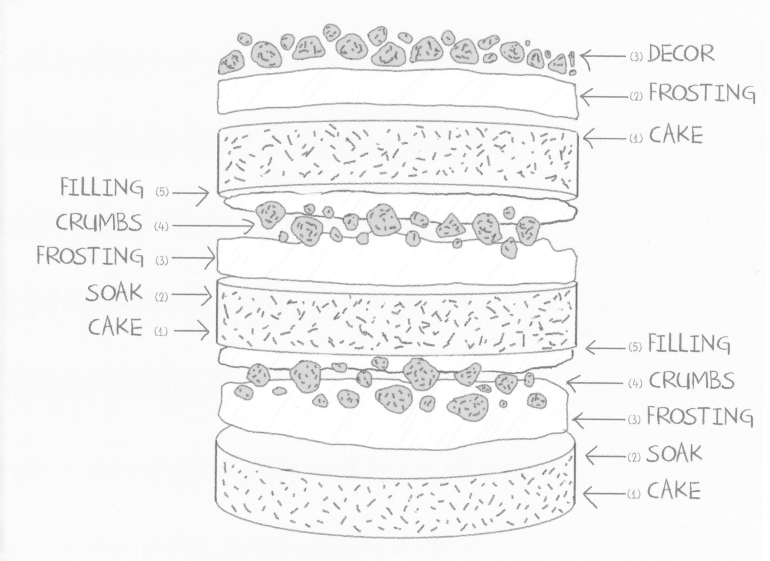

(3) DECOR

(2) FROSTING

(1) CAKE

FILLING (5)

CRUMBS (4)

FROSTING (3)

SOAK (2)

CAKE (1)

(5) FILLING

(4) CRUMBS

(3) FROSTING

(2) SOAK

(1) CAKE

key lime pie layer cake

makes one 6-inch layer cake, 5 to 6 inches tall/serves 8 to 12

Only the realest of real-deal Milk Bar patrons ever got a nibble of our key lime pie layer cake, the brainchild of Leslie Discher, the first cook we hired after opening Milk Bar. At the time, it was just Helen Jo, Marian Mar, James Mark, and me and we were turning into crazy people. We held an open call for pastry cooks and Leslie Discher walked through our door. She lived in the neighborhood and liked waking up early, which made her the perfect candidate for an a.m. pastry cook, call time: 4:30 a.m. She would show up with the biggest smile on her face and bake cornflake chocolate chip cookies next to me. Leslie had worked for many great pastry chefs but she never had a chance to innovate, and she quickly expressed to me that she wanted to create a layer cake that revolved around her love for key lime pie. After months of testing, it finally made it to the menu: a graham cracker cake, layered with sour cream filling, key lime curd, graham crust, and graham buttercream. It's Leslie's first creation and one I really love.

1 recipe	**graham cracker cake** (page 218)	
65g	**key lime juice**	¼ cup + 1 T
200g	**sour cream frosting** (page 117)	1 cup
190g	**graham crumbs** (page 219)	1½ cups
1 recipe	**key lime curd** (page 220)	
1 recipe	**graham buttercream** (page 220)	

special equipment:

1	**6-inch cake ring**
2	**strips acetate, each 3 × 20 inches**

cupcake assembly instructions

Put a piece of parchment paper or a silicone baking mat on the counter. Invert the cake onto it and peel off the parchment or mat from the bottom of the cake. Use the cake ring to stamp out 2 rounds from the cake. These are your top 2 cake layers. The remaining cake "scraps" will come together to make the bottom layer.

layer 1, the bottom

1. Clean the cake ring and place it in the center of a sheet pan lined with clean parchment or a silicone baking mat. Use 1 strip of acetate to line the inside of the cake ring.

2. Put the cake scraps together inside the ring and use the back of your hand to tamp the scraps together into a flat even layer.

3. Dunk a pastry brush in the key lime juice (or use a spoon) and give the cake a good, healthy bath of half of the juice.

4. Use the back of a spoon to spread one-half of the sour cream frosting in an even layer over the cake.

When we say "graham crumbs," we are referring to our recipe for graham crumbs (see page 219), *not* to store-bought graham crackers that have been pulverized into fine sand.

(recipe continues)

5. Sprinkle one-quarter of the graham crumbs evenly over the frosting. Use the back of your hand to press them lightly into the frosting, anchoring them in place.

6. Use the back of a spoon to spread half of the key lime curd as evenly as possible over the crumbs.

layer 2, the middle

1. With your index finger, gently tuck the second strip of acetate between the cake ring and the top ¼ inch of the first strip of acetate, to make a ring of acetate 5 to 6 inches tall, high enough to support the height of the finished cake.

2. Set a cake round on top of the curd (if one of your cake rounds is jankier than the other, use it here in the middle and save the prettier one for the top). Repeat the layering: lime juice, sour cream frosting, crumbs, and curd.

layer 3, the top

1. Nestle the remaining cake round into the curd. Cover the top of the cake with the graham buttercream. Give it volume and swirls, or do as we do and opt for a perfectly flat top. Garnish the frosting with the remaining graham crumbs.

2. Transfer the sheet pan to the freezer and freeze for a minimum of 12 hours to set the cake and filling. The cake will keep, well wrapped in plastic, in the freezer for up to 2 weeks.

3. At least 3 hours before you are ready to serve the cake, pull the sheet pan out of the freezer and, using your fingers and thumbs, pop the cake out of the cake ring. Gently peel off the acetate and transfer the cake to a platter or cake stand. Let it defrost in the fridge for a minimum of 3 hours. (Wrapped well in plastic, the cake can be refrigerated for up to 5 days.)

4. Slice the cake into wedges and serve.

graham cracker cake

makes 1 quarter-sheet pan of cake

115g	unsalted butter, softened	1 stick (8 T)
325g	sugar	1⅔ cups
3	large eggs	
140g	buttermilk	⅔ cup
50g	key lime juice	¼ cup
40g	grapeseed or other neutral oil	¼ cup
150g	cake flour	1¼ cups
50g	graham cracker crumbs	⅓ cup
5g	baking powder	1¼ tsp
4g	kosher salt	1 tsp

"Graham cracker crumbs" are graham crackers that have been pulverized into a fine sand in a blender or food processor.

1. Heat the oven to 350°F. Pan-spray a quarter-sheet pan and line it with parchment paper, or just line the pan with a silicone baking mat.

2. Combine the butter and sugar in the bowl of a stand mixer fitted with the paddle attachment and cream together on medium-high for 2 to 3 minutes, until light and fluffy. Scrape down the sides of the bowl halfway through this process, and again at the end.

3. Add the eggs, one at a time, beating on medium-high for 1 minute after each addition. After you add the last egg, scrape down the sides of the bowl, then beat on high for 4 more minutes. Scrape down the sides of the bowl again.

4. Combine the buttermilk, key lime juice, and oil and with the mixer on medium speed, stream them in very slowly. It should take you approximately 3 minutes to add these liquids. Scrape down the sides of the bowl, increase the mixer speed to medium-high, and paddle for an additional 2 to 3 minutes, until the mixture is practically white, twice the size of your original fluffy butter-and-sugar mixture, and completely homogeneous. Stop the mixer and scrape down the sides of the bowl.

5. Whisk the cake flour, graham cracker crumbs, baking powder, and salt in a bowl.

6. With the mixer on very low speed, slowly add the dry ingredients and mix for 45 to 60 seconds, just until your batter comes together. Scrape down the sides of the bowl, then mix on low for an additional 45 seconds to make sure no lumps of cake flour get left behind.

7. Pour the cake batter into the sheet pan and, using a spatula, spread the batter in an even layer in the pan.

8. Bake for 25 to 30 minutes, rotating the pan front to back halfway through baking. The cake will rise and puff, doubling in size, but will remain slightly buttery and dense. At 25 minutes, gently poke the edge of the cake with your finger. The cake should bounce back slightly and the center should no longer be jiggly. If it doesn't pass these tests, leave the cake in the oven for an additional 3 to 5 minutes.

9. Let the cake cool in the pan on a wire rack or, in a pinch, in the fridge or freezer (don't worry, it's not cheating). The cooled cake can be stored in the fridge, wrapped in plastic wrap, for up to 5 days.

graham crumbs

makes about 375g (3 cups)

190 g	graham cracker crumbs	1½ cups
20g	milk powder	¼ cup
25g	sugar	2 T
3g	kosher salt	¾ tsp
85g	unsalted butter, melted	6 T
55g	heavy cream	¼ cup

"Graham cracker crumbs" are graham crackers that have been pulverized into a fine sand in a blender or food processor.

1. Heat the oven to 250°F. Line a sheet pan with parchment paper or a silicone baking mat.

2. Toss the graham cracker crumbs, milk powder, sugar, and salt together in a medium bowl.

3. Whisk the butter and heavy cream together. Add these to the dry ingredients and toss again to evenly distribute. The butter will act as glue, adhering to the dry ingredients and turning the mixture into a bunch of small clusters.

4. Spread the clusters on the lined sheet pan and bake until they've darkened in color and smell like toasted, buttery graham heaven, about 20 minutes.

5. Let the crumbs cool completely before using them in a recipe. The crumbs will keep in an airtight container for 1 week in the fridge or in the freezer for up to 1 month.

(recipe continues)

key lime curd

makes about 460g (2 cups)

110g	key lime juice	½ cup
100g	sugar	½ cup
4	large eggs	
½	silver gelatin sheet	
115g	unsalted butter, very cold, cut into chunks	1 stick (8 T)
1g	kosher salt	¼ tsp

1. Combine the key lime juice and sugar in a blender and blend until the sugar granules have dissolved. Add the eggs and blend on low until you have a bright-yellow mixture. Transfer the contents of the blender to a medium pot or saucepan. Clean the blender canister.

2. Bloom the gelatin (see page 27).

3. Set the pot of key lime mixture over low heat and whisk regularly as it heats up. Keep a close eye on it as it begins to thicken. Once the mixture starts to bubble up and begin to boil, remove it from the heat and transfer it to the blender. Add the bloomed gelatin, butter, and salt and blend until the mixture is thick, shiny, and super smooth.

4. Pour the mixture through a fine-mesh sieve into a heatproof container and put it in the fridge until the key lime curd has cooled completely, at least 30 minutes. The curd can be refrigerated for up to 1 week; do not freeze.

You can substitute ¼ teaspoon powdered gelatin for the sheet gelatin.

graham buttercream

makes about 215g (1 cup)

80g	graham crumbs (page 219)	⅔ cup
100g	whole milk	⅓ cup + 2 T
20g	unsalted butter, softened	1½ T
8g	confectioners' sugar	1 T
5g	light brown sugar	1 tsp (packed)
0.5g	kosher salt	⅛ tsp

1. Put the graham crumbs in a blender. Add the milk and puree the two together until you have a smooth-as-silk graham puree. Put the puree in the fridge to chill.

2. Combine the butter, confectioners' sugar, brown sugar, and salt in a small bowl and, using a spatula, briskly stir everything together until the mixture is smooth and fluffy.

3. Stir in the chilled graham puree until the concoction is evenly mixed together.

4. Use the frosting immediately or store it in an airtight container in the fridge for up to 1 week. If you store it in the refrigerator, be sure to loosen it up before using, otherwise it will be impossible to spread. The easiest way to do this is by putting the frosting in the bowl of a stand mixer fitted with the paddle attachment and beating it on medium speed for 3 to 4 minutes.

When we say "graham crumbs," we are referring to our recipe on page 219—*not* to pulverized graham crackers.

strawberry-lemon layer cake

makes one 6-inch layer cake, 5 to 6 inches tall/serves 8 to 12

Inspired in equal parts by strawberry shortcake, lemon chiffon pie, and New York cheesecake, this was the result of one of my first "what kind of cake do you want for your birthday" games I used to play with friends, before Milk Bar was even a twinkle in my eye.

I have a big love affair with Tristar strawberries. They are a vintage strawberry breed that a handful of folks farm in upstate New York and New Jersey. They are also tiny little jewels from heaven. Naturally I had to use them in this cake. I made pickled Tristar strawberry jam and layered it with lemon juice–soaked vanilla cake, lemon cheesecake, and milk crumbs. The frosting for the top is the same pickled strawberry jam paddled into a standard frosting of unsalted butter, confectioners' sugar, and a little bit of salt. It's one of my favorite frostings because it's so out there. Who makes a pickled strawberry jam frosting? It's acidic, it's sweet, and the jam holds a lot of structure.

It was such a smart combination of flavors, I knew it had a home on the menu at Milk Bar. It rotates on and off seasonally depending on how things go with Tristar season. In midsummer, at the height of the season, we'll go through about twenty cases of jamming Tristars a day (that's the overripe, bruised selection of Tristars no one else wants, but we love). That's like a JILLION pieces of fruit. The entire kitchen smells like fresh strawberries and everyone's fingers are stained red.

It's okay if you can't get your hands on Tristars. Ask a local farmer if he/she has any "seconds" or "jamming" strawberries of any variety. You'll probably make their day—most folks only want the prettiest firm strawberries, but the more red, ripe, and bruised, the better for this recipe. If you're at the grocery store, choose the smallest, reddest strawberries you can find; they'll have the most flavor.

1 recipe	**vanilla cake** (page 190)	
60g	**lemon juice**	¼ cup
100g	**pickled strawberry jam** (page 222)	½ cup
155g	**milk crumbs** (page 129)	1¼ cups
1 recipe	**lemon cheesecake** (page 224)	
1 recipe	**pickled strawberry frosting** (page 225)	

special equipment:

1	**6-inch cake ring**
2	**strips acetate, each 3 × 20 inches**

cake assembly instructions

Put a piece of parchment paper or a silicone baking mat on the counter. Invert the cake onto it and peel off the parchment or mat from the bottom of the cake. Use the cake ring to stamp out 2 rounds from the cake. These are your top 2 cake layers. The remaining cake "scraps" will come together to make the bottom layer of the cake.

layer 1, the bottom

1. Clean the cake ring and place it in the center of a sheet pan lined with clean parchment or a silicone baking mat. Use 1 strip of acetate to line the inside of the cake ring.

(recipe continues)

2. Put the cake scraps together inside the ring and use the back of your hand to tamp the scraps together into a flat even layer.

3. Dunk a pastry brush in the lemon juice (or use a spoon) and give the layer of cake a good, healthy bath of half of the juice.

4. Use the back of a spoon to spread about 50g (¼ cup) of the pickled strawberry jam in an even layer over the cake.

5. Sprinkle one-third of the milk crumbs evenly over the pickled strawberry jam. Use the back of your hand to press them lightly into the jam, anchoring them in place.

6. Use the back of a spoon to spread one-half of the lemon cheesecake as evenly as possible over the crumbs.

layer 2, the middle

1. With your index finger, gently tuck the second strip of acetate between the cake ring and the top ¼ inch of the first strip of acetate, to make a ring of acetate 5 to 6 inches tall, high enough to support the height of the finished cake. Set a cake round on top of the lemon cheesecake (if one of your cake rounds is jankier than the other, use it here in the middle and save the prettier one for the top).

2. Repeat the layering: lemon juice, jam, milk crumbs, and lemon cheesecake.

layer 3, the top

1. Nestle the remaining cake round into the cheesecake. Cover the top of the cake with the pickled strawberry frosting. Give it volume and swirls, or do as we do and opt for a perfectly flat top. Garnish the frosting with the remaining milk crumbs.

2. Transfer the sheet pan to the freezer and freeze for a minimum of 12 hours to set the cake and filling. The cake will keep, well wrapped in plastic, in the freezer for up to 2 weeks.

3. At least 3 hours before you are ready to serve the cake, pull the sheet pan out of the freezer and, using your fingers and thumbs, pop the cake out of the cake ring. Gently peel off the acetate, and transfer the cake to a platter or cake stand. Let it defrost in the fridge for a minimum of 3 hours. (Wrapped well in plastic, the cake can be refrigerated for up to 5 days.)

4. Slice the cake into wedges and serve.

pickled strawberry jam

makes about 685g (2 cups)

450g	ripe strawberries	1 pound
200g	sugar	1 cup
8g	pectin NH	2 tsp
2g	kosher salt	½ tsp
15g	sherry vinegar	1 T
7g	white wine vinegar	1½ tsp

Read up on pectin NH (see page 16).

If making jam at home isn't your jam, use your favorite store-bought strawberry jam instead and whisk the vinegars into it. Use the quantities listed here for 2 cups of store-bought jam.

1. Wash and hull the strawberries. Put them in a blender and puree until they are fully broken down. Strain through a fine-mesh sieve.

(recipe continues)

2. Whisk together the sugar, pectin, and salt in a medium pot or saucepan. Slowly whisk in the strawberry puree, sherry vinegar, and white wine vinegar and bring to a full, rolling boil over medium heat, stirring occasionally with a heatproof spatula. Reduce the heat and cook at a low boil for 2 minutes to activate the pectin and turn the puree into a beautiful jam.

3. Once the jam coats the back of a spoon, remove the jam from the heat and cool completely. The jam will keep in the refrigerator in an airtight container for up to 2 weeks.

lemon cheesecake

makes about 230g (1 cup)

130g	**liquid cheesecake** (at right)	½ cup + 2 T
100g	**lemon curd** (page 133)	¼ cup + 3 T

In a mixer fitted with the paddle attachment, mix the liquid cheesecake and lemon curd together until well combined. Use immediately.

liquid cheesecake

makes about 460g (2 cups)

320g	**cream cheese, softened**	11 ounces
200g	**sugar**	1 cup
10g	**cornstarch**	1 T
3g	**kosher salt**	¾ tsp
35g	**whole milk**	2 T + 2 tsp
1	**large egg**	
1	**large egg yolk**	

1. Heat the oven to 300°F. Pan-spray a 9 x 5-inch loaf pan.

2. Put the cream cheese in the bowl of a stand mixer fitted with the paddle attachment and mix on low speed for 2 minutes. Scrape down the sides of the bowl with a spatula. Add the sugar and mix for 1 to 2 minutes, until the sugar has been completely incorporated. Scrape down the sides of the bowl.

3. Whisk together the cornstarch and salt in a medium bowl. Whisk in the milk in a slow, steady stream, then whisk in the whole egg and egg yolk until the slurry is homogenous.

4. With the mixer on medium-low speed, stream in the egg slurry. Paddle for 3 to 4 minutes, until the mixture is smooth and loose. Scrape down the sides of the bowl.

5. Pour the cheesecake batter into the loaf pan.

6. Bake for 25 minutes. Gently shake the pan. The cheesecake should be firmer and more set toward the outer boundaries of the pan but still be jiggly and loose in the dead center. What you're looking for is a nearly set but underbaked cheesecake. If the cheesecake is still jiggly all over, give it 5 minutes more—and another 5 minutes if it needs it, but it's never taken me more than 35 minutes. And if the cheesecake rises more than ¼ inch or begins to brown, take it out of the oven immediately.

7. Cool the cheesecake completely, to finish the baking process and allow the cheesecake to set. The final product will resemble a cheesecake, but it will be pipeable and pliable enough to easily spread or smear, while still having body and volume.

pickled strawberry frosting

makes about 250g (1 cup)

115g	unsalted butter, softened	1 stick (8 T)
40g	confectioners' sugar	¼ cup
100g	pickled strawberry jam (page 222)	½ cup
1g	kosher salt	¼ tsp
0.5g	citric acid	⅛ tsp

1. Combine the butter and confectioners' sugar in the bowl of a stand mixer fitted with the paddle attachment and cream together on medium-high for 2 to 3 minutes, until light and fluffy.

2. Meanwhile, whisk together the pickled strawberry jam, salt, and citric acid.

3. Scrape down the sides of the bowl with a spatula. With the mixer on low speed, gradually stream in the strawberry mixture.

4. Use the frosting immediately or store it in an airtight container in the fridge for up to 1 week. If you store it in the refrigerator, be sure to loosen it up before using, otherwise it will be impossible to spread. The easiest way to do this is by putting the frosting in the bowl of a stand mixer fitted with the paddle attachment and beating it on medium speed for 3 to 4 minutes.

dulce de leche layer cake

makes one 6-inch layer cake, 5 to 6 inches tall/serves 8 to 12

This cake has been around since the beginning of Milk Bar, and its milky, caramel flavor has remained a cult favorite to this day. But the dulce de leche cake was actually invented long before Milk Bar opened, when I was only making cakes for fun. I'm a huge fan of caramel. As a dorky pastry person, I love the thought of taking sugar and melting it down in a pan with nothing else until it reaches the perfect shade of amber, creating an extraordinary flavor. It's the reason I fell in love with science and the different states a single ingredient can take at different temperatures. So caramel is a flavor that I like to incorporate into my desserts as often as possible. It's a tricky thing because caramel *goes* with a lot of things, but it doesn't often get to be the *star* of the dish; it's often an afterthought.

I wanted to make a layer cake ode to caramel; but on its own, caramel can be cloyingly sweet, so I needed something with a rich, milky base to offset it. I love exploring the different grocery store aisles and one day, years ago, I found La Lechera dulce de leche in a can. Dulce de leche is basically sweetened condensed milk that has been caramelized. It's the perfect secret ingredient and it's used in almost every element of this cake. I mixed the dulce de leche into plain cake batter and it turned out amazing. It added a milkiness to the flavor of the cake, and gave the texture an extra bounce; it was less spongy and more dense. I then used straight dulce de leche as a layer when assembling the cake and I also mixed it into the frosting. With the addition of milk crumbs and an evaporated milk soak, I suppose you could say this cake is actually a love letter to both caramel and milk with different degrees of flavor playing between them.

Read up on dulce de leche (see page 14).

1 recipe	dulce de leche cake (page 185)	
65g	whole milk	¼ cup + 1 T
275g	dulce de leche	1 cup
155g	milk crumbs (page 129)	1¼ cups
1 recipe	dulce de leche frosting (page 229)	

special equipment:

1	6-inch cake ring
2	strips acetate, each 3 × 20 inches

cake assembly instructions

Put a piece of parchment paper or a silicone baking mat on the counter. Invert the cake onto it and peel off the parchment or mat from the bottom of the cake. Use the cake ring to stamp out 2 rounds from the cake. These are your top 2 cake layers. The remaining cake "scraps" will come together to make the bottom layer.

(recipe continues)

layer 1, the bottom

1. Clean the cake ring and place it in the center of a sheet pan lined with clean parchment or a silicone baking mat. Use 1 strip of acetate to line the inside of the cake ring.

2. Put the cake scraps together inside the ring and use the back of your hand to tamp the scraps together into a flat even layer.

3. Dunk a pastry brush in the milk (or use a spoon) and give the cake a good, healthy bath of half of the milk.

4. Use the back of a spoon to spread one-half of the dulce de leche in an even layer over the cake.

5. Sprinkle one-third of the milk crumbs evenly over the dulce de leche. Use the back of your hand to press them lightly into the dulce de leche, anchoring them in place.

6. Use the back of a spoon to spread one-third of the dulce de leche frosting as evenly as possible over the crumbs.

layer 2, the middle

1. With your index finger, gently tuck the second strip of acetate between the cake ring and the top ¼ inch of the first strip of acetate, to make a ring of acetate 5 to 6 inches tall, high enough to support the height of the finished cake. Set a cake round on top of the frosting (if one of your cake rounds is jankier than the other, use it here in the middle and save the prettier one for the top).

2. Repeat the layering: milk, dulce de leche, milk crumbs, and dulce de leche frosting.

layer 3, the top

1. Nestle the remaining cake round into the frosting. Cover the top of the cake with the remaining frosting. Give it volume and swirls, or do as we do and opt for a perfectly flat top. Garnish the frosting with the remaining milk crumbs.

2. Transfer the sheet pan to the freezer and freeze for a minimum of 12 hours to set the cake and filling. The cake will keep, well wrapped in plastic, in the freezer for up to 2 weeks.

3. At least 3 hours before you are ready to serve the cake, pull the sheet pan out of the freezer and, using your fingers and thumbs, pop the cake out of the cake ring. Gently peel off the acetate, and transfer the cake to a platter or cake stand. Let it defrost in the fridge for a minimum of 3 hours. (Wrapped well in plastic, the cake can be refrigerated for up to 5 days.)

4. Slice the cake into wedges and serve.

dulce de leche frosting

makes about 550g (2 cups)

Read up on dulce de leche (see page 14).

325g	**dulce de leche**	1 cup + 1 T
225g	**unsalted butter, softened**	2 sticks (16 T)
1g	**kosher salt**	¼ tsp

1. Combine the dulce de leche, butter, and salt in the bowl of a stand mixer fitted with the paddle attachment and cream together on medium-high for 6 to 8 minutes, scraping the bowl down once to make sure there are no butter lumps, until the mixture is smooth and fluffy.

2. Use the frosting immediately or store it in an airtight container in the fridge for up to 1 week. If you store it in the refrigerator, be sure to loosen it up before using, otherwise it will be impossible to spread. The easiest way to do this is by putting the frosting in the bowl of a stand mixer fitted with the paddle attachment and beating it on medium speed for 3 to 4 minutes.

popcorn layer cake

makes one 6-inch layer cake, 5 to 6 inches tall/serves 8 to 12

Jena Derman developed this cake in the dead of winter. We were at a brainstorming meeting and were sharing stories of being heavy into hibernation and spending too many days at the movie theater. Naturally, this led to the decision to make a movie theater cake. We wanted to include the elements of popcorn, gummy bears, and Coca-Cola, because all those things taste amazing when you're eating them together in a dark theater. As we started to R&D the cake, though, it got weird *really* quick.

We decided to focus on popcorn. We ground buttered popcorn to a flour and used it to replace some of the flour in our standard cake recipe; and with the addition of our favorite sidekick, powdered freeze-dried corn, the cake tasted just like popcorn! We soaked it with popcorn milk, which, as you've probably guessed, is buttery popcorn steeped in milk, then strained. We layered it with a dense white chocolate popcorn fudge, corn pudding, and a gooey caramel that's similar to the caramel in our candy bar pie. We decorated it with caramel corn and served it with a dollop of pickled strawberry jam. Corn and strawberry is a classic Milk Bar combo, especially during the summer season, and that pickled strawberry jam elevates the entire cake to a whole new level. The combination made all the popcorn elements taste even more like popcorn somehow.

This recipe involves some extra legwork in the form of pulverizing popcorn in a blender and sifting it, but it's the only way to get that popcorn flavor to stand out, so don't lose your cool on this step. Bring your grocer a slice if he/she looks at you like a loony when you buy the store out of popcorn. We also found packaged, already popped buttered popcorn, though not great at the movies, is the PERFECT popcorn to use here!

---

1 recipe	**popcorn cake** (page 182)	
30g	**popcorn milk** (page 183)	2 T
30g	**milk**	2 T
1 recipe	**popcorn pudding** (page 233)	
1 recipe	**popcorn crumbs** (page 233)	
1 recipe	**salted caramel filling** (page 234)	
1 recipe	**corn fudge** (page 234)	

1 recipe	**caramel corn** (page 235)	
100g	**pickled strawberry jam** (page 222), **for serving**	½ cup

special equipment:

1	**6-inch cake ring**
2	**strips acetate, each 3 × 20 inches**

cake assembly instructions

Put a piece of parchment paper or a silicone baking mat on the counter. Invert the cake onto it and peel off the parchment or mat from the bottom of the cake. Use the

(recipe continues)

cake ring to stamp out 2 rounds from the cake. These are your top 2 cake layers. The remaining cake "scraps" will come together to make the bottom layer.

layer 1, the bottom

1. Clean the cake ring and place it in the center of a sheet pan lined with clean parchment or a silicone baking mat. Use 1 strip of acetate to line the inside of the cake ring.

2. Put the cake scraps together inside the ring and use the back of your hand to tamp the scraps together into a flat even layer.

3. Combine the popcorn milk and the milk and dunk a pastry brush in the popcorn milk mixture (or use a spoon) and give the cake a good, healthy bath of half of the milk mixture.

4. Use the back of a spoon to spread one-half of the popcorn pudding in an even layer over the cake.

5. Sprinkle one-half of the popcorn crumbs evenly over the popcorn pudding. Use the back of your hand to press them lightly into the pudding, anchoring them in place.

6. Use the back of a spoon to spread one-half of the salted caramel filling as evenly as possible over the crumbs.

layer 2, the middle

1. With your index finger, gently tuck the second strip of acetate between the cake ring and the top ¼ inch of the first strip of acetate, to make a ring of acetate 5 to 6 inches tall, high enough to support the height of the finished cake. Set a cake round on top of the salted caramel filling (if one of your cake rounds is jankier than the other,

use it here in the middle and save the prettier one for the top).

2. Repeat the layering: popcorn milk, pudding, crumbs, and salted caramel filling.

layer 3, the top

1. Nestle the remaining cake round into the salted caramel filling. Warm the corn fudge in the microwave in 10-second increments, stirring in between, until it becomes easily spreadable, about 20 seconds. Cover the top of the cake with corn fudge and give it volume and swirls, or do as we do and opt for a perfectly flat top. Garnish the fudge with the caramel corn (reserve some for serving).

2. Transfer the sheet pan to the freezer and freeze for a minimum of 12 hours to set the cake and filling. The cake will keep, well wrapped in plastic, in the freezer for up to 2 weeks.

3. At least 3 hours before you are ready to serve the cake, pull the sheet pan out of the freezer and, using your fingers and thumbs, pop the cake out of the cake ring. Gently peel off the acetate, and transfer the cake to a platter or cake stand. Let it defrost in the fridge for a minimum of 3 hours. (Wrapped well in plastic, the cake can be refrigerated for up to 5 days.)

4. Slice the cake into wedges and serve with 1 tablespoon of pickled strawberry jam dolloped on top, or spread or swooshed on each plate alongside a small handful of extra caramel corn.

popcorn pudding

makes about 550g (2½ cups)

50g	popcorn milk (page 183)	¼ cup
6g	cornstarch	3 tsp
180g	popcorn milk (page 183)	¾ cup + 2 T
2	large egg yolks	
150g	sugar	¾ cup
20g	corn powder (see page 14)	3 T + 1 tsp
10g	kosher salt	2½ tsp
110g	unsalted butter, cold, cubed	1 stick (8 T)
2	silver gelatin sheets	

1. Whisk the 50g (¼ cup) popcorn milk and the cornstarch together in a small bowl. Set the slurry aside.

2. Whisk the 180g (¾ cup + 2T) popcorn milk and the egg yolks together in a small bowl. Whisk the sugar, corn powder, and salt into the yolk mixture in a steady stream, then transfer everything to a small saucepan. Add the butter to the saucepan.

3. Bloom the gelatin (see page 27).

4. Heat the milk-egg mixture over low heat, whisking regularly as it heats up. Keep a close eye on it. Once it just starts to boil, whisk in the popcorn-and-cornstarch slurry. Bring it back to a boil, then remove it from the stove and add the bloomed gelatin. Whisk until the gelatin has dissolved.

5. Pour the mixture through a fine-mesh sieve into a heatproof container and put it in the fridge until the popcorn pudding has cooled completely, at least 30 minutes. The pudding can be refrigerated for up to 1 week; do not freeze.

popcorn crumbs

makes about 190g (1¼ cups)

45g	milk powder	½ cup
45g	ap flour	⅓ cup
25g	sugar	2 T
10g	cornstarch	1 T
8g	corn powder (see page 14)	1 T + 1½ tsp
3g	kosher salt	¾ teaspoon
70g	unsalted butter, melted	¼ cup + 1 T

1. Heat the oven to 250°F. Line a sheet pan with parchment paper or a silicone baking mat.

2. Combine the milk powder, flour, sugar, cornstarch, corn powder, and salt in a medium bowl. Toss with your hands to mix. Add the melted butter and toss, using a spatula, until the mixture starts to come together and form small clusters.

3. Spread the clusters on the lined sheet pan. Bake for 20 minutes. The crumbs should be sandy, but still clumped together at that point, and your kitchen should smell like buttery heaven. Cool the crumbs completely. The crumbs will keep in an airtight container in the fridge for up to 1 week or in the freezer for up to 1 month.

Read up on corn powder (see page 14).

You can substitute 1 teaspoon powdered gelatin for the sheet gelatin.

(recipe continues)

salted caramel filling

makes about 350g (1½ cups)

110g	**sugar**	½ cup + 2½ tsp
35g	**light corn syrup**	2 T
1	**silver gelatin sheet**	
190g	**heavy cream**	¾ cup + 2 T
20g	**unsalted butter**	1 T + 1½ tsp
3g	**vanilla extract**	¾ tsp
3g	**kosher salt**	¾ tsp

1. Heat the sugar and corn syrup in a heavy-bottomed medium saucepan over medium-high heat. As soon as the sugar starts to melt, use a heatproof spatula to move it constantly around the pan—you want it all to melt and caramelize evenly. Cook and stir, cook and stir, until the caramel is a deep dark amber, 3 to 5 minutes.

2. Meanwhile, bloom the gelatin (see page 27).

3. Once the caramel has reached the target color, remove the saucepan from the heat. Very slowly and very carefully, pour in the heavy cream. The caramel will bubble up and steam—stand away until the steam dissipates. Use the spatula to vigorously stir the mixture together. If it is at all lumpy or if there are any clumps of hardened caramel floating around the cream, put the saucepan back over medium heat and heat the mixture, stirring constantly, until all the caramel has dissolved and the mixture is smooth. Remove the pan from the heat.

4. Stir the bloomed gelatin into the caramel. Once the gelatin has dissolved, stir in the butter, vanilla extract, and salt. Pour the caramel through a fine-mesh sieve to make sure there are no lumps of sugar or gelatin in it.

5. Let the caramel cool to room temperature, then let it cool covered in the fridge for at least 8 hours before using. It will keep in the refrigerator, in an airtight container, for up to 3 weeks.

6. When you are ready to assemble the cake, remove the caramel from the fridge and paddle it in the bowl of a stand mixer on low speed to loosen it up and make it spreadable.

You can substitute ½ teaspoon powdered gelatin for the sheet gelatin.

corn fudge

makes about 115g (⅔ cup)

25g	**heavy cream**	1 T + 2 tsp
15g	**light corn syrup**	2¼ tsp
10g	**sugar**	2½ tsp
45g	**white chocolate, chopped**	1½ ounces
15g	**unsalted butter, cubed**	1 T
6g	**corn powder** (see page 14)	1 T
.25g	**kosher salt**	pinch

1. Combine the heavy cream, corn syrup, and sugar in a small, microwave-safe container and heat in the microwave for 45 seconds, until it is very hot to the touch.

2. Add the white chocolate, butter, corn powder, and salt and stir vigorously to combine. Keep stirring until the white chocolate and butter have melted. If it seems like the white chocolate and butter are not going to fully melt, heat the mixture

Read up on corn powder (see page 14).

in the microwave in 10-second intervals, stirring in between, until everything has melted together. Give the mixture one more vigorous stir to make sure everything is evenly incorporated.

3. Use the corn fudge immediately, while it is still warm, to top the cake.

caramel corn

makes about 280g (5 cups)

1 bag (3.3 oz)	**plain microwave popcorn, freshly popped**	
135g	**sugar**	½ cup + 3 T
20g	**light corn syrup**	1 T
30g	**unsalted butter, cubed**	2 T
2g	**baking soda**	½ tsp
.25g	**kosher salt**	pinch

1. Pour half (about 5 cups) of the popped popcorn into a large bowl and set it aside. Save the leftover popcorn in the bag for a late-night snack attack.

2. Heat the sugar and corn syrup in a small heavy-bottomed saucepan over medium-high heat. As soon as the sugar starts to melt, use a heatproof spatula to move it constantly around the pan—you want it all to melt and caramelize evenly. Cook and stir, cook and stir, until the caramel has reached 375°F.

3. Once the caramel has reached the target temperature, remove the saucepan from the heat. Very slowly and very carefully, add the butter to the caramel. The caramel will bubble up and steam—stand away until the steam dissipates.

4. Sift in the baking soda and whisk the mixture together. If it is at all lumpy, put the saucepan back over medium heat and heat the mixture, whisking constantly, until all of the caramel has dissolved and the mixture is smooth. Remove the pan from the heat.

5. Pour the caramel over the popcorn in the bowl and carefully toss it together using a heatproof spatula. Sprinkle the popcorn with the salt as you toss it.

6. Continue to toss the popcorn every few minutes until it has cooled completely. Use however much you want to decorate the cake and eat the rest as a snack.

pineapple upside-down layer cake

makes one 6-inch layer cake, 5 to 6 inches tall/serves 8 to 12

The pineapple upside-down (PUD) layer cake is a proper Courtney McBroom–Christina Tosi collaboration. It came into this world because of Jim Meehan of PDT, a killer cocktail bar in NYC. One of his bartenders, who frequented Milk Bar often, was leaving for some sort of tropical location and we were put in charge of making her a going-away cake. All we knew was that she loved making tiki-inspired cocktails and was moving somewhere warm and sunny. We immediately realized the obvious, which is that we needed to make a PUD cake with the Milk Bar palate.

We started with a plain vanilla cake, but we added shredded, unsweetened coconut. We soaked the cake with maraschino cherry juice and layered it with yellow cake crumbs, poached pineapple, and PUD cake frosting. What is PUD cake frosting you ask? Let me elaborate. When thinking of PUD cake, most people's brains generally turn to the version that grandma made with the boxed mix. It's such a classic flavor, and that thought was what guided us—we used pineapple juice and yellow cake mix in the frosting to make the *frosting* taste like that nostalgic *cake*. It's like cake *Inception*!

So if you take anything away from this layer cake recipe, let it be the idea that any box cake mix plus butter, plus confectioners' sugar, a pinch of salt, and some liquid equals an entire universe of delicious frostings that have never existed before. With this technique, you can make brownie-flavored frosting with brownie mix as the base, you can make yellow cake frosting, blueberry muffin frosting . . . let your imagination run with it!

---

1 recipe	coconut cake (page 194)	
1 recipe	maraschino cherry soak (page 239)	
300g	poached pineapple (page 239), **cut into ¼-inch cubes**	1½ cups
1 recipe	pineapple upside-down frosting (page 240)	
1 recipe	yellow cake crumbs (page 111)	

special equipment:

1	6-inch cake ring
2	strips acetate, each 3 × 20 inches

cake assembly instructions

Put a piece of parchment paper or a silicone baking mat on the counter. Invert the cake onto it and peel off the parchment or mat from the bottom of the cake. Use the cake ring to stamp out 2 rounds from the cake. These are your top 2 cake layers. The remaining cake "scraps" will come together to make the bottom layer.

The poaching process for the pineapple takes a while, so do that in advance to save yourself from a last-second time crunch.

(recipe continues)

layer 1, the bottom

1. Clean the cake ring and place it in the center of a sheet pan lined with clean parchment or a silicone baking mat. Use 1 strip of acetate to line the inside of the cake ring.

2. Put the cake scraps together inside the ring and use the back of your hand to tamp the scraps together into a flat even layer.

3. Dunk a pastry brush in the maraschino cherry soak (or use a spoon) and give the cake a good, healthy bath of half of the soak.

4. Spread one-half of the poached pineapple chunks in an even layer over the cake.

5. Use the back of a spoon to spread one-fifth of the pineapple upside-down frosting as evenly as possible over the pineapple.

6. Sprinkle one-third of the yellow cake crumbs evenly over the frosting. Use the back of your hand to press them lightly into the frosting, anchoring them in place.

7. Use the back of a spoon to spread one-fifth of the pineapple upside-down frosting as evenly as possible over the crumbs.

layer 2, the middle

1. With your index finger, gently tuck the second strip of acetate between the cake ring and the top ¼ inch of the first strip of acetate, to make a ring of acetate 5 to 6 inches tall, high enough to support the height of the finished cake. Set a cake round on top of the pineapple upside-down frosting (if one of your cake rounds is jankier than the other, use it here in the middle and save the prettier one for the top).

2. Repeat the layering: soak, pineapple chunks, pineapple upside-down frosting, cake crumbs, and pineapple upside-down frosting.

layer 3, the top

1. Nestle the remaining cake round into the frosting. Cover the top of the cake with the remaining frosting. Give it volume and swirls, or do as we do and opt for a perfectly flat top. Garnish the frosting with the remaining yellow cake crumbs.

2. Transfer the sheet pan to the freezer and freeze for a minimum of 12 hours to set the cake and filling. The cake will keep, well wrapped in plastic, in the freezer for up to 2 weeks.

3. At least 3 hours before you are ready to serve the cake, pull the sheet pan out of the freezer and, using your fingers and thumbs, pop the cake out of the cake ring. Gently peel off the acetate, and transfer the cake to a platter or cake stand. Let it defrost in the fridge for a minimum of 3 hours. (Wrapped well in plastic, the cake can be refrigerated for up to 5 days.)

4. Slice the cake into wedges and serve.

maraschino cherry soak

makes about 60g (¼ cup)

20g	**pineapple poaching liquid** (from poached pineapple recipe below)	1 T + 1 tsp
20g	**grenadine**	1 T + 1 tsp
10g	**buttermilk**	2 tsp
10g	**whole milk**	2 tsp

Whisk everything together in a small bowl. Use immediately.

poached pineapple

makes about 1kg (1 pineapple's worth)

1	**pineapple, peeled, cored, and quartered lengthwise**	
225g	**water**	1 cup
190g	**sauvignon blanc, the cheap stuff**	¾ cup + 2 T
100g	**sugar**	½ cup
1	**Thai long peppercorn (or a few white peppercorns)**	
2	**green cardamom pods**	
0.5g	**vanilla extract**	⅛ tsp

1. Heat the oven to 350°F.

2. Lay the pineapple quarters flat in a large (approximately 3½-quart) Dutch oven.

3. Whisk the water, wine, sugar, peppercorn, cardamom, and vanilla extract together and pour the liquid over the pineapple pieces. They should be almost completely covered with liquid, but it's okay if some of the pineapple sticks out a little bit above the liquid.

4. Cover the pot and bake for 2 hours. They're done when they turn a deep yellow and you can slide a paring knife through them with ease.

5. Remove the pineapple from the oven and let them cool completely before using in a recipe. Keep them stored in their poaching liquid, in the refrigerator. (Reserve some of the liquid for the maraschino cherry soak.) They will keep for up to 2 weeks.

(recipe continues)

pineapple upside-down frosting

makes about 650g (3 cups)

60g	yellow cake mix	¼ cup + 1 T
370g	poached pineapple (page 239)	12 ounces
200g	unsalted butter, softened	1¾ sticks (14 T)
115g	confectioners' sugar	½ cup + 3 T
2g	kosher salt	½ tsp
0.5g	citric acid	⅛ tsp

1. Heat the oven to 250°F. Line a sheet pan with parchment paper or a silicone baking mat.

2. Spread the cake mix on the lined sheet pan and bake for 20 minutes. Cool the toasted cake mix completely before using.

3. Meanwhile, puree the cooled, poached pineapple in a blender and strain it through a fine-mesh sieve (discard the solids). Measure out 275g (1¼ cups) of the puree. If you don't have enough, puree a little bit more until you get this amount. Set the puree aside.

4. Combine the butter, confectioners' sugar, salt, citric acid, and the cooled toasted yellow cake mix in the bowl of a stand mixer fitted with the paddle attachment and cream together on medium-high for 6 to 8 minutes, scraping the bowl down once to make sure there are no butter lumps, until the mixture is smooth and fluffy.

5. With the mixer on low, stream in the pineapple puree and continue creaming until the puree is fully emulsified and the frosting is smooth and fluffy again.

6. Use the frosting immediately or store it in an airtight container in the fridge for up to 1 week. If you store it in the refrigerator, be sure to loosen it up before using, otherwise it will be impossible to spread. The easiest way to do this is by putting the frosting in the bowl of a stand mixer fitted with the paddle attachment and beating it on medium speed for 3 to 4 minutes.

There is a yellow cake mix that reigns supreme for this recipe: It's Pillsbury (see page 17)!

german chocolate jimbo layer cake

makes one 6-inch layer cake, 5 to 6 inches tall/serves 8 to 12

The inspiration for this cake came into our lives through my friend and cowriter Courtney McBroom. A very near and dear friend of *hers* worked under Jim Nelson, the editor in chief of *GQ* magazine. Jim is a lovely man with excellent taste. It was Jim's birthday, and all of a sudden, we were catapulted into this crazy life of coming up with a cake for the ultimate tastemaker. We did some sleuthing and discovered that he loves chocolate cake, specifically *German* chocolate cake. Traditionally, German chocolate cake is a milk chocolate cake layered with an ooey-gooey coconut filling with pecans or walnuts and chocolate frosting. In our world, ooey-gooey = crack pie, so we immediately pulled some raw crack pie filling from the walk-in and underbaked it without the oat crust, so it remained ooey and gooey. We folded in some shredded, sweetened coconut, and turned it into the world's best German chocolate cake filling.

For the nut element, we turned to our roots. *The Momofuku Milk Bar* cookbook has an entire chapter dedicated to the nut crunch, which is basically a combination of some crunchy crepes or crispy cereal, a nut paste, and sometimes a nut brittle. So we made a nut crunch by toasting pecans, blending them into a pecan butter, then folding that butter into crispies. Needless to say, Jim loved his birthday cake and we loved naming the German Chocolate Jimbo after him.

---

1 recipe	**chocolate cake** (page 166)	
1 recipe	**malt cake soak** (page 244)	
1 recipe	**coconut-crack filling** (page 244)	
115g	**pecan crunch** (page 150)	¾ cup
1 recipe	**chocolate frosting** (page 245)	
15g	**shredded, sweetened coconut, toasted**	3 T

special equipment:

1	**6-inch cake ring**
2	**strips acetate, each 3 × 20 inches**

cake assembly instructions

Put a piece of parchment paper or a silicone baking mat on the counter. Invert the cake onto it and peel off the parchment or mat from the bottom of the cake. Use the cake ring to stamp out 2 rounds from the cake. These are your top 2 cake layers. The remaining cake "scraps" will come together to make the bottom layer of the cake.

layer 1, the bottom

1. Clean the cake ring and place it in the center of a sheet pan lined with clean parchment or a silicone baking mat. Use 1 strip of acetate to line the inside of the cake ring.

(recipe continues)

2. Put the cake scraps together inside the ring and use the back of your hand to tamp the scraps together into a flat even layer.

3. Dunk a pastry brush in the malt cake soak (or use a spoon) and give the layer of cake a good, healthy bath of half of the soak.

4. Use the back of a spoon to spread half of the coconut-crack filling in an even layer over the cake.

5. Sprinkle half of the pecan crunch evenly over the coconut-crack filling. Use the back of your hand to press the pieces lightly into the filling, anchoring them in place.

6. Use the back of a spoon to spread one-third of the chocolate frosting over the pecan crunch layer.

layer 2, the middle

1. With your index finger, gently tuck the second strip of acetate between the cake ring and the top ¼ inch of the first strip of acetate, to make a ring of acetate 5 to 6 inches tall, high enough to support the height of the finished cake. Set a cake round on top of the frosting (if one of your cake rounds is jankier than the other, use it here in the middle and save the prettier one for the top).

2. Repeat the layering: soak, filling, pecan crunch, and frosting.

layer 3, the top

1. Nestle the remaining cake round into the frosting. Cover the top of the cake with the remaining frosting. Give it volume and swirls, or do as we do and opt for a perfectly flat top. Garnish the frosting with toasted shredded coconut.

2. Transfer the sheet pan to the freezer and freeze for a minimum of 12 hours to set the cake

and fillings. The cake will keep, well wrapped in plastic, in the freezer for up to 2 weeks.

3. At least 3 hours before you are ready to serve the cake, pull the sheet pan out of the freezer and, using your fingers and thumbs, pop the cake out of the cake ring. Gently peel off the acetate, and transfer the cake to a platter or cake stand. Let it defrost in the fridge for a minimum of 3 hours. (Wrapped well in plastic, the cake can be refrigerated for up to 5 days.)

4. Slice the cake into wedges and serve.

malt cake soak

makes 65g (¼ cup + 1 tablespoon)

55g	**whole milk**	¼ cup
10g	**Ovaltine, classic malt**	2 T

Whisk together the milk and Ovaltine in a small bowl. Use immediately.

coconut-crack filling

makes about 280g (1½ cups)

75g	**sugar**	⅓ cup
45g	**light brown sugar**	3 T (packed)
6g	**corn powder** (see page 14)	1 T
5g	**milk powder**	1 T
2g	**kosher salt**	½ tsp
55g	**unsalted butter, melted**	½ stick (4 T)
40g	**heavy cream**	3 T
1g	**vanilla extract**	¼ tsp
2	**large egg yolks**	
100g	**shredded, sweetened coconut**	1 cup (packed)

1. Heat the oven to 325°F. Generously pan-spray a 9 x 5-inch loaf pan.

2. Combine the sugar, brown sugar, corn powder, milk powder, and salt in the bowl of a stand mixer fitted with the paddle attachment and mix on low speed until evenly blended.

3. Add the melted butter and paddle for 1 minute, until all the dry ingredients are moist.

4. Add the heavy cream and vanilla extract and continue mixing on low for 1 minute until any white streaks from the cream have completely disappeared into the mixture. Scrape down the sides of the bowl with a spatula.

5. Add the egg yolks, paddling them into the mixture just to combine; be careful not to aerate the mixture, but be certain the mixture is glossy and homogenous. Mix on low speed until it is.

6. Pour the crack pie filling into the loaf pan and bake for 20 to 25 minutes. At 20 minutes, gently shake the pan. The crack pie filling should be firmer and more set toward the outer boundaries of the baking pan but slightly jiggly and loose in the center. If it's jiggly all over, give it 2 to 3 minutes more. It should just start to brown on top.

7. Let the crack pie filling cool to room temperature.

8. Once cooled, mix the crack pie filling with the sweetened shredded coconut. This filling can be used immediately or stored in the refrigerator in an airtight container for up to 1 week.

chocolate frosting

makes about 320g (1½ cups)

115g	unsalted butter, softened	1 stick (8 T)
120g	confectioners' sugar	1 cup
20g	cocoa powder	3 T
2g	kosher salt	½ tsp
25g	whole milk	2 T

1. Combine the butter, sugar, cocoa powder, and salt in the bowl of a stand mixer fitted with the paddle attachment and cream together on medium-high for 5 to 7 minutes, until smooth and fluffy. Scrape down the sides of the bowl.

2. With the mixer on its lowest speed, stream in the milk. Crank the mixer up to medium-high and beat for 2 to 3 minutes, until the mixture is silky smooth and glossy. Scrape down the sides of the bowl.

3. Use the frosting immediately or store it in an airtight container in the fridge for up to 1 week. If you store it in the refrigerator, be sure to loosen it up before using, otherwise it will be impossible to spread. The easiest way to do this is by putting the frosting in the bowl of a stand mixer fitted with the paddle attachment and beating it on medium speed for 3 to 4 minutes.

pretzel layer cake

makes one 6-inch layer cake, 5 to 6 inches tall/serves 8 to 12

The first few years that Milk Bar was open, it grew quickly. Each of our hardbodies was an incredible baker, but the business needed more, and so I expected more. In order to keep a focus, each staff member became a specialist in a given area of the business. Some ran operations, others finance, others our team culture. In 2011, Helen Jo, managing HR, came to me one day desperately needing a creative outlet. She wanted to make a cake. Her now-husband loves snack foods; he loves gummy bears, he loves popcorn, but more than anything else, he loves pretzels, so she wanted to make a pretzel cake. We brainstormed a list of things that go well with pretzels and came up with mustard and beer. Off Helen Jo went. Three or four months later, we realized that mustard, though delicious, is a little weird in cake form. We noted that honey pairs well with mustard, so therefore it must also pair well with pretzel. We also remembered that most people love chocolate and pretzels especially when the former is covering the latter.

After a few more months of testing, Helen Jo had crafted the perfect pretzel cake. She toasted the pretzels, then ground them into the consistency of flour and replaced some of the flour in the cake with it, making it salty, dark, and malty. She soaked the cake with stout beer, which rounded it out perfectly, then layered it with pretzel crumbs and honey frosting. The pretzel crumbs are perfectly crunchy, and the umami flavors in the honey frosting bring out the salty maltiness of the pretzels. This seems like a labor-intensive cake, but all it really takes is a food processor and a few extra steps. If you want to make an alcohol-free version, you don't *have* to use the stout beer as a soak, you can use straight-up milk instead. And for the stout ganache, just sub in an equal amount—70g (⅓ cup)—heavy cream in lieu of the stout.

---

1 recipe	**pretzel cake** (page 201)	
65g	**chocolate stout**	¼ cup
1 recipe	**stout ganache** (opposite)	
1 recipe	**pretzel crumbs** (page 248)	
1 recipe	**honey frosting** (page 248)	

special equipment:

1	**6-inch cake ring**
2	**strips acetate, each 3 × 20 inches**

cake assembly instructions

Put a piece of parchment paper or a silicone baking mat on the counter. Invert the cake onto it and peel off the parchment or mat from the bottom of the cake. Use the cake ring to stamp out 2 rounds from the cake. These are your top 2 cake layers. The remaining cake "scraps" will come together to make the bottom layer of the cake.

layer 1, the bottom

1. Clean the cake ring and place it in the center of a sheet pan lined with clean parchment or a silicone baking mat. Use

1 strip of acetate to line the inside of the cake ring.

2. Put the cake scraps together inside the ring and use the back of your hand to tamp the scraps together into a flat even layer.

3. Dunk a pastry brush in the chocolate stout (or use a spoon) and give the layer of cake a good, healthy bath of half of the stout.

4. Use the back of a spoon to spread one-fifth of the honey frosting in an even layer over the cake.

5. Sprinkle one-third of the pretzel crumbs evenly over the frosting. Use the back of your hand to anchor them in place.

6. Use the back of a spoon to spread one-fifth of the honey frosting as evenly as possible over the crumbs.

layer 2, the middle

1. With your index finger, gently tuck the second strip of acetate between the cake ring and the top ¼ inch of the first strip of acetate, to make a ring of acetate 5 to 6 inches tall, high enough to support the height of the finished cake. Set a cake round on top of the honey frosting (if one of your cake rounds is jankier than the other, use it here in the middle and save the prettier one for the top).

2. Repeat the layering: stout, stout ganache, pretzel crumbs, and honey frosting.

layer 3, the top

1. Nestle the remaining cake round into the frosting. Cover the top of the cake with the remaining honey frosting. Give it volume and swirls, or do as we do and opt for a perfectly flat top. Garnish the frosting with the remaining pretzel crumbs.

2. Transfer the sheet pan to the freezer and freeze for a minimum of 12 hours to set the cake and filling. The cake will keep, well wrapped in plastic, in the freezer for up to 2 weeks.

3. At least 3 hours before you are ready to serve the cake, pull the sheet pan out of the freezer and, using your fingers and thumbs, pop the cake out of the cake ring. Gently peel off the acetate, and transfer the cake to a platter or cake stand. Let it defrost in the fridge for a minimum of 3 hours. (Wrapped well in plastic, the cake can be refrigerated for up to 5 days.)

4. If you're feeling wacky, cover the top of the cake with more pretzels before slicing it into wedges and serving.

stout ganache

makes about 350g (1 cup)

70g	chocolate stout	⅓ cup
45g	heavy cream	3 T
250g	72% chocolate, melted	9 ounces

1. Combine the beer and heavy cream in a small saucepan and bring to a boil over medium heat.

2. Once the liquid has boiled, pour it over the melted chocolate in a heatproof bowl and use a spatula to stir the concoction together until it is completely smooth.

3. Use the ganache immediately or, if you choose to make it ahead of time and refrigerate it, microwave it in 15-second intervals, stirring in between until it's pliable enough to spread.

(recipe continues)

4. The ganache will keep in the refrigerator, in an airtight container, for up to 2 weeks.

pretzel crumbs

makes about 540g (4½ cups)

55g	pretzels	½ cup
85g	sugar	⅓ cup + 1 T
80g	cake flour	⅔ cup
45g	malt powder	¼ cup + 1½ tsp
30g	light brown sugar	2 T (packed)
2g	baking powder	½ tsp
1g	baking soda	¼ tsp
1g	kosher salt	¼ tsp
35g	grapeseed or other neutral oil	3 T + 2 tsp
20g	Ovaltine, classic malt	¼ cup
190g	white chocolate, melted	6¾ ounces

1. Heat the oven to 300°F. Line a sheet pan with parchment paper or a silicone baking mat.

2. Blitz the pretzels in a blender until they are a fine powder. Set it aside.

3. Whisk together the sugar, cake flour, malt powder, brown sugar, baking powder, baking soda, and salt in a large bowl.

4. Add the oil and use your hands or a spatula to mix everything until you have clumpy crumbs.

5. Spread the crumbs on the lined sheet pan and bake for 15 to 20 minutes.

6. Let the crumbs cool completely, then toss them with the ground pretzels and Ovaltine.

7. Pour the white chocolate over the crumbs and toss until your clusters are enrobed. Then continue tossing them every 5 minutes, until the white chocolate hardens and the clusters are no longer sticky. The crumbs will keep in an airtight container in the fridge for up to 1 week or in the freezer for up to 1 month.

honey frosting

makes about 490g (2 cups)

230g	unsalted butter, softened	2 sticks (16 T)
80g	confectioners' sugar	½ cup + 2 T
185g	honey	½ cup
2g	kosher salt	½ tsp

1. Combine the butter and confectioners' sugar in the bowl of a stand mixer fitted with the paddle attachment and cream together on medium-high for 4 to 5 minutes, until fluffy.

2. Scrape down the bowl, then add the honey and salt and continue to cream for 30 seconds, until light and combined.

3. Use the frosting immediately or store it in an airtight container in the fridge for up to 1 week. If you store it in the refrigerator, be sure to loosen it up before using, otherwise it will be impossible to spread. The easiest way to do this is by putting the frosting in the bowl of a stand mixer fitted with the paddle attachment and beating it on medium speed for 3 to 4 minutes.

Find malt powder (this recipe's secret weapon) in a gourmet food store or online!

If you're making this without the stout ganache, bump up the Honey Frosting amounts to total 740g (3 cups):
340g unsalted butter, softened (3 sticks)
120g confectioners' sugar (1 cup)
275g honey (¾ cup)
3g salt (¾ tsp)

pumpkin pie layer cake

makes one 6-inch layer cake, 5 to 6 inches tall/serves 8 to 12

Let's face it, not many people (besides my mom), really loooooove pumpkin pie. It's just one of those things that's always on the table around the holidays because people love the *idea* of it.

It was November 2012. And we were brainstorming for the upcoming Thanksgiving holiday. We'd made an awesome pumpkin pie soft serve the year before, but you can't really bring soft serve to the dessert table (it barely makes it out the front door)! We were adamant about folks being able to bring Milk Bar home, but pumpkin crack pie seemed too easy. So we took that idea and made it into a layer cake! Yes! The result is like bringing cake AND pie to the party!

We deconstructed the bits and pieces of pumpkin pie that just needed a little more attention to make it gooey and guilty and delicious. We made a pumpkin cake. We played around with a cream cheese frosting, but it proved to be a little too sweet and big and bright. What we really needed was something a bit richer, so we made a brown butter cheesecake layer that ended up a better play with its deep nuttiness and richness. From there, we decided to go back to one of my favorite things, an item we have been making even before Milk Bar existed: pumpkin ganache. To tie everything together with a nice little bow, we bring the pie element in with our classic pie crumbs and add some pepitas (pumpkin seeds) as a fun and delicious textural element.

---

1 recipe	**pumpkin cake** (page 250)	
65g	**whole milk**	¼ cup + 1 T
1 recipe	**brown butter graham cheesecake** (page 251)	
155g	**pie dough crumbs** (page 252)	1¼ cups
1 recipe	**pumpkin ganache** (page 253)	
1 recipe	**toasted pepitas** (page 253)	

special equipment:

1	**6-inch cake ring**
2	**strips acetate, each 3 × 20 inches**

cake assembly instructions

Put a piece of parchment paper or a silicone baking mat on the counter. Invert the cake onto it and peel off the parchment or mat from the bottom of the cake. Use the cake ring to stamp out 2 rounds from the cake. These are your top 2 cake layers. The remaining cake "scraps" will come together to make the bottom layer of the cake.

layer 1, the bottom

1. Clean the cake ring and place it in the center of a sheet pan lined with clean parchment or a silicone baking mat. Use 1 strip of acetate to line the inside of the cake ring.

(recipe continues)

2. Put the cake scraps together inside the ring and use the back of your hand to tamp the scraps together into a flat even layer.

3. Dunk a pastry brush in the milk (or use a spoon) and give the layer of cake a good, healthy bath of half of the milk.

4. Use the back of a spoon to spread half of the brown butter graham cheesecake in an even layer over the cake.

5. Sprinkle one-third of the pie dough crumbs evenly over the cheesecake. Use the back of your hand to press them lightly into the cheesecake, anchoring them in place.

6. Use the back of a spoon to spread one-third of the pumpkin ganache as evenly as possible over the pie dough crumbs.

layer 2, the middle

1. With your index finger, gently tuck the second strip of acetate between the cake ring and the top ¼ inch of the first strip of acetate, to make a ring of acetate 5 to 6 inches tall, high enough to support the height of the finished cake. Set a cake round on top of the ganache (if one of your cake rounds is jankier than the other, use it here in the middle and save the prettier one for the top).

2. Repeat the layering: milk, cheesecake, crumbs, and ganache.

layer 3, the top

1. Nestle the remaining cake round into the ganache. Cover the top of the cake with the remaining ganache. Give it volume and swirls, or do as we do and opt for a perfectly flat top. Garnish the ganache with the remaining pie dough crumbs and the toasted pepitas.

2. Transfer the sheet pan to the freezer and freeze for a minimum of 12 hours to set the cake and filling. The cake will keep, well wrapped in plastic, in the freezer for up to 2 weeks.

3. At least 3 hours before you are ready to serve the cake, pull the sheet pan out of the freezer and, using your fingers and thumbs, pop the cake out of the cake ring. Gently peel off the acetate, and transfer the cake to a platter or cake stand. Let it defrost in the fridge for a minimum of 3 hours. (Wrapped well in plastic, the cake can be refrigerated for up to 5 days.)

4. Slice the cake into wedges and serve.

pumpkin cake

makes 1 quarter-sheet pan cake

115g	unsalted butter, softened	1 stick (8 T)
150g	sugar	¾ cup
150g	light brown sugar	⅔ cup (packed)
1	large egg	
175g	Libby's pumpkin puree	⅔ cup + 1 T
110g	buttermilk	½ cup
25g	grapeseed or other neutral oil	2 T + 1 tsp
1g	vanilla extract	¼ tsp
210g	cake flour	2¼ cups
12g	kosher salt	1 T
4g	baking powder	1 tsp
2g	baking soda	¼ tsp
4g	ground cinnamon	2 tsp
2g	ground ginger	1 tsp
0.5g	ground nutmeg	½ tsp

1. Heat the oven to 350°F. Pan-spray a quarter-sheet pan and line it with parchment paper, or just line the pan with a silicone baking mat.

2. Combine the butter and both sugars in the bowl of a stand mixer fitted with the paddle attachment and cream together on medium-high for 2 to 3 minutes, until light and fluffy. Scrape down the sides of the bowl halfway through this process, and again at the end of it.

3. Add the egg and beat on medium-high for 1 minute. Scrape down the sides of the bowl, then beat on high for 4 more minutes. Scrape down the sides of the bowl again.

4. Combine the pumpkin puree, buttermilk, oil, and vanilla extract and with the mixer on medium speed, stream them into the cake batter very slowly. It should take you approximately 3 minutes to add these liquids. Scrape down the sides of the bowl, increase the mixer speed to medium-high, and paddle for an additional 2 to 3 minutes, until the mixture is a pale orange, twice the size of your original fluffy butter-and-sugar mixture, and completely homogeneous. Don't rush the process. You're basically forcing too much liquid into an already fatty mixture that doesn't want to make room for that liquid. There should be no streaks of fat or liquid. Stop the mixer and scrape down the sides of the bowl.

5. Whisk together the flour, salt, baking powder, baking soda, cinnamon, ginger, and nutmeg.

6. With the mixer on very low speed, slowly add the dry ingredients and mix for 45 to 60 seconds, just until your batter comes together. Scrape down the sides of the

bowl, then mix on low for an additional 45 seconds to make sure no lumps of cake flour get left behind.

7. Pour the cake batter into the sheet pan and, using a spatula, spread the batter in an even layer in the pan.

8. Bake for 30 to 35 minutes, rotating the pan front to back halfway through baking. The cake will rise and puff, doubling in size, but will remain slightly buttery and dense. At 30 minutes, gently poke the edge of the cake with your finger: The cake should bounce back slightly and the center should no longer be jiggly. If it doesn't pass these tests, leave the cake in the oven for an additional 3 to 5 minutes.

9. Let the cake cool in the pan on a wire rack or, in a pinch, in the fridge or freezer (don't worry, it's not cheating). The cooled cake can be stored in the fridge, wrapped in plastic wrap, for up to 5 days.

brown butter graham cheesecake

makes about 360g (1¾ cups)

1 recipe	**brown butter graham crust** (page 252)	
240g	**liquid cheesecake** (page 224)	1 cup + 1 T

Combine the brown butter graham crust and liquid cheesecake in a medium bowl. Use immediately or store in an airtight container in the fridge for up to 1 week.

(recipe continues)

brown butter graham crust

makes about 130g (¾ cup)

"Graham cracker crumbs" are graham crackers that have been pulverized into a fine sand in a blender or food processor.

70g	graham cracker crumbs	½ cup + 2 tsp
10g	sugar	2½ tsp
8 g	milk powder	1 T + 1 tsp
1g	kosher salt	¼ tsp
20g	brown butter (see box, page 174)	1 T + 1 tsp
20g	heavy cream	1 T + 1 tsp

1. Toss the graham cracker crumbs, sugar, milk powder, and salt with your hands in a medium bowl to evenly distribute the dry ingredients.

2. Whisk the brown butter and heavy cream together in a small bowl. Add them to the dry ingredients and toss again to evenly distribute. They will act as a glue, adhering to the dry ingredients and turning the mixture into a bunch of small clusters. The mixture should hold its shape if squeezed tightly in the palm of your hand. If it is not moist enough to do so, melt an additional 15 to 25g (1 to 1½ tablespoons) butter and mix it in.

pie dough crumbs

makes about 300g (2½ cups)

240g	ap flour	1¾ cups
15g	sugar	1 T + 1 tsp
2g	kosher salt	½ tsp
80g	cold unsalted butter, cubed	6 T
40 to 60g	cold water	3 to 4 T

1. Heat the oven to 350°F. Line a sheet pan with parchment paper or a silicone baking mat.

2. Combine the flour, sugar, and salt in the bowl of a stand mixer fitted with the paddle attachment and paddle on low speed until everything is well mixed.

3. Add the butter and 40g (3 tablespoons) water and paddle on low speed until the mixture starts to come together in small clusters. If necessary, add another tablespoon of water in a very slow stream, using just enough to get the clusters to come together.

4. Spread the clusters on the lined sheet pan and bake for 30 minutes. Take them out of the oven and use a heatproof spatula to break them apart and toss them around. Put the crumbs back in the oven and bake until they are a nice, super-duper deep brown. Most ovens bake differently, so keep a close eye on them; it could take as little as 15 and up to 30 minutes more to reach this point. They will still be slightly moist to touch, but don't worry, they will dry and harden as they cool.

5. Let the crumbs cool completely before using in a recipe or eating. The crumbs will keep for 1 week at room temperature or 1 month in the fridge or freezer.

pumpkin ganache

makes about 330g (1½ cups)

Oh, the wonders pumpkin ganache holds! It will elevate any baked good, dessert, or snack attack. Pipe it atop a sugar cookie or square of blondie, enrobe it in chocolate for a seasonal bonbon, or pull my favorite move and smear it on some Ritz crackers and with slices of pears, and some Stilton cheese crumbled on top.

150g	white chocolate	5½ ounces
25g	unsalted butter	2 T
25g	light corn syrup	1 T + ¾ tsp
55g	heavy cream, as cold as possible	¼ cup
75g	Libby's pumpkin puree	⅓ cup
2g	kosher salt	½ tsp
1g	ground cinnamon	½ tsp

1. Combine the white chocolate and butter in a microwave-safe dish and gently melt them in the microwave in 15-second bursts, stirring between blasts. The result should be barely warm to the touch and totally homogenous.

2. Transfer the chocolate mixture to a container that can accommodate a hand blender—something tall and narrow, like a 1-quart plastic deli container. Warm the corn syrup in the microwave for 15 seconds, then immediately add it to the chocolate mixture and buzz with the hand blender. After a minute, stream in the heavy cream, with the hand blender running—it's okay if the mixture looks weird and broken. Don't give up hope! It will come back together as you continue blending.

3. Blend in the pumpkin puree, salt, and cinnamon. Put the ganache in the fridge to firm up before using, for at least 4 hours, or, ideally, overnight. The pumpkin ganache will keep in the refrigerator, in an airtight container, for up to 1 week.

toasted pepitas

makes about 65g (½ cup)

65g	pepitas (hulled pumpkin seeds)	¼ cup
4g	kosher salt	1 tsp

1. Heat the oven to 325°F.

2. Toss the pepitas with the salt, spread them on a baking sheet, and toast them in the oven until they just start to brown, 10 to 15 minutes. Let them cool completely before using them to garnish the cake.

pancake layer cake

makes one 6-inch layer cake, 5 to 6 inches tall/serves 8 to 12

The idea of a pancake cake originated in 2008, from Minor Brinkley, who became one of our opening cake slicers and cashiers after he'd been fired multiple times as a server from both Ssäm Bar *and* Noodle Bar. He was quite an endearing, yet tricky person. He gave each of the early Milk Bar employees nicknames revolving around butter, perfect for a bakery full of it. Mine was Tiger Butter (to this day, he still calls me that). But when he worked shifts, I always made sure to hang by the register to make sure he was describing the food properly to customers. Once, someone asked him what was in the pistachio cake and he actually answered, "I dunno, like probably passion fruit and some chocolate and, you know, some other stuff, whatever you want it to be." "That's absolutely the wrong answer," I roared. For some reason, he kept his job, probably because he made people smile, and he loved to help come up with ridiculous Milk Bar ideas.

Early one morning, he said to me, "Hey, Tiger Butter, how come you don't make a pancake cake? I would like a pancake cake for breakfast. I'd also eat that pancake cake for lunch and for dinner and probably a late-night snack, too. That's basically all the hours we are open here." That's all we needed for it to became a project for the Sunday night team, which consisted of Yewande Komolafe and me. I would bring in my nonstick pancake griddle and we'd make pancakes in every possible way to try to figure out how we could create the perfect pancake cake. This went on for approximately two years to no avail.

Many years after that, Jena Derman found the handwritten notes for the abandoned pancake cake project stashed in a binder and decided to take this cake on as her new R&D project. She made a wetter, puffier batter that bakes up somewhere between a crepe, a pancake, and a sheet cake in texture. We layer it up with a maple gel and a miso curd (which brings an eggy, umami vibe), then top it off with a zingy raspberry jam. Serve this cake warm (zap it in the microwave or in a hot oven) with a pat of black pepper butter to make it savory, sweet, and more intriguing. (It's also great with a fried egg and a few slabs of bacon on top.)

1 recipe	**pancake cake** (page 257)
1 recipe	**pancake soak** (page 257)
1 recipe	**maple gel** (page 258)
1 recipe	**miso curd** (page 258)
1 recipe	**raspberry jam** (page 259)

1 recipe	**black pepper butter** (page 259), **for serving**

special equipment:

1	**6-inch cake ring**
2	**strips acetate,** **each 3 × 20 inches**

(recipe continues)

cake assembly instructions

Put a piece of parchment paper or a silicone baking mat on the counter. Invert the cake onto it and peel off the parchment or mat from the bottom of the cake. Use the cake ring to stamp out 4 rounds from the cake. These are your top 4 cake layers. The remaining cake "scraps" will come together to make the bottom layer.

layer 1, the bottom

1. Clean the cake ring and place it in the center of a sheet pan lined with clean parchment or a silicone baking mat. Use 1 strip of acetate to line the inside of the cake ring.

2. Put the cake scraps together inside the ring and use the back of your hand to tamp the scraps together into a flat even layer.

3. Dunk a pastry brush in the pancake soak (or use a spoon) and give the cake a good, healthy bath of one-quarter of the soak.

4. Use the back of a spoon to spread one-half of the maple gel in an even layer over the cake.

layer 2, the middle

1. Nestle another cake round on top of the maple gel and repeat the soaking process with another one-quarter of the pancake soak.

2. Use the back of a spoon to spread one-half of the miso curd in an even layer over the cake.

layer 3, still the middle

1. Nestle another cake round on top of the miso curd and repeat the soaking process with yet another one-quarter of the pancake soak.

2. Use the back of a spoon to spread all of the raspberry jam in an even layer over the cake.

layer 4, yep, still the middle

1. With your index finger, gently tuck the second strip of acetate between the cake ring and the top ¼ inch of the first strip of acetate, to make a ring of acetate 5 to 6 inches tall, high enough to support the height of the finished cake. Set a cake round on top of the jam (if one of your 2 remaining cake rounds is jankier than the other, use it here in the middle and save the prettier one for the top).

2. Repeat the layering as for layer 2: pancake soak and miso curd.

layer 5, the top

1. Nestle the remaining cake round into the miso curd. Cover the top of the cake with the remaining maple gel.

2. Transfer the sheet pan to the freezer and freeze for a minimum of 12 hours to set the cake and filling. The cake will keep, well wrapped in plastic, in the freezer for up to 2 weeks.

3. At least 3 hours before you are ready to serve the cake, pull the sheet pan out of the freezer and, using your fingers and thumbs, pop the cake out of the cake ring. Gently peel off the acetate, and transfer the cake to a platter or cake stand. Let it defrost in the fridge for a minimum of 3 hours. (Wrapped well in plastic, the cake can be refrigerated for up to 5 days.)

4. Slice the cake into wedges and heat each slice in the microwave for 15 seconds before serving with 1 tablespoon of black pepper butter dolloped on top.

pancake cake

makes 1 half-sheet pan of cake

480g	egg yolks	from 25 large eggs
160g	sugar	¾ cup + 1 T
200g	whole milk	¾ cup + 2 T
110g	maple syrup	½ cup + 1 T
50g	unsalted butter, melted and cooled	4 T
160g	ap flour	1 cup + 3 T
10g	kosher salt	2½ tsp
4g	baking powder	1 tsp
3g	baking soda	¾ tsp

1. Heat the oven to 350°F. Pan-spray a half-sheet pan and line it with parchment paper, or just line the pan with a silicone baking mat.

2. Combine the egg yolks and sugar in the bowl of a stand mixer fitted with the whisk attachment and whip together on medium-high for 2 to 3 minutes, until the mixture becomes thick and ribbony.

3. Scrape down the sides of the bowl. With the mixer on low, first stream in the milk, then the maple syrup, then the melted butter. Turn the mixer up to high speed and continue to whip for an additional minute.

4. Combine the flour, salt, baking powder, and baking soda in a small bowl.

5. With the mixer on very low speed, slowly add the dry ingredients and mix for 45 to 60 seconds, just until your batter comes together. Scrape down the sides of the bowl, then mix on low for an additional 45 seconds to make sure no lumps of AP flour get left behind.

6. Pour the cake batter into the half-sheet pan and, using a spatula, spread the batter in an even layer in the pan. The cake batter will be much thinner than the consistency of the other cake batters in this chapter, and the batter will rise almost to the top of the pan.

7. Bake for 20 to 25 minutes. The cake will rise and puff, doubling in size, but will remain slightly buttery and dense. At 20 minutes, gently poke the edge of the cake with your finger. The cake should bounce back slightly and the center should no longer be jiggly. The cake should be evenly browned on top with no discernable yellow spots. If it doesn't pass these tests, leave the cake in the oven for an additional 2 to 5 minutes.

8. Let the cake cool in the pan on a wire rack or, in a pinch, in the fridge or freezer (don't worry, it's not cheating). The cooled cake can be stored in the fridge, wrapped in plastic wrap, for up to 5 days.

pancake soak

makes 130g (½ cup + 1 tablespoon)

110g	whole milk	½ cup
20g	maple syrup	1 T

Whisk together the milk and maple syrup in a small bowl. Use immediately.

Heads up! This cake makes batter that is spread over 1 half-sheet pan (as opposed to 1 quarter-sheet pan like all the other cakes). That's because this layer cake is wicked cool, and wildly different (in all the best ways!).

Check out page 74 for an angelic way to use the extra egg whites you'll have!

(recipe continues)

maple gel

makes about 245g (1 cup)

240g	maple syrup	1 cup
6g	pectin NH	1½ tsp

1. Heat the maple syrup in a small saucepan over low heat. As the syrup begins to heat up, sprinkle in the pectin a little at a time, stirring vigorously as you do it to prevent the pectin from clumping.

2. Once the pectin is fully incorporated, bring the maple syrup up to a boil. (Feel free to dial the heat up if you want to speed up the process.)

3. Remove the pan from the heat and transfer the contents to a blender. Blend on high for 1 minute, then strain the mixture through a fine-mesh sieve.

4. Let the gel cool slightly before using. It shouldn't be hot, but should be warm enough so that it spreads easily. If it has cooled too much by the time you are ready to use it, you can warm it in the microwave in 10-second increments until it is easily spreadable. Do not make ahead.

Read up on pectin NH (see page 16).

miso curd

makes about 420g (1¾ cups)

20g	shiro miso	1 T + 1 tsp
80g	unsalted butter, melted	6 T
60g	light brown sugar	¼ cup (packed)
40g	whole milk	2 T + 2 tsp
30g	shiro miso	2 T
2	large eggs	
2	large egg yolks	
1	silver gelatin sheet	

1. Heat the oven to 400°F. Line a baking sheet with a silicone baking mat.

2. Spread the 20g (1 tablespoon + 1 teaspoon) miso out ¼ inch thick on the lined baking sheet. This is a tiny amount of miso—no need to cover the entire sheet, just shoot for an even smear. Bake it until the miso is browned and quite burnt around the edges, 10 to 15 minutes. Don't be a ninny; really burn those edges! Remove it from the oven and let it cool slightly.

3. Bloom the gelatin (see page 27).

4. Whisk together the melted butter, baked miso, brown sugar, milk, the 30g (2 tablespoons) shiro miso, the whole eggs, and egg yolks in a medium bowl.

5. Pour this mixture into a medium saucepan and stir it regularly over low heat as it heats up. Keep a close eye on it as it begins to thicken. Once the mixture starts to bubble up and begin to boil, remove it from the heat and transfer it to a blender. Add the bloomed gelatin and blend until the mixture is thick, shiny, and super smooth.

This curd gives a savory, eggy profile to the pancake cake. We found too many sweet layers threw the final, perfect bite of the cake off, so we developed this edgy, savory layer as a spreadable filling.

You can substitute ½ teaspoon powdered gelatin for the sheet gelatin.

6. Pour the mixture through a fine-mesh sieve into a heatproof container and put it in the fridge until the miso curd has cooled completely, at least 30 minutes. The curd can be refrigerated for up to 1 week; do not freeze.

raspberry jam

makes about 110g (½ cup)

225g	**raspberries**	8 ounces
30g	**sugar**	2 T + 1 tsp
1.5g	**pectin NH**	¼ tsp + ⅛ tsp
10g	**lemon juice**	2 tsp

1. Wash the raspberries. Put them in a blender and puree until they are fully broken down. Strain them through a fine-mesh sieve and weigh out 85g (⅓ cup) of puree. If you have any left over, save it for a smoothie or something clever. If you don't have enough, blend and strain some more raspberries until you do.

2. Whisk together the sugar and pectin in a small pot or saucepan. Slowly whisk in the raspberry puree and lemon juice and bring it to a full, rolling boil over medium heat. Reduce the heat and cook at a low boil for 2 minutes to activate the pectin and turn the puree into a beautiful jam.

3. Once the jam coats the back of a spoon, remove the jam from the heat. The jam can be stored in an airtight container in the fridge for up to 2 weeks.

Read up on pectin NH (see page 16).

black pepper butter

makes about 110g (½ cup)

95g	**unsalted butter, softened**	7 T
10g	**sugar**	3 tsp
4g	**kosher salt**	1 tsp
3.5g	**black pepper, freshly ground**	1½ tsp

Do not go easy on the black pepper! It seems like a LOT of it, but the butter and sugar can hold it, I promise!

1. Combine the butter, sugar, salt, and pepper in the bowl of a stand mixer fitted with the paddle attachment and cream together on medium-high for 2 to 3 minutes, until fluffy. Scrape down the sides of the bowl, and cream for an additional minute.

2. The black pepper butter will keep in the refrigerator, in an airtight container, for up to 1 month. Let it soften to room temperature before using it.

mint cookies and cream layer cake

makes one 6-inch layer cake, 5 to 6 inches tall/serves 8 to 12

It's surprisingly difficult to innovate around the holidays because most people have an exact idea of what they think "holiday flavor" is: fruitcake, eggnog, mulled spices—all of the clichés. Now, I'm down for all of those flavors, but they've been done already. Like, a million times done. So how do you come up with a great seasonal cake that's not typical? I did some soul searching and recognized that one of the things I love most over the holidays (and anytime of year, really) is mint cookies and cream. Specifically, mint cookies and cream in the style of . . . OREO. So we set off to reverse-engineer the chocolate cookie tops and bottoms, and of course the creamy, white centers. And reverse-engineer it we did. We reverse-engineered the shizzle out of it until we had a mint cookies and cream cake on our hands. (Please note that the official name of this cake does not include the word "Oreo" for legal reasons.)

Basically what I'm saying is, when you make this frosting, you may think to yourself, *Hmm, this seems an awful lot like the middle of my favorite childhood sandwich cookie. I feel like a kid again! I'm finally ALIVE! Does anyone have a glass of milk I can dunk this frosting into?*

---

1 recipe	chocolate chip cake (opposite)	
65g	whole milk	¼ cup + 1 T
1 recipe	cookies and cream frosting (page 262)	
175g	chocolate crumbs (page 147)	1¼ cups
1 recipe	mint liquid cheesecake (page 205)	

special equipment:

1	6-inch cake ring
2	strips acetate, each 3 x 20 inches

....

cake assembly instructions

Put a piece of parchment paper or a silicone baking mat on the counter. Invert the cake onto it and peel off the parchment or mat from the bottom of the cake. Use the cake ring to stamp out 2 rounds from the cake. These are your top 2 cake layers. The remaining cake "scraps" will come together to make the bottom layer of the cake.

layer 1, the bottom

1. Clean the cake ring and place it in the center of a sheet pan lined with clean parchment or a silicone baking mat. Use 1 strip of acetate to line the inside of the cake ring.

2. Put the cake scraps together inside the ring and use the back of your hand to tamp the scraps together into a flat even layer.

3. Dunk a pastry brush in the milk (or use a spoon) and give the layer of cake a good, healthy bath of half of the milk.

4. Take one-third of the cookies and cream frosting and form it into a ball with your hands. Gently flatten it into a pancake-like shape and lay it down in the center of the cake. Press to the edges using your fingertips.

5. Sprinkle one-third of the chocolate crumbs evenly over the cookies and cream frosting. Use the back of your hand to press them lightly into the frosting, anchoring them in place.

6. Use the back of a spoon to spread half of the mint liquid cheesecake as evenly as possible over the crumbs.

layer 2, the middle

1. With your index finger, gently tuck the second strip of acetate between the cake ring and the top ¼ inch of the first strip of acetate, to make a ring of acetate 5 to 6 inches tall, high enough to support the height of the finished cake. Set a cake round on top of the cheesecake (if one of your cake rounds is jankier than the other, use it here in the middle and save the prettier one for the top).

2. Repeat the layering: milk, flattened cookies and cream frosting, chocolate crumbs, and mint cheesecake.

layer 3, the top

1. Nestle the remaining cake round into the mint cheesecake. Cover the top of the cake with the remaining cookies and cream frosting, and spread evenly. Garnish the frosting with the remaining chocolate crumbs.

2. Transfer the sheet pan to the freezer and freeze for a minimum of 12 hours to set the cake and filling. The cake will keep, well wrapped in plastic, in the freezer for up to 2 weeks.

3. At least 3 hours before you are ready to serve the cake, pull the sheet pan out of the freezer and, using your fingers and thumbs,

pop the cake out of the cake ring. Gently peel off the acetate, and transfer the cake to a platter or cake stand. Let it defrost in the fridge for a minimum of 3 hours. (Wrapped well in plastic, the cake can be refrigerated for up to 5 days.)

4. Slice the cake into wedges and serve.

chocolate chip cake

makes 1 quarter-sheet pan of cake

115g	unsalted butter, softened	1 stick (8 T)
250g	sugar	1¼ cups
60g	light brown sugar	¼ cup (packed)
3	large eggs	
110g	buttermilk	½ cup
75g	grapeseed or other neutral oil	½ cup
12g	vanilla extract	1 T
185g	cake flour	1½ cups
4g	baking powder	1 tsp
4g	kosher salt	1 tsp
150g	mini chocolate chips	¾ cup

1. Heat the oven to 350°F. Pan-spray a quarter-sheet pan and line it with parchment paper, or just line the pan with a silicone baking mat.

2. Combine the butter, sugar, and brown sugar in the bowl of a stand mixer fitted with the paddle attachment and cream together on medium-high for 2 to 3 minutes, until light and fluffy. Scrape down the sides of the bowl halfway through this process, and again at the end of it.

(recipe continues)

3. Add the eggs, one at a time, beating on medium-high for 1 minute after each addition. After you add the last egg, scrape down the sides of the bowl, then beat on high for 4 more minutes. Scrape down the sides of the bowl again.

4. Combine the buttermilk, oil, and vanilla extract and with the mixer on medium speed, stream them into the cake batter very slowly. It should take you approximately 3 minutes to add these liquids. Scrape down the sides of the bowl, increase the mixer speed to medium-high, and paddle for an additional 2 to 3 minutes, until the mixture is practically white, twice the size of your original fluffy butter-and-sugar mixture, and completely homogenous. Don't rush the process. You're basically forcing too much liquid into an already fatty mixture that doesn't want to make room for the liquid. There should be no streaks of fat or liquid. Stop the mixer and scrape down the sides of the bowl.

5. Whisk together the flour, baking powder, and salt in a medium bowl.

6. With the mixer on very low speed, slowly add the dry ingredients and mix for 45 to 60 seconds, just until your batter comes together. Scrape down the sides of the bowl, then mix on low for an additional 45 seconds to make sure no lumps of cake flour get left behind.

7. Pour the cake batter into the sheet pan and, using a spatula, spread the batter in an even layer in the pan. Sprinkle the chocolate chips evenly over the cake batter.

8. Bake for 30 to 35 minutes. The cake will rise and puff, doubling in size, but will remain slightly buttery and dense. At 30 minutes, gently poke the edge of the cake with your finger: The cake should bounce back slightly and the center should no longer be jiggly. If it doesn't pass these tests, leave the cake in the oven for an additional 3 to 5 minutes.

9. Let the cake cool in the pan on a wire rack or, in a pinch, in the fridge or freezer (don't worry, it's not cheating). The cooled cake can be stored in the fridge, wrapped in plastic wrap, for up to 5 days.

cookies and cream frosting

makes about 525g (2½ cups)

250g	confectioners' sugar	2 cups + 1 T
95g	vegetable shortening	½ cup
70g	light corn syrup	¼ cup
25g	cornstarch	2 T + 1 tsp
12g	clear vanilla extract	1 T
1g	kosher salt	¼ tsp
70g	chocolate crumbs (page 147)	½ cup

Clear vanilla extract gives this frosting a solid nod to the cream filling of an Oreo. Regular vanilla extract just won't do here. Read up on why clear vanilla extract is so special (see page 15).

1. Combine the confectioners' sugar, shortening, corn syrup, cornstarch, vanilla extract, and salt in the bowl of a stand mixer fitted with the paddle attachment and cream together on medium-low for 2 to 3 minutes, until well combined.

2. Use a spatula to fold in the chocolate crumbs and use immediately.

all about
ice cream cakes

makes one 6-inch layer cake, 5 to 6 inches tall/serves 8 to 12

You know what's better than regular cake? Regular cake with ice cream in it! And you know what's even better than that? Milk Bar layer cake with ice cream in it, and, if you've mastered the recipes here, it's easy as pie to make.

First, head to the store and buy a delicious pint of ice cream (or make your own). It can be any kind of frozen treat—ice cream, sorbet, heck, even sherbet. It can be smooth or full of swirls and mix-ins—just make sure you like the flavor. Then, pick a cake from our layer cake or truffle chapter that goes well with the ice cream. From there, mix and match a crumb and a filling or two and follow the assembly procedure below, substituting ice cream for frosting or filling #1!

Here are a few of my favorite flavor combos to get those creative juices flowing:

caramel corn ice cream cake: popcorn cake (page 182), caramel ice cream, popcorn crumbs (page 233), dulce de leche frosting (page 229)

black and white ice cream cake: chocolate cake (page 166), vanilla ice cream, chocolate crumbs (page 147), fudge sauce (page 110), chocolate frosting (paging Fudgy the Whale!) (page 245)

grasshopper ice cream cake: chocolate chip cake (page 261), mint chip ice cream, chocolate crumbs (page 147), mint liquid cheesecake (page 205), cookies and cream frosting (page 262)

simply the best ice cream cake: vanilla cake (page 190), strawberry ice cream, graham crumbs (page 219), sour cream frosting (page 117).

No need to use a soak in any of your ice cream cakes; the softened ice cream takes care of all the soaking you could ever hope for.

If the spreadable filling you choose is NOT a frosting, plan to make a small amount of frosting for the very top of the cake.

Work quickly when assembling this cake, lest you end up with a soggy cake and a puddle of melted ice cream on the floor.

1 recipe	**Milk Bar cake from the layer cake or truffle section**	
1 pint	**ice cream, sorbet or sherbet, softened (but not already melty)**	
155g	**[fill-in-the-blank crumbs]**	1¼ cups
360g	**your favorite filling (or frosting)**	1⅓ cups

180g	**your favorite frosting for the top**	⅔ cup

special equipment:

1	**6-inch cake ring**
2	**strips acetate, each 3 × 20 inches**

cake assembly instructions

Put a piece of parchment paper or a silicone baking mat on the counter. Invert the cake onto it and peel off the parchment or mat from the bottom of the cake. Use the cake ring to stamp out 2 rounds from the cake. These are your top 2 cake layers. The remaining cake "scraps" will come together to make the bottom layer.

layer 1, the bottom

1. Clean the cake ring and place it in the center of a sheet pan lined with clean parchment or a silicone baking mat. Use 1 strip of acetate to line the inside of the cake ring.

2. Put the cake scraps together inside the ring and use the back of your hand to tamp the scraps together into a flat even layer.

3. Use the back of a spoon to spread one-half of the softened ice cream in an even layer over the cake.

4. Sprinkle one-third of the crumbs evenly over the ice cream. Use the back of your hand to press them lightly into the ice cream, anchoring them in place.

5. Use the back of a spoon to spread one-third of the filling as evenly as possible over the crumbs.

layer 2, the middle

1. With your index finger, gently tuck the second strip of acetate between the cake ring and the top ¼ inch of the first strip of acetate, to make a ring of acetate 5 to 6 inches tall, high enough to support the height of the finished cake.

2. Set a cake round on top of the filling (if one of your cake rounds is jankier than the other, use it here in the middle and save the prettier one for the top). Repeat the layering: ice cream, crumbs, and filling.

layer 3, the top

1. Nestle the remaining cake round into the filling. Cover the top of the cake with the frosting. Give it volume and swirls, or do as we do and opt for a perfectly flat top. Garnish the frosting with the remaining crumbs.

2. Transfer the sheet pan to the freezer and freeze for a minimum of 12 hours to set the cake and filling. The cake will keep, well wrapped in plastic, in the freezer for up to 2 weeks.

3. When you are ready to serve the cake, pull the sheet pan out of the freezer and, using your fingers and thumbs, pop the cake out of the cake ring. Gently peel off the acetate and transfer the cake to a platter or cake stand. Let it sit at room temperature for 5 minutes to soften slightly.

4. With a warm cloth or towel and sharp knife, slice the cake into wedges, warming and wiping down the blade of the knife between each cut, and serve immediately.

all about large format and wedding cakes

Hey there! I'm assuming you are here because you love a challenge. But the joke's on you, because making giant tiered cakes isn't really that hard. Just follow the pro tips listed below and you'll be on a one-way train to Weddingcakesville in no time. YOU GOT THIS!

scaling a cake up (or down)

All of the cakes and fillings in this book are easily scalable; it's just a matter of simple math. If you need or want to make an 8-inch or 10-inch cake, double the layer cake recipe and bake the cakes in a half-sheet pan. Use an 8-inch or 10-inch cake circle to cut the cake rounds and assemble the cakes using the same procedure as you would a 6-inch layer cake. Be sure to scale those fillings up as well! I recommend doubling the filling recipes to be safe—any extras can be kept in the fridge or freezer for another use.

If you are making cakes larger than 10 inches, you will need to quadruple the recipe and bake the cake in a full sheet pan. You will also need a very large oven to hold that sheet pan. If you've made it this far in the book, I'm guessing you have access to an oven that size and the math skills to scale all of the recipes up appropriately. YAAAAAASSSSS!!!

If you need to scale a cake down, follow the recipes and procedures for the 6-inch layer cake, just use a smaller cake ring and know that you will have some leftover fillings and cake scraps.

And if you're making more than one larger size cake, it's probably because you want to stack one on top of the other. Maybe for a wedding? Or because someone in your life is just THAT awesome. Read on!

how to stack and serve a wedding cake (and serving sizes)

Wedding cakes can be all shapes and sizes, with as many tiers as you dare to stack. The general rule of thumb is to make each cake progressively smaller in diameter by 2 to 4 inches as you stack upward to the sky. To assemble a three-tier wedding cake, we usually start with a 14-inch cake for the base, followed by a 10-inch cake in the middle, and top it off with a 6-inch showstopper. If you use this as your guide, you can go anywhere from this point. You can make a four-tier wedding cake by stacking a 4-inch cake on top of the 6-inch. Or you can do a smaller two-tier cake with a 10-inch and a 6-inch. All you need to know are a few infrastructure secrets that you will apply to all cake stacking situations. Once you know these, you can stack all the way to the moon. THE MOON, I TELL YA!

My wedding cake, as demanded by my sweet, wonderful husband, was seven layers of Mint Cookies and Cream Layer Cake (page 260)—the tallest in Milk Bar history!!! And we had so much fun eating and dancing the night of, we actually ended up serving the cake for breakfast the next morning. Which is my way of telling you, YOU DO YOU!

You will need to decide how large you want your cake to be based on how many people you are feeding. Refer to the chart on page 274 for help. Once you know how big you want to go, bake, assemble, and freeze your individual cakes. When stacking cakes, they *must be fully frozen* and with the acetate strips still on until you have reached part 5 on page 273!! So give yourself plenty of time (and plenty of freezer space). The individual cakes will need to sit in the freezer for at least one full day after you assemble them and before you stack them.

You will need the following supplies, all of which you'll be able to find at your neighborhood hardware store and/or specialty cake shop.

all you need is:

- **1 small handsaw**
- **1 vise grip**
- **wooden dowels, 2 feet long and $5/16$ inch in diameter. You will need one dowel for each assembled cake (except the top layer).**
- **If you're planning a cake that is three-tiered or larger, you'll need *one more* wooden dowel 2 feet long and $5/16$ inch in diameter (which you will cut to the height of the entire cake). You will thread this through the center of the entire tiered cake. If you're planning a cake that will be taller than 2 feet high, get a longer dowel—you'll need this dowel to be as tall as the entire cake.**
- **1-foot ruler or measuring tape**
- **sandpaper**
- **cardboard cake rounds. You will need 1 round for each assembled cake tier, each one 2 inches smaller in diameter than the cake itself. For example, if you want to stack a tiered cake with a 14-inch, 10-inch, and 6-inch layer, you will need one each of a 12-inch, 8-inch, and 4-inch cardboard round.**
- **1 sturdy round tray or platter that is 2 inches larger than the bottom cake. This will be what holds the entire cake, so be sure to use something that will hold up to the weight of the cake. We use metal pizza trays. If you are unsure what to use, ask the lovely person at the cake shop.**
- **½ cup (at most) light corn syrup. This is used as a glue to help the cakes stick to their cardboard rounds.**

Remember, leave the acetate strips on all of the cakes until you have reached part 5!!

here's what to do
part 1: dowel the frozen cakes

This process involves measuring, cutting, and inserting wooden dowels into all of the cakes except for the top tier. By doing this, you create structure and support within each stacked cake so that each cake doesn't sink in or collapse under the pressure of all of the other cakes stacked on top.

1. Remove the largest cake from the freezer. This will be your bottom.

2. Take one wooden dowel, line it up against the cake and note where you should cut it so that it is just long enough to go through the cake, from the bottom to *just under* the top, by a millimeter or two. It is important that the cut dowel not peek up above the top of the cake or it will cause the cake that is stacked on top of it to be wobbly and crooked.

3. Once you have the length of the dowel figured out, use the vise grip and handsaw to cut it. Use the newly cut dowel as a length guide to cut two more dowels for that layer.

4. After cutting the dowels, use the sandpaper to sand down the rough ends of each one and use a damp paper towel to wipe away any leftover dust from the sanding process.

5. Use your fingers to press straight down onto the dowels to insert them into the cake, positioning them in a triangular formation. (The goal here is to insert them close enough to the center of the cake so that they are hidden by the cake that will be stacked on top of them, but not so close to the center that they can't support the cake; see at left). If you have a little trouble getting the dowel to go in, it may be because you hit a crumb or filling that blocked it; just try to

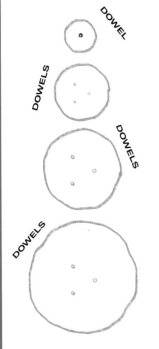

push through. If you have a bunch of trouble, remove the dowel and try, try, try again!

6. Once the dowels are inserted, use another dowel or the very tips of your fingers to push the inserted dowels all the way to the bottom of the cake, making sure their tops sit just below the surface of the cake. Return this cake to the freezer until you are ready to stack your tiers.

Repeat steps 2 through 6 with every cake except for the smallest, top tier cake.

part 2: prep the cardboard rounds

1. (Skip this step if you are making a two-tier cake; go directly to step 2). Use a ruler or measuring tape and an X-Acto blade or a sharp pair of scissors to cut a hole in the dead center of each cardboard round you are going to use. Make the holes large enough for the larger, center dowel to pass through it easily. After you center and stack the cakes on top of one another, you won't be able to see the holes when you insert the dowel, so give yourself a little room for error.

2. Set the cardboard rounds on a flat surface and smear the top of each one generously with corn syrup. Remove the cakes from the freezer and set each cake on top of its corresponding cardboard round. A 6-inch cake will sit on a 4-inch round, a 10-inch cake will sit on an 8-inch round, and so on. Once the cakes have been placed on the cardboard rounds, the cardboard rounds should no longer be visible.

part 3: stack those cakes!!

It is important to do these steps while the cakes are still frozen solid. It will make your life so much easier and the cakes will look cleaner and more professional. If the cakes have defrosted in the time it took you to put them on the cardboard in part 2, put them back in the freezer for 30 minutes, or until they have frozen firmly again.

1. Schmear some corn syrup in the center of the large base tray and place the bottom tier of the cake (already on a cardboard round) right on top of it. Double-check that all of the dowels are firmly and evenly in place.

2. Take the next largest cake and stack it on top of the base cake. Make sure it is centered (use a ruler to help guide you) and flat. You may need to pick it up and rotate it until you find the perfect fit. This is a little bit like playing Tetris. If the bottom cake slopes slightly downward on the left and the top cake slopes slightly upward on the right, you want to piece them together so that the sum of the parts equals a perfectly flat stacked cake. This is a game that's all about alternating angles to create balance.

Once you've stacked your first cake, step back and really look at it. Does it sit on top of the bottom cake and not sink in? Is it perfectly centered? If you cut holes in the cardboard rounds because you're making a three-tier or larger cake, will the center holes line up? Is it flat and even? Once it's passed all of these tests, move on to stacking the next tier. Repeat step 2 until you've stacked every cake *but the very top layer*. If you are only making a two-tiered cake, skip the next part and go straight to part 5.

part 4: thread the center dowel

If you are stacking a three-tier cake or more, you have to thread the center dowel through the entire cake. This keeps each tier aligned and provides the safety of additional structure and support. The goal is for the dowel to go from the very bottom of the base cake all the way through each cake and ending halfway through the top tier. Double-check that the cakes don't need to be adjusted or tilted before you run the final dowel through it. Once this step is finished, it will be quite difficult to move the cakes around.

1. Take the dowel reserved for the center and line it up against the entire cake. Eyeball where you want to cut it. Again, it should run through the entire cake *and* be tall enough to run halfway up through the top tier, which you haven't stacked yet.

2. Cut, sand, and wipe the edge of the dowel clean, then push the dowel straight through the whole cake, making sure it reaches the very bottom of the cake. Press down firmly to make sure the dowel has gone as far as it will go and that it is securely in place.

part 5: crown and decorate your tiered cake!

1. Place the final cake on top. If you are making a three-tier cake or higher, center the cake directly over the center dowel and grasp your hands around the side, on the acetate, pressing down gently to secure the cake on the dowel. Stand back and revel in the satisfaction of placing the smallest cake on the very top. You crushed it!!!!

2. Remove the acetate from all of the cake layers and use the corresponding decor crumbs used in each individual layer cake to decorate the top of each tier.

decorating tips

Decorating a wedding cake serves two purposes. It makes the wedding cake look beautiful, polished, and put together, but most important, it hides any imperfections or seams that may be lurking about. We always use

Pro tip: If your beautiful cakes baked off a little wonky and they just won't stack to make a perfectly flat tiered cake, you can use little bits of cardboard cake rounds to prop up the cakes under each separate layer to even the playing field.

the crumbs that correspond to the cake and fit them snugly in the seams where the two cakes are stacked on top of each other.

how to slice cakes of various sizes

Slicing cake correctly isn't always a piece of cake, which is why we're sharing these super cool cake-cutting grids as reference. In addition to the grids, here are a couple of helpful hints to make it even easier:

1. Always use a warm, clean knife. This means dipping the entire blade of the knife in a pitcher of hot water and using a towel to wipe and dry the blade between each cut. You will probably think you can get away with skipping this step and only wiping the knife after every other cut, but I assure you, this is a bad decision. If you want a professional-looking slice of cake, you MUST wipe the blade clean each time.

2. Cakes are much easier to slice if they are cold. Cutting a warm cake is a one-way ticket to catastrophe. If you have trouble making neat, clean slices and the cake is super crumbly or the frosting is running everywhere, put the cake in the freezer for 30 minutes, then recommence with the cutting. That said, when you slice cold cake, give it a few minutes to come to room temperature before serving. These are true cake-slicing secrets no one ever talks about!

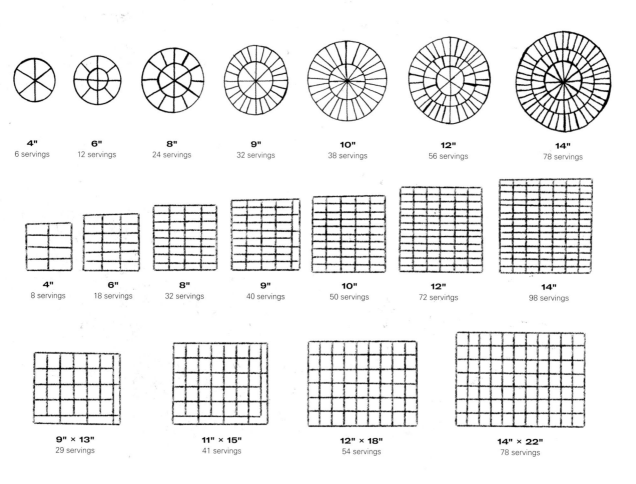

4"
6 servings

6"
12 servings

8"
24 servings

9"
32 servings

10"
38 servings

12"
56 servings

14"
78 servings

4"
8 servings

6"
18 servings

8"
32 servings

9"
40 servings

10"
50 servings

12"
72 servings

14"
98 servings

9" × 13"
29 servings

11" × 15"
41 servings

12" × 18"
54 servings

14" × 22"
78 servings

VEGANITY

Well, my friends, you've finally reached the end of Milk Bar's *All About Cake*. I can only assume that you are here because you've made every other recipe in the book and you're looking for something more, something different, something . . . VEGAN. If that's the case, we've got you covered. And why wouldn't we?

Butter, milk, cream, eggs—well, they're my friends most days, but sometimes they can be my enemies, too. My frenemies. A few years after we opened the doors of the first Milk Bar, it became clear that we would need to create some delicious vegan options, either because we needed a break or because you did. So we put on our vegan thinking caps (made of synthetic material, NOT leather) and got to work.

We HATE vegan recipes that TASTE like they're vegan. YUCK. If we wouldn't crave it on our least-vegan day, we aren't going to try and sell it to you, that's for sure. We developed a delicious line of vegan and gluten-free cookies—the LIFE cookies that we sell in all of our stores—and we developed a few extra bonus recipes in case we ever got a special request. Well, turns out, lots of people are vegan and we got a lot of special requests. Here, you'll find a vegan vanilla cake and a vegan chocolate cake that you can sub in for any of the chocolate or vanilla cake recipes in this book. Feel free to get creative. (That's the first time you've heard me say that, right?!) Punch up the vegan vanilla cake with some shredded coconut or lemon zest. Give the vegan chocolate cake some earthy vibes with ginger and molasses. If gluten-free baking really turns you on, by all means, go for it with these cakes! (See gluten-free flour notes, page 15.) We tested them as such, too.

There is also a recipe for lemon jam and chocolate ganache in this section. Both are vegan and both are delicious. Use them, along with all of the other accidental vegan recipes throughout the book, to make your very own vegan creations. Use the other recipes in this book as a guide for ratios of fillings to use.

surprise! there are tons of incidental / accidental vegan recipes throughout the book:

I don't know if you noticed, but the birthday crumbs are on this list. This is the best accidental vegan recipe ever. You can make these crumbs without the rainbow sprinkles and use them in any cake for added crunch, or ground down as a truffle coating. Add orange extract or peppermint extract (or any extract) for cool flavor combos.

bitter tea soak
(page 120)

bourbon mint soak
(page 48)

vanilla-orange soak
(page 208)

raspberry jam
(page 259)

pickled strawberry jam
(page 222)

rhubarb-elderflower jam
(page 60)

tangerine confit
(page 195)

jammy blueberry sauce
(page 116)

apple compote
(page 175)

poached pineapple
(page 239)

pickled celery
(page 71)

maple gel
(page 258)

strawberry jam
(page 143)

bourbon-lemon glaze
(page 48)

grapefruit glaze
(page 38)

lemon-honey glaze
(page 35)

toasted pepitas
(page 253)

sesame seed brittle
(page 57)

birthday crumbs
(page 106)

birthday sand
(page 163)

here are some ideas for fun combinations to get the ball rolling:

coconut-tangerine dark chocolate cake truffle: vegan vanilla cake (page 278), tangerine confit (page 195), dark chocolate coating (make white chocolate coating on page 163 but with dark chocolate instead), toasted coconut

chocolate on chocolate cake: vegan chocolate cake (page 279), vegan chocolate ganache (page 280), birthday crumbs (use chocolate sprinkles instead of rainbow) (page 106)

vegan arnold palmer sheet cake: vegan vanilla cake (page 278) (x2), bitter tea soak (page 120), vegan lemon jam (page 281), birthday crumbs (add tea leaves instead of sprinkles) (page 106)

vegan vanilla cake

makes 1 quarter-sheet pan of cake

As a not-so-vegan eater, I always assume that I won't like vegan baked goods as much as the baked goods full of butter and eggs and cream. Every time I make this cake, I think to myself that there's just no way it is going to bake into delicious results. *Every time* I think this, and I've made this cake A LOT of times. And every time, it comes out of the oven, I put that first bite in my chompers and I'm shocked at how good it is. It 100 percent stacks up against any cake in this book. It walks the walk and talks the talk, delicious bite for delicious bite.

460g	plain unsweetened nondairy milk	2 cups
140g	grapeseed or other neutral oil	⅔ cup + 1 T
50g	vanilla extract	¼ cup
12g	distilled white vinegar	2 tsp
360g	ap flour	2½ cups
320g	sugar	1½ cups + 2 T
105g	light brown sugar	⅓ cup + 2 T (packed)
8 g	kosher salt	2 tsp
4g	baking powder	1 tsp

1. Heat the oven to 350°F. Pan-spray a quarter-sheet pan and line it with parchment paper, or just line the pan with a silicone baking mat.

2. Whisk the nondairy milk, oil, vanilla extract, and vinegar together in a large bowl.

3. Whisk the flour, sugar, brown sugar, salt, and baking powder together in a separate large bowl.

4. Pour the wet ingredients into the dry ones and stir to combine. If the batter looks lumpy, use a whisk to break up all the lumps.

5. Pour the cake batter into the sheet pan and, using a spatula, spread the batter in an even layer in the pan.

6. Bake for 30 to 35 minutes, rotating the pan front to back halfway through baking. The cake will rise and puff, doubling in size, but will remain rich and rather dense. At 30 minutes, gently poke the edge of the cake with your finger: The cake should bounce back slightly and the center should no longer be jiggly. If it doesn't pass these tests, leave the cake in the oven for an additional 3 to 5 minutes.

7. Let the cake cool in the pan on a wire rack or, in a pinch, in the fridge or freezer (don't worry, it's not cheating). The cooled cake can be stored in the fridge, wrapped in plastic wrap, for up to 5 days.

Not only is this cake vegan, but it can also be gluten-free! If you choose to go the gluten-free flour route, add an additional 2g (½ teaspoon) salt to the dry ingredients.

This cake makes delicious cupcakes too! Just pour the batter into a cupcake pan according to the instructions for the White Album Cupcakes (page 127). Be aware that they will be more dense, but they will still be just as moist and tasty. The yield is also higher; you'll get about 20 cupcakes out of this batch.

vegan chocolate cake

makes 1 quarter-sheet pan of cake

Did you read what I wrote in the vegan vanilla cake intro? Ditto for this one!

460g	plain unsweetened nondairy milk	2 cups
140g	grapeseed or other neutral oil	⅔ cup + 1 T
12g	vanilla extract	1 T
12g	distilled white vinegar	2 tsp
420g	sugar	2 cups + 2 T
300g	ap flour	2¼ cups
60g	cocoa powder	½ cup
12g	kosher salt	1 T
4g	baking powder	1 tsp

1. Heat the oven to 350°F. Pan-spray a quarter-sheet pan and line it with parchment paper, or just line the pan with a silicone baking mat.

2. Whisk the nondairy milk, oil, vanilla extract, and vinegar together in a large bowl.

3. Whisk the sugar, flour, cocoa powder, salt, and baking powder together in a separate large bowl.

4. Pour the wet ingredients into the dry ones and stir to combine. If the batter looks lumpy, use a whisk to break up all the lumps.

5. Pour the cake batter into the sheet pan and, using a spatula, spread the batter in an even layer in the pan.

6. Bake for 30 to 35 minutes, rotating the pan front to back halfway through baking. The cake will rise and puff, doubling in size, but will remain rich and rather dense. At 30 minutes, gently poke the edge of the cake with your finger: The cake should bounce back slightly and the center should no longer be jiggly. If it doesn't pass these tests, leave the cake in the oven for an additional 3 to 5 minutes.

7. Let the cake cool in the pan on a wire rack or, in a pinch, in the fridge or freezer (don't worry, it's not cheating). The cooled cake can be stored in the fridge, wrapped in plastic wrap, for up to 5 days.

Watch the oven diligently when baking this cake. It's already brown, so it's tricky to gauge visually when it's overbaked. (If you overbake it, it becomes crumbly and far less tasty.)

vegan chocolate ganache

makes about 350g (1½ cups)

Our vegan chocolate ganache tastes like pure, liquid chocolate, which isn't a surprise because that's basically what it is. This version is the perfect consistency for a dense, gooey filling in a layer or sheet cake. It's also great whipped as a frosting or as a replacement for Fudge Sauce (page 110) in any recipe. If you want to make it thinner or thicker, you can do so by taking away or adding water, 5g (1 teaspoon) at a time, until you get to a consistency that you love.

40g	cocoa powder	⅓ cup + 2 T
100g	dark chocolate chips	½ cup
120g	sugar	½ cup + 2 T
95g	water	⅓ cup + 1 T + 2 tsp

1. Put the cocoa powder and chocolate chips in a large heatproof bowl.

2. Combine the sugar and water in a medium saucepan and bring to a boil. Carefully pour the boiling syrup over the cocoa powder and chocolate. Wait 1 minute, then whisk the mixture, starting slowly in the center of the bowl and getting faster, with broader strokes, until you have a thick, glossy chocolate ganache on your hands.

3. The ganache can be refrigerated for up to 1 week; do not freeze.

vegan lemon jam

makes about 560g (2½ cups)

The addition of coconut and soy milk rounds out the tartness of this jam perfectly. It sets a tad looser than a lemon curd, but can be used in any application where you would use a lemon curd. It goes great as a filling mixed with the vegan vanilla cake for lemon cake truffles or as a spreadable layer on a cake.

8	lemons	
100g	coconut milk	½ cup
50g	plain unsweetened soy milk	¼ cup
3g	lemon extract	¾ tsp
200g	sugar	1 cup
20g	cornstarch	2 T
3g	kosher salt	¾ tsp

1. Using a Microplane or the finest-toothed side of a box grater, zest the lemons. Do your best to grate only as far down as the yellow part of the skin; the white pith has less lemon flavor and can be bitter. You should have about 35g (¼ cup) lemon zest. Set the zest aide and squeeze 155g (¾ cup) juice from the lemons.

2. Stir the lemon juice, coconut milk, soy milk, and lemon extract together in a medium, heavy-bottomed saucepan.

3. Whisk together the lemon zest, sugar, cornstarch, and salt in a medium bowl. Slowly stream the dry mixture into the lemon juice, whisking constantly.

4. Set the lemon mixture over low heat and whisk regularly as it heats up. Keep a close eye on it as it begins to thicken. When it starts to bubble up and come to a boil, continue to cook it, stirring constantly for an additional 20 seconds. Remove it from the heat and let the jam cool to room temperature. Store in the fridge in an airtight container until it has chilled and set completely, at least 30 minutes. The jam can be refrigerated for up to 1 week; do not freeze.

acknowledgments

To Courtney McBroom: My sister from another mister. My counterpart in all things cookbook. My bicycle riding OG HARDBODY. Thank you for putting up with all the terrible and wonderful things I bring to our friendship. You are brilliant. An outstanding human being. And an incredible Texan.

To those who *got in there* as we mixed, baked, shot, tested, and tasted *All About Cake*: Peter Meehan, Gabriele Stabile, Mark Ibold, Walter Green, Jonathan Santiago, Hannah Clark, Bradley Goodman, East Village Community School, New York City Hall and its beautiful brides and grooms, Café Altro Paradiso and team, Annie Leonard, Hilary Fann, Tess Mahoney, Lydia Yeakel, Tarran Hatton, Sarah Wimberly, Sarah Heasley, Katya Ekimoto, Marisa Iapicco, Stephany Cruz. Thank you for pushing through the many tummy aches too much cake surely brings. For your insane dedication, for embracing TMI, for crushing and for loving cake as much as I do.

To my Milk Bar family: You put up with and embrace my obsession with cake. You make it your own, and oftentimes make it better. You bring the thunder every day and continue to inspire, create, and change the world of dessert. Thank you for your ride-or-die mentality. I am one proud cake mom.

To Kim Witherspoon: For always ensuring my crazy ideas come to life through the pages of words and photos we dream up.

To the honorary hardbodies at Clarkson Potter: Francis Lam, for believing in 200+ pages of cake and putting up with our bad jokes, and to Rica Allannic for picking up this project from the start—and running with the first two cookbook dreams I brought to her doorstep. (I'm pretty sure the rest of the world already knows this, but still.) To copyeditor Kate Slate, for every gram, ounce, and scant pinch. You put my attention to detail to shame, you saint! To Jen Wang, for helping wrangle the design. Marysarah Quinn, for her courage in working alongside us once more and bringing her angelic attitude to the madness of making a book!

To our most generous and awesome bakeware friends: Adele Schober and Breville and Gretchen Holt and OXO. We would be lost without your killer mixers, bowls, baking pans, and beyond. You both win Best Supporting Role in a Cookbook/Documentary. Thank you for your kindness, friendship, and bigheartedness.

To my family: Why is it that writing ANOTHER cookbook amid building and growing an insane business while trying to remain a stand-up daughter, niece, sister, aunt, and wife seems like a good idea? Your guess is probably as good, if not better, than mine. Thank you for always doing your best to understand, but never question the "why" in what I do. Thank you for teaching me to love, and to pursue love. And for eating all the cake scraps that I leave a trail of so loyally.

To cake: The boring old stuff, and the exciting new wave of it happening in our kitchen, and hopefully at this point in yours. Never say never, my friend. As long as you have a whisk and some sugar, something great is just a few (cup)cakes away.

index

Note: Page references in *italics* indicate photographs.

Acetate, 19
Almond butter, in Jimbo Soak, 199
Angel Food Cake, Mommala's (from Heaven), 74–75
Apple Cider:
    Caramel, 94
    Donut Crock-Pot Pudding, *92, 93*–94
Apple(s):
    Burnt Miso Pound Cake, *66, 67*–68
    Compote, 175
    Green, Matchsticks, 80
    -Oatmeal–Brown Sugar Microwave Mug Cake, *78, 79*–80
    Pie Cake Truffles, *172, 173*–76
Arnold Palmer Sheet Cake, 118–21, *121*

Baking pans/vehicles, 19–20
Baller Birthday Sheet Cake, *102, 103*–6
Banana extract, 15
Banana(s):
    -Chocolate-Hazelnut Cupcakes, *152, 153*–55
    -Chocolate–Peanut Butter Crock-Pot Cake, 90–91, *91*
    Cupcakes, 153–54
    Green Curry Pound Cake, 69
    ripening, 13–14
B'day Truffles, *160, 161*–63
Birthday Crumbs, 106
Birthday Frosting, 106
Birthday Sand, 163
Birthday Sheet Cakes, 104–5, 162–63
Black Pepper Butter, 259
Black Sesame Crock-Pot Cake, 88–89, *89*
Blueberry:
    and Corn Sheet Cake, *112, 113*–17

Sauce, Jammy, 116
Bourbon:
    -Lemon Glaze, 48
    Mint Julep Bundt Cake, 47–48, *49*
    Mint Soak, 48
Brittle, Sesame Seed, 57
Brown Sugar Glaze, 80
Bundt Cakes:
    Cherry Cola, *40, 41*–42
    Lemon Poppy Seed, 34–35
    Mint Julep, 47–48, *49*
    Molasses-Rye, *50, 51*–52
    Pistachio, *44, 45*–46
    Raspberry, *36, 37*–38
Bundt pans, 19
Butter:
    Barely-Brown, Cake, 174–75
    Black Pepper, 259
    brown, making, 174
    for recipes, 14
Buttercream, Graham, 220
Butter extract, 15

Cake flour, 15
Cake rings, 20
Cakes. *See also specific types of cakes*
    freshness and storage, 28
    interchangeability of batters, 27–28
Cake Truffles:
    Apple Pie, *172, 173*–76
    B'day, *160, 161*–63
    Chocolate Chip–Passion Fruit, 170–71
    Chocolate Malt, *164, 165*–67
    Coconut-Tangerine, *192, 193*–95
    Croquembouches, 210, *211*
    Dulce de Leche, 184–86
    formula for, 159
    German Chocolate Jimbo, 198–99
    Liam's #toughcookie, *206, 207*–8
    Mint Cookies and Cream, 204–5, *205*

Pineapple Upside-Down, 196–97
Popcorn, *180, 181*–83
Pretzel, 200–202
Strawberry-Lemon, *188, 189*–91
Caramel:
    Apple Cider, 94
    Corn, 235
    Salted, Filling, 234
Celery, Pickled, 71, *72*
Celery Root Pound Cake, 70–71, *72–73*
Cheese. *See* Cream cheese
Cheesecake:
    Brown Butter Graham, 251–52
    Lemon, 224
    Liquid, 224–25
    Mint Liquid, 205
Cherry Cola Bundt Cake, *40, 41*–42
Cherry Cola Glaze, 42
Chocolate. *See also* White Chocolate
    -Banana-Hazelnut Cupcakes, *152, 153*–55
    -Banana–Peanut Butter Crock-Pot Cake, 90–91, *91*
    Cake, Vegan, 279
    Chip Cake, 261–62
    Chip Mint Molten Microwave Mug Cake, 82, *83*
    Chip–Passion Fruit Cake Truffles, 170–71
    chips, mini, buying, 14
    Compost Pound Cake, 61–62, *63*
    Cookies and Cream Frosting, 262
    Crumbs, 147
    Cupcake, No One Hates on a, *144*, 145–47
    Cupcake Frosting, 147
    Cupcakes, 145–46
    Frosting, 245
    Fudge Sauce, 110
    Ganache, Vegan, 280
    German, Cupcakes, *148*, 149–50

German, Jimbo Cake Truffles, 198–99
German, Jimbo Layer Cake, *242*, 243–45
Hazelnut Frosting, 155
Malt Cake Truffles, *164, 165*–67
Milk Soak, 111
Mint Cookies and Cream Cake Truffles, 204–5, *205*
Mint Cookies and Cream Layer Cake, 260–62, *263*
Molten, Microwave Mug Cake, *84*, 85
for recipes, 14
Sand, 205
Sheet Cakes, 108–10, 166–67
Stout Ganache, 247–48
-Yellow Sheet Cake, Inside-Out, 107–11, *109*
Citric or ascorbic acid, 14
Citrus Milk Crumbs, 120–21
Clear vanilla extract, 15
Coating, White Chocolate, 163
Coconut:
    Cake, 194–95
    -Crack Filling, 244–45
    Crack Pie Frosting, 149–50
    Cupcakes, 141–42
    German Chocolate Jimbo Cake Truffles, 198–99
    German Chocolate Jimbo Layer Cake, *242*, 243–45
    Pineapple Upside-Down Cake Truffles, 196–97
    Pineapple Upside-Down Layer Cake, *236*, 237–40, *241*
    -Strawberry Cupcakes, *140*, 141–43
    -Tangerine Cake Truffles, *192, 193*–95
Cola extract, 15
Compost Pound Cake, 61–62, *63*
Confit, Tangerine, 195
Cookies and Cream Frosting, 262
Cookies and Cream Mint Layer Cake, 260–62, *263*

Corn flour, 15
Corn powder:
  about, 14
  Corn and Blueberry Sheet
    Cake, *112,* 113–17
  Corn Crumbs, 117
  Corn Fudge, 234–35
  Corn Sheet Cake, 115
  making your own, 14
  Popcorn Crumbs, 233
  Popcorn Pudding, 233
  Popcorn Sand, 183
Crack Pie Frosting, 149–50
Cream cheese:
  Creamsicle Swirl, 87
  Liquid Cheesecake, 224–25
  Peanut Butter Goo, 91
Creamsicle Crock-Pot Cake,
  86–87
Creamsicle Swirl, 87
Crock-Pot Cakes:
  Banana-Chocolate–Peanut
    Butter, 90–91, *91*
  Black Sesame, 88–89, *89*
  Creamsicle, 86–87
Crock-Pot Pudding, Apple
  Cider Donut, *92,* 93–94
Crock-pots, 19
Croquembouches, Cake Truffle,
  210, *211*
Crumbs:
  Birthday, 106
  Chocolate, 147
  Citrus Milk, 120–21
  Corn, 117
  interchangeability of, 27–28
  Milk, 129
  Pie Dough, 252
  Popcorn, 233
  Pretzel, 248
  Yellow Cake, 111
Crunch, Pecan, 150
Cupcake pans, 19
Cupcakes:
  Banana, 153–54
  Chocolate, 145–46
  Coconut, 141–42
  Graham Cracker, 137–38
  Lemon, 131–32
  Vanilla, 127–28
Cupcakes (decorated):
  Banana-Chocolate-Hazelnut,
    152, 153–55
  Chocolate, No One Hates on
    a, *144,* 145–47

German Chocolate, *148,*
  149–50
Key Lime Pie, *136,* 137–39
Lemon Meringue, *130,*
  131–33
Strawberry-Coconut, *140,*
  141–43
White Album, *126,* 127–29
Curd:
  Key Lime, 220
  Lemon, 133
  Miso, 258–59

Donut, Apple Cider, Crock-Pot
  Pudding, *92,* 93–94
Dulce de Leche:
  about, 14–15
  Cake, 185–86
  Cake Truffles, 184–86
  Frosting, 229
  Layer Cake, *226,* 227–29
  making your own, 14–15
  Soak, 186

Elderflower:
  -Rhubarb Goo, 60
  -Rhubarb Jam, 60
  -Rhubarb Pound Cake, *58,*
    59–60
Equipment, 19–25
Extracts, 15

Fillings. *See also* Curd;
  Ganache; Jam
  Coconut-Crack, 244–45
  interchangeability of, 27–28
  Salted Caramel, 234
Flour, sifting, note about, 28
Flours, 15
Food coloring, 15
Frostings. *See also* Ganache
  Birthday, 106
  Chocolate, 245
  Chocolate Cupcake, 147
  Chocolate Hazelnut, 155
  Cookies and Cream, 262
  Crack Pie, 149–50
  Dulce de Leche, 229
  Graham Buttercream, 220
  Honey, 248
  interchangeability of, 27–28
  Lemon, 121

Pickled Strawberry, 225
Pineapple Upside-Down, 240
Sour Cream, 117
Strawberry, 143
Yellow Cake, 111
Fruit purees. *See* Purees
Fudge, Corn, 234–35
Fudge Sauce, 110

Ganache:
  Chocolate, Vegan, 280
  Pumpkin, 253
  Stout, 247–48
Gel, Maple, 258
Gelatin:
  blooming, 27
  sheet and powdered, 16
German Chocolate Cupcakes,
  148, 149–50
German Chocolate Jimbo
  Cake Truffles, 198–99
German Chocolate Jimbo
  Layer Cake, *242,* 243–45
Glazes:
  Bourbon-Lemon, 48
  Brown Sugar, 80
  Burnt Honey, 65
  Cherry Cola, 42
  Grapefruit, 38
  Lemon-Honey, 35
  Molasses-Stout, 52
  Peanut Butter Goo, 91
  Pistachio, 46
  Rhubarb-Elderflower Goo, 60
Gloves, latex, 20
Gluten-free flour, 15
Graham cracker crumbs. *See
  also* Graham Crumbs
  Brown Butter Graham Crust,
    252
  Compost Pound Cake, 61–62,
    63
  Graham Cracker Cake,
    218–19
  Graham Cracker Cupcakes,
    137–38
Graham Crumbs:
  Graham Buttercream, 220
  Key Lime Pie Layer Cake,
    216, 217–20
  recipe for, 219
Grapefruit Glaze, 38
Green Curry Banana Pound
  Cake, 69

Hazelnut:
  -Banana-Chocolate
    Cupcakes, *152,* 153–55
  Chocolate Frosting, 155
Heatproof rubber spatulas, 24
Honey:
  Burnt, Glaze, 65
  Frosting, 248
  -Lemon Glaze, 35

Ice cream cakes:
  assembling, 266–67
  favorite flavor combos, 266

Jam:
  Lemon, Vegan, 281
  Pickled Strawberry, 222–24
  Raspberry, 259
  Rhubarb-Elderflower, 60
  Strawberry, 143
Jimbo Cake Truffles, German
  Chocolate, 198–99
Jimbo Layer Cake, German
  Chocolate, *242,* 243–45
Jimbo Soak, 199

Key Lime:
  Curd, 220
  Graham Cracker Cake,
    218–19
  Pie Cupcakes, *136,* 137–39
  Pie Layer Cake, *216,* 217–20
  Whipped Cream, 139

Large format cakes, 268–74
Layer Cakes:
  Dulce de Leche, *226,* 227–29
  formula for, 214
  German Chocolate Jimbo,
    242, 243–45
  Key Lime Pie, *216,* 217–20
  Mint Cookies and Cream,
    260–62, *263*
  Pancake, *254,* 255–59
  Pineapple Upside-Down,
    236, 237–40, *241*
  Popcorn, *230,* 231–35
  Pretzel, 246–48
  Pumpkin Pie, 249–53
  Strawberry-Lemon, 221–25,
    223

Lemon:
  -Bourbon Glaze, 48
  Cheesecake, 224
  Cupcakes, 131–32
  Curd, 133
  Frosting, 121
  -Honey Glaze, 35
  Jam, Vegan, 281
  Meringue, 132–33
  Meringue Cupcakes, *130,*
    131–33
  Poppy Seed Bundt Cake,
    34–35
  -Strawberry Cake Truffles,
    188, 189–91
  -Strawberry Layer Cake,
    221–25, *223*
  -Tea Sheet Cake, 119–20
Lemon extract, 15
Lime, key. *See* Key Lime
Lipton tea and tea powder:
  about, 16
  Bitter Tea Soak, 120
  Lemon-Tea Sheet Cake,
    119–20
Loaf or pound cake pans, 20

Malt Cake Soak, 244
Malted milk powder. *See*
  Ovaltine
Malted Milk Sand, 167
Malted Milk Soak, 167
Maple syrup:
  Maple Gel, 258
  Pancake Soak, 257
Maraschino Cherry Soak, 239
Measuring cups and spoons,
  23
Meringue:
  Lemon, 132–33
  Lemon, Cupcakes, *130,*
    131–33
  note about, 133
Microwave Mug Cakes:
  Mint Chocolate Chip Molten,
    82, *83*
  Molten Chocolate, *84,* 85
  mugs for, 20
  Oatmeal-Apple–Brown
    Sugar, *78,* 79–80
Microwave ovens, 23
Milk Crumbs, 129
Milk powder, about, 16
Milk Sand, 183

Mint:
  Bourbon Soak, 48
  Chocolate Chip Molten
    Microwave Mug Cake,
    82, *83*
  Cookies and Cream Cake
    Truffles, 204–5, *205*
  Cookies and Cream Layer
    Cake, 260–62, *263*
  Julep Bundt Cake, 47–48, *49*
  Liquid Cheesecake, 205
Miso:
  Burnt, Pound Cake, *66,* 67–68
  Curd, 258–59
  Pancake Layer Cake, *254,*
    255–59
Mixers, 23
Molasses:
  -Rye Bundt Cake, *50,* 51–52
  -Stout Glaze, 52
Mugs, for microwave cake
  recipes, 20

Nonfat milk powder, about, 16
Nuts. *See* Hazelnut; Pecan;
  Pistachio

Oatmeal-Apple–Brown Sugar
  Microwave Mug Cake, *78,*
  79–80
Offset spatulas, 23
Oils, 16
Orange:
  Creamsicle Crock-Pot Cake,
    86–87
  Liam's #toughcookie Cake
    Truffles, *206,* 207–8
  -Vanilla Sand, 208
  -Vanilla Soak, 208
Ovaltine:
  Malt Cake Soak, 244
  Malted Milk Sand, 167
  Malted Milk Soak, 167
  Pretzel Crumbs, 248
Ovens, 23
Oven thermometers, 23

Pancake Cake, 257
Pancake Layer Cake, *254,*
  255–59
Pancake Soak, 257
Pan spray, 24

Parchment paper, 24
Passion Fruit–Chocolate Chip
  Cake Truffles, 170–71
Peanut Butter:
  –Banana-Chocolate Crock-
    Pot Cake, 90–91, *91*
  Goo, 91
Pecan(s):
  Crunch, 150
  German Chocolate Jimbo
    Layer Cake, *242,* 243–45
Pectin NH, 16–17
Pepitas, Toasted, 253
Peppermint extract, 15
Pickled Celery, 71, *72*
Pickled Strawberry Frosting,
  225
Pickled Strawberry Jam,
  222–24
Pie Dough Crumbs, 252
Pie Dough Sand, 176
Pineapple:
  Poached, 239
  Upside-Down Cake Truffles,
    196–97
  Upside-Down Frosting, 240
  Upside-Down Layer Cake,
    236, 237–40, *241*
Pistachio:
  Bundt Cake, *44,* 45–46
  Glaze, 46
Popcorn:
  Cake, 182–83
  Cake Truffles, *180,* 181–83
  Caramel Corn, 235
  Crumbs, 233
  Layer Cake, *230,* 231–35
  Milk, 183
  Pudding, 233
  Sand, 183
Poppy Seed Lemon Bundt
  Cake, 34–35
Pound cake pans, 20
Pound Cakes:
  Banana Green Curry, 69
  Burnt Miso, *66,* 67–68
  Celery Root, 70–71, *72–73*
  Compost, 61–62, *63*
  Pretzel, 64–65
  Rhubarb-Elderflower, *58,*
    59–60
  Sesame, 56–57
Pretzel(s):
  Cake, 201–2
  Cake Truffles, 200–202

Compost Pound Cake, 61–62,
  63
Crumbs, 248
Layer Cake, 246–48
Pound Cake, 64–65
Sand, 202
Pudding:
  Apple Cider Donut Crock-Pot,
    92, 93–94
  Popcorn, 233
Pumpkin:
  Cake, 250–51
  Ganache, 253
  Pie Layer Cake, 249–53
Purees:
  about, 17
  Raspberry, 38

Rainbow sprinkles:
  Birthday Cake, 162–63
  Birthday Crumbs, 106
  Birthday Sheet Cake, 104–5
Raspberry(ies):
  Bundt Cake, *36,* 37–38
  Jam, 259
  Pancake Layer Cake, *254,*
    255–59
  Puree, 38
Rhubarb:
  -Elderflower Goo, 60
  -Elderflower Jam, 60
  -Elderflower Pound Cake, *58,*
    59–60
  Rye-Molasses Bundt Cake, *50,*
    51–52

Salt, for recipes, 17
Salted Caramel Filling, 234
Sand:
  Birthday, 163
  Chocolate, 205
  Malted Milk, 167
  Milk, 183
  Pie Dough, 176
  Popcorn, 183
  Pretzel, 202
  Strawberry, 191
  Vanilla-Orange, 208
Sauces. *See also* Ganache
  Fudge, 110
  Jammy Blueberry, 116
Scales, 24
Sesame Pound Cake, 56–57

Sesame Seed Brittle, 57
Sheet Cakes:
    Barely-Brown Butter, 174–75
    Birthday, 104–5, 162–63
    Chocolate, 108–10, 166–67
    Chocolate, Vegan, 279
    Chocolate Chip, 261–62
    Coconut, 194–95
    Corn, 115
    Dulce de Leche, 185–86
    Graham Cracker, 218–19
    Lemon-Tea, 119–20
    Pancake, 257
    Popcorn, 182–83
    Pretzel, 201–2
    Pumpkin, 250–51
    Vanilla, 190
    Vanilla, Vegan, 278
Sheet Cakes (decorated):
    Arnold Palmer, 118–21, 121
    Baller Birthday, 102, 103–6
    Corn and Blueberry, 112,
        113–17
    formula for, 98
    Inside-Out Chocolate-Yellow,
        107–11, 109
Sheet pans, 20
Silicone baking mat/silpat, 24
Soaks:
    Bitter Tea, 120
    Bourbon Mint, 48

Chocolate Milk, 111
Dulce de Leche, 186
interchangeability of,
    27–28
Jimbo, 199
Malt Cake, 244
Malted Milk, 167
Maraschino Cherry, 239
Pancake, 257
Vanilla Milk, 105
Vanilla-Orange, 208
Sour Cream:
    Frosting, 117
    Sour Whipped Cream, 68
Spatulas, heatproof, 24
Spatulas, offset, 23
Spoons, 25
Stand mixers, 23
Stout:
    Ganache, 247–48
    -Molasses Glaze, 52
    Pretzel Layer Cake, 246–48
Strawberry:
    -Coconut Cupcakes, 140,
        141–43
    Frosting, 143
    Jam, 143
    -Lemon Cake Truffles, 188,
        189–91
    -Lemon Layer Cake, 221–25,
        223

Pickled, Frosting, 225
Pickled, Jam, 222–24
Sand, 191
Whipped Cream, 71
Swirl, Creamsicle, 87

Tangerine:
    -Coconut Cake Truffles, 192,
        193–95
    Confit, 195
Tasting, and adjusting, 28
Techniques, 27–28
Timer, 25

Vanilla:
    Cake, 190
    Cake, Vegan, 278
    Cupcakes, 127–28
    extract, for recipes, 15
    Milk Soak, 105
    -Orange Sand, 208
    -Orange Soak, 208
Vegan recipes:
    additional, list of, 277
    fun cake flavor combos,
        277
    Vegan Chocolate Cake, 279
    Vegan Chocolate Ganache,
        280

Vegan Lemon Jam, 281
Vegan Vanilla Cake, 278

Wedding cakes, 268–74
Whipped Cream:
    Key Lime, 139
    Sour, 68
    Strawberry, 71
White Album Cupcakes, 126,
    127–29
White Chocolate:
    about, 14
    Coating, 163
    Corn Fudge, 234–35
    Pretzel Crumbs, 248
    Pumpkin Ganache, 253

Yellow cake mix:
    Chocolate Chip–Passion Fruit
        Cake Truffles, 170–71
    choosing, 17
    Pineapple Upside-Down
        Cake Truffles, 196–97
    Pineapple Upside-Down
        Frosting, 240
    Yellow Cake Crumbs, 111
    Yellow Cake Frosting, 111

CHRISTINA TOSI is the two-time James Beard Award–winning chef, founder, and owner of Milk Bar. Known for baking outside of the lines and turning dessert on its head, Christina has been a judge on Fox's *MasterChef* series and is featured on the hit Netflix docu-series *Chef's Table: Pastry*. She is also the author of the cookbooks *Momofuku Milk Bar* and *Milk Bar Life*.